Beautiful Beginnings

Beautiful Beginnings

A Developmental Curriculum for Infants and Toddlers

by

Helen H. Raikes

and

Jane McCall Whitmer

·P·A·U·L·H·
BROOKES
PUBLISHING CO. ®

Baltimore • London • Sydney

Paul H. Brookes Publishing Co.
Post Office Box 10624
Baltimore, Maryland 21285-0624
U.S.A.

www.brookespublishing.com

Typeset by Erin Geoghegan.
Manufactured in China by JADE PRODUCTIONS.

This curriculum contains activities and suggestions that should be used in the child care center, classroom, home, or other environments only when children are receiving proper supervision. It is the caregiver's or teacher's responsibility to provide a safe, secure environment for all children and to know each child's individual circumstances (e.g., allergies to food or other substances, medical needs). The authors and publisher disclaim any liability arising directly or indirectly from the use of this book.

Every effort has been made to ascertain proper ownership of copyrighted materials and obtain permissions for their use. Any omission is unintentional and will be corrected in future printings upon proper notification.

Individuals described herein are composites or fictional accounts based on the authors' actual experiences. Individuals' names have been changed and identifying details have been altered to protect confidentiality.

Additional stickers are available in packages of four sets of six sheets (24 sheets total), and may be ordered from Paul H. Brookes Publishing Co. (1-800-638-3775, 410-337-9580, or www.brookespublishing.com).

Library of Congress Cataloging-in-Publication Data

Raikes, Helen H.
    Beautiful beginnings : a developmental curriculum for infants and toddlers / by Helen H. Raikes and Jane McCall Whitmer.—1st ed.
        p.   cm.
    ISBN-13: 978-1-55766-820-2
    ISBN-10: 1-55766-820-5 (alk. paper)
    1. Infants—Development.   2. Toddlers—Development.   3. Day care centers—Activity programs.   4. Creative activities and seat work.   5. Education, Preschool—Curricula.   I. Whitmer, Jane McCall.   II. Title.
    HQ774.R33 2006
    372.21'6—dc22
                                                                                          2005021415

British Library Cataloguing in Publication data are available from the British Library.

Contents

Section I   Getting to Know Beautiful Beginnings

Section II   Beautiful Beginnings Experiences

0–6 Months

18–24 Months

CD-ROM CONTENTS

About the Authors

About this CD-ROM

Blank Goals Sheet

Beautiful Beginnings Experiences & Overview Goals Charts

    0–6 Months

    6–12 Months

    12–18 Months

    18–24 Months

    24–30 Months

    30–36 Months

About the Authors

Helen H. Raikes, Ph.D., Professor, Family and Consumer Sciences, and Associate, Center on Children, Families, and the Law, University of Nebraska–Lincoln, 3221 South 76th Street, Lincoln, Nebraska 68506

Dr. Raikes is an associate at the Center on Children, Families and the Law at the University of Nebraska–Lincoln in addition to holding a professorship in the Family and Consumer Sciences Department and is an associate with The Gallup Organization, Omaha, Nebraska. Previously, she was a Society for Research in Child Development Executive Policy Fellow at the U.S. Administration for Children and Families, where she had responsibilities for the Early Head Start National Research and Evaluation Project. *Beautiful Beginnings* began when Dr. Raikes and Jane McCall Whitmer were directors at the SRI/Saint Elizabeth Child Development Center, serving employees of Selection Research, Inc., The Gallup Organization, and Saint Elizabeth Community Health Center. She focuses on understanding optimal environments for infants and toddlers and closing the gap between "what we know" and "what we do."

Jane McCall Whitmer, M.S., Early Intervention and Prevention Specialist, Salida, Colorado 81201

Ms. Whitmer is an educator and early intervention and prevention specialist. She holds master's degrees in educational administration and human development and the family. Ms. Whitmer has taught children of every age, has served as an elementary school administrator, and has traveled extensively to provide training and technical assistance for Early Head Start and Head Start programs. Today she works primarily with parents and teachers, consulting on a variety of early childhood topics. In addition to curricula, a topic she is particularly passionate about is teacher development and renewal in the area of early childhood education.

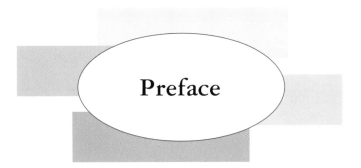

Preface

The development of *Beautiful Beginnings: A Developmental Curriculum for Infants and Toddlers* has been a labor of love for more than two decades. In the 1980s, its forerunner was a "homegrown" curriculum developed for the early childhood program staff at SRI/Saint Elizabeth Child Development Center. We were excited about all that was known about infant development and wanted a way to bring the new knowledge about infant development to teachers and providers, to close the gaps between what we knew about infants and young children and what we practiced, and those between general approaches to curricula and those tailored to individuals. Other programs in our area heard about our program and asked to use it, so we expanded it somewhat. Still, *Beautiful Beginnings* remained homegrown until Jane McCall Whitmer began training for Early Head Start and came back with requests to reproduce the curriculum. The teachers in these programs told her that the *Beautiful Beginnings* seemed to fill another gap—for a specific curriculum to help them plan for individual children.

For many good reasons, professionals, parents, and policy makers alike approach the idea of a *curriculum* for infants and toddlers with some caution. Every infant and toddler is unique, with his or her own needs and preferences. When it comes to early learning, there is no one size that fits all. Most would agree, however, that sensitive, responsive, fun-filled interactions synchronized with each baby's developing abilities are important for optimal infant/toddler development; thus, it is important that a curriculum be approached within that context.

PURPOSES OF *BEAUTIFUL BEGINNINGS*

We designed *Beautiful Beginnings* to fulfill three essential purposes: 1) to enrich the early day-to-day experiences of infants and toddlers; 2) to ensure that needed and timely experiences occur with infants and toddlers, especially those who are vulnerable, so that the children have the greatest opportunity to reach their potential; and 3) to give those who care for infants and toddlers a menu of experiences to select from and a way to do so.

What we love most about *Beautiful Beginnings* is that it directs caregivers to watch for children's strengths and emerging developments. We don't want caregivers to focus on helping young children "master" the many Experiences (as we call them, with a capital E) offered in this curriculum; we do want them to watch the infants and toddlers and offer Experiences that provide each child with opportunities to practice what he or she seems to be most passionate about or interested in at the moment. We think that if infants and toddlers are offered appropriate Experiences, mastery will follow in its own time.

COMPONENTS OF *BEAUTIFUL BEGINNINGS*

Beautiful Beginnings is composed of this book, stickers (one set bound in the book), and a CD-ROM affixed to the inside back cover. Each is described here briefly, and Chapter 3 gives more detailed information on how to use the curriculum:

- **Beautiful Beginnings manual:** This book includes

    —Three introductory chapters describing the curriculum and how to use it

    —A materials list broken down into age groups, so that users may equip their centers or other environments with all they will need to carry out the curriculum

    —A bibliography with references and resources

    —All of the Experiences, divided into age ranges

- **Sticker sheets:** This manual includes one set of six sheets of stickers corresponding to the Goals Chart for each of the six age ranges (0–6 months, 6–12 months, 12–18 months, 18–24 months, 24–30 months, and 30–36 months). Additional stickers can be purchased by contacting Paul H. Brookes Publishing Co., Post Office Box 10624, Baltimore, Maryland 21285-0624 (1-800-638-3775, 410-337-9580, http://www.brookespublishing.com).

- **CD-ROM:** The CD-ROM is included so that users can print out and copy pages from the curriculum to use in their programs. The CD-ROM contains instructions for using the CD-ROM, information about the authors, all of the Experiences for each age range that are included in the book, all Overview Goals Charts, and a blank Goals Sheet.

PRIOR USES OF *BEAUTIFUL BEGINNINGS*

We have had a great deal of fun in developing, implementing, and sharing *Beautiful Beginnings* with many different groups. *Beautiful Beginnings* has been carried out in different settings—in centers, in home visiting programs where it has been used by both home visitors and parents, and in school-based programs for teen parents. Several dozens of teachers in various settings have worked collaboratively for years in administering, observing, and planning with *Beautiful Beginnings*. Now, we are excited to make this developmentally appropriate and specific curriculum available on a wider scale. We hope that it will help to fill gaps and meet your program goals. But most of all, we hope that *Beautiful Beginnings* will increase your sense of wonder and joy about infants and toddlers because early development is a wonder to behold. Meeting young children's development with playful, respectful, well-timed opportunities for interaction is a gift to infants and toddlers as well as to the adults who care for them. Enjoy the dance!

Acknowledgments

We acknowledge the support and assistance of many in preparation of this curriculum. First, we pay tribute to the late Dr. Donald O. Clifton (1924–2003), former President of The Gallup Organization and the inspirational figure for whom the Donald O. Clifton Child Development Center is named. The American Psychological Association considers Dr. Clifton the Father of Strengths-Based Psychology. He provided brilliant inspiration to us and many others in teaching us how to intentionally build on children's gifts and talents, starting from when they are very young. Dr. Clifton wrote several books and served as co-author of *Soar with Your Strengths* (with Paula Nelson, Delacorte Press, 1992); *Now, Discover Your Strengths* (with Marcus Buckingham, The Free Press, 2001); and *How Full Is Your Bucket? Positive Strategies for Work and Life* (with Tom Rath, Gallup Press, 2004). Each of these works describes an approach to supporting development that begins with identifying individual strengths.

Next, we recognize the teachers and director at the Donald O. Clifton Child Development Center. From 1981 to 1991, the authors of this curriculum were program directors of this program's predecessor, the SRI/Saint Elizabeth Child Development Center. We salute the amazing staff who implemented the earliest versions of what was then known as *Best Beginnings*. The teachers who worked with *Best Beginnings* are too numerous to name; however, we single out Cindy Cerny and Brenda John, who provided support in producing the first version of the curriculum, and teachers Kelly Baumgartner, Jane Bromfield, Sharon Hunter, Nancy Janike, Susie Johnson, Julie Jones-Branch, Diann Kroos, Diana Miller, Chris Moudry, Sharon Otto, Sue Pace, Pat Putney, Carla Pyle, Kristi Welch, Kim Wright, and Shirley Young, who creatively applied the curriculum through several "generations" of families in this infant/toddler program. We further acknowledge the parents and children who engaged collaboratively with us in month-in, month-out observation and planning and the creative and joyful offering of what you see in this curriculum.

In moving the curriculum from its early stages to its present form, we thank Jim Krieger, Mary Reckmeyer, and The Gallup Organization for recognizing the curriculum's potential if published, particularly for programs serving infants and toddlers from low-income families. We also thank Julie Jones-Branch for last-minute assistance; the University of Nebraska's "Getting Ready" project for implementing the curriculum in a rigorous research study; and Heather Raikes and AnnieLaurie Erickson (our daughters, who happen to be astounding artists), who produced a *Beautiful Beginnings* video. And, we thank Ron Raikes and Ron Ferris for their continual support throughout the entire process.

The photographs used in *Beautiful Beginnings* were graciously provided by AnnieLaurie

Erickson, the Montessori School for Young Children, Prairie Hill Learning Center, Cedars Youth Services, and several staff members of Paul H. Brookes Publishing Co.

Finally, we acknowledge the staff with whom we have worked at Brookes Publishing. Jessica Allan, Leslie Eckard, Erin Geoghegan, Sarah Shepke, and other staff members have been tremendous. We had heard that we would have a high-quality experience working with professional staff at Brookes, and it was all true.

To the people who most completely taught us
the wonder of children's beginnings
(and all that follows), our children:

Heather, Abbie, and Justin Raikes

and

Ellie and AnnieLaurie Erickson

Getting to Know
Beautiful
Beginnings

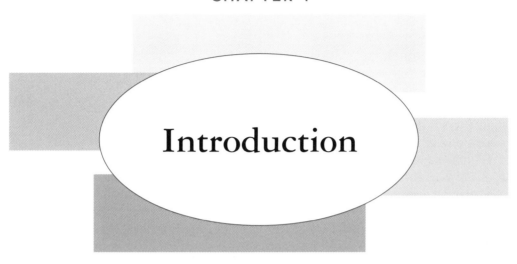

CHAPTER 1

Introduction

Makesha is a teacher in an infant care center. Four infants have been assigned to her, and they constitute her "family." At the center, she is considered their primary caregiver. Makesha is fascinated by, and engaged in, watching and thinking about these four babies, all of whom are between 7 and 10 months old. She loves observing their new developments and finding ways for the babies to exercise their emerging skills. They develop so fast! Makesha often consults the curriculum used by the center for new ideas she can implement for each emerging stage. The curriculum also helps her look for things the babies can do that she might not have noticed.

Layla has just started working in a small child care center operating out of a community center. She is working in the infant room with the young infants, ages 6 weeks to 6 months. She admires their tiny fingers and toes and how the older ones struggle so mightily to master rolling over and sitting up. Layla tries to follow the example set by her coworkers, but sometimes they are busy. To tell the truth, other than carrying the babies around, she's not always sure what to do with them. She wonders how she can help them learn and develop.

Rick is a teacher in a toddler center that uses the *Beautiful Beginnings* curriculum. The toddlers he cares for compose a rambunctious group of four to six, depending on the day of the week. Rick develops a daily schedule that includes new *Beautiful Beginnings* Experiences for the children that are based on their development and individual differences. His classroom is ready—all of the materials for a curriculum of toys and materials for children from 18 to 36 months are on hand, carefully arranged in baskets, trays, and bins, with their location in the classroom pictorially marked so children can find and return materials. Some are

---

To be fair to both genders in describing individuals in this book, pronouns are alternated.

in shelves that only open when Rick can carefully supervise their use, whereas others are available at all times.

Looking around the classroom, an observer sees 28-month-old Tommy pouring water from one container to another, working within the water table to contain any spills as he begins this new Experience of controlled pouring. In another part of the classroom, Zia is carefully carrying a basket of beads to a mat. She sits on the mat and begins to string these large beads. Andrew and Alan are placing large blocks end to end. Rick brings them a basket of two small cars and illustrates pretending that the cars drive down a roadway. The boys' eyes light up and they begin to imitate him. He is pleased because "pretending" was an Experience he had planned this week for these boys. He'd observed them putting the blocks end to end several times and thought they might be ready for the new pretending Experiences. He made a mental note to bring out the large steering wheel tomorrow to see if they expanded "pretending to drive" from today to this new arena. As Tommy finishes, Rick shows him how to put the two small containers back on the shelf and to select something else.

These stories illustrate why using a curriculum such as *Beautiful Beginnings* is so important in working with young children. Teachers, home visitors, program directors, and parents may ask, "Isn't it enough just to offer lots of toys and a lot of love and affection? Why is such a curriculum necessary?"

WHY A CURRICULUM IS NEEDED

Researchers and experts agree that an environment rich in opportunities helps infants and young children develop optimally. Several of the reasons why are detailed here.

Development Happens Quickly and Continually

Babies develop very, very quickly. At each new developmental stage, parents and teachers have opportunities to offer enriching experiences to babies. These experiences create foundations for the next stages of development. *Beautiful Beginnings* suggests appropriate experiences for infants and toddlers at each stage of development.

Brain Development Is Fostered by Rich Experiences

A well-researched, tested curriculum offers experiences that are well matched to development. Experiences of this nature are believed to stimulate neural connections in a baby's rapidly developing brain.

The Planning Is Begun

It is difficult for loving, adult caregivers, despite all they may know about child development, to plan for new experiences in every area of development because developmental changes are so many and so frequent. A curriculum keeps developmental expectations in front of teachers, caregivers, and parents and leads them to understand child development and their own special children more deeply. The next section expands on each of these reasons for using a curriculum with infants and toddlers.

AN OVERVIEW OF THE *BEAUTIFUL BEGINNINGS* CURRICULUM

Some may still believe that curricula should be used in schools with older children, not with babies. Experienced infant/toddler teachers and directors may be concerned about babies being pushed to do things they do not want to do rather than following their own natural rhythms. The *Beautiful Beginnings* curriculum for infants and toddlers does not overly structure experiences for babies—just the opposite. Our curriculum provides experiences (to be capitalized as Experiences when describing the Experiences that make up this curriculum) that are to be fitted to very young children's natural rhythms. This curriculum is designed to be individualized to meet the needs of each child in a child care center, home visiting program, teen parenting program, other parenting education program, or home. The Experiences in *Beautiful Beginnings* are designed to build on each child's strengths and naturally emerging competencies and interests. But the curriculum can also be used as a safety net for children who may require extra enrichment. For example, some programs may use *Beautiful Beginnings* in conjunction with a screening system such as the Ages & Stages Questionnaires® (ASQ; Bricker & Squires, 1999) to ensure that children who are vulnerable receive needed developmental experiences.

The *Beautiful Beginnings* curriculum features six modules (one for each 6-month period from birth to age 3) that include developmentally appropriate activities (Experiences) organized by areas of development (Communication, Gross Motor, Fine Motor, Intellectual, Discovery, and Social for all children, and, for infants and toddlers 6 months and older, the addition of Self-Help and then Pretend at 18 months). These Experiences are easy and inexpensive to administer and may be carried out by caregivers, home visitors, or parents. They are generally grouped according to children's ages but are not designed to be followed rigidly. Rather, they provide a "menu" of ideas, generally corresponding to developmental sequences. Each child is unique in his development, so Experiences may be selected across age spans as well as within.

Expanding on Our Curriculum

Let us return to the three reasons we stated earlier for an infant–toddler curriculum: to enrich infants' and toddlers' experiences, to support early development in all areas, and to provide a guide for adults who care for infants and toddlers. Here, we expand on each of these.

Enrich Infants' and Toddlers' Opportunities

Babies seek activities that correspond to their development. Each new stage of infant development offers opportunities for rich interactions with people and objects that also provide foundations for the next stages. Most people have observed that babies seem to want opportunities to practice in areas in which they are developing. Many people notice how babies who are learning to crawl can't seem to be on the floor enough, how a baby wants the adult to pop the jack-in-the-box again and again, and how toddlers want the same story read over and over in exactly the same way. Many toddlers will even correct an adult if a word is omitted from a beloved story line. Many people have noted that children almost seem to "lust" for the opportunities to practice their new skills; in the German language, there is a term that captures this quality that translates to *function lust.* Observers will note that babies sometimes practice the old skills they learned at earlier stages; however, for the most part, they are attracted to opportunities to practice emerging developmental skills. Part of the allure is that these are skills young children can partially master—but another reason is that they also gravitate toward the challenge and novelty.

Nature has equipped babies to be motivated to practice just what they need to become proficient. After they become good at one skill, they are attracted to the next more difficult stage, enabling one stage to build on the next. A curriculum helps us—the adults who care so much about the babies in our charge—to find good things to put in front of them at just the right time.

Development occurs very quickly in babies. The windows of opportunity are short and require quick responses. Today's new skill is boring to the baby a week later because of her development. The baby masters one challenge and is then quickly attracted to a new novelty. A curriculum helps caregivers find the experiences that match what the baby is attracted to *today, this week.* A curriculum helps caregivers provide the richness of experiences that meets the baby's rapid (sometimes exploding) development.

Several decades ago, Dr. Burton White (1975) helped parents and caregivers understand the importance of such richness of experience for older infants and toddlers. His study of notably well-developing toddlers in the Boston area, conducted in the 1960s, demonstrated that parents of these children continually expanded on the toddlers' thinking, events, and conversations. Parents offered the "next idea" to the toddlers. Parents didn't sit down and formally "teach" their children (although they did this to some extent), but rather, they mostly taught "on the fly." When their child brought them something to show or asked for help, the parent would typically expand on the concept, idea, word, or child's action. Most of these lessons took about 30 seconds, but they occurred hundreds of time in the course of a normal day. Naturally, parents had to be very attuned to their child's development to know what was the "next idea." These parents were also great architects of their child's environment and experiences, providing experiences in the home and outside the home that allowed the child to explore and practice newly emerging developments. Newer work by Hart and Risley (1995) further illustrated the role of richness of experiences (in this case, of language) provided to children by attentive caregivers. These researchers found that effective parents provide small "bites" of language enrichment hundreds of times on a daily basis. Each day and in all areas of development, little windows of opportunity open for brief moments. During these opportune moments, adults can provide experiences that enrich, nourish, and delight the developing infant. A good curriculum can help them be somewhat prepared with new experiences to offer the baby.

Support Early Development

Child development literature is rich with early and more recent findings that support the importance of appropriately timed responses and stimulation to enhance children's early development. Most early childhood teachers, providers, and parents have now heard about the importance of early brain development. They know that the most rapid phase for brain development in the lifespan is the period from birth to age 3. During this time, new neurons are forming in the brain (more so now than during any other phase) and extensions of the neurons are growing that make it possible for one neuron to "talk to" another one, forming pathways of neural connections. What is particularly exciting to early childhood educators and parents is that newer evidence suggests that the growth in extensions and connections seems to occur in the context of experience. That is, when a baby first makes a connection between two ideas (e.g., "If I use this stick to reach, I can get that toy I want"), experts believe that a neural connection is also formed. When the baby practices a new skill, an initially delicate connection becomes stronger and more robust. Thus, most early childhood experts now agree that stimulation, appropriately timed and matched to the child's readiness, is an important ingredient in differentiation of neural connections. Some of these ideas are well expressed in an important book called *From Neurons to Neighborhoods* that interprets what we know about early childhood development (Shonkoff & Phillips, 2000). New knowledge also demonstrates that a television set that blares "language" is not an effective teacher of language development (Vandewater et al., 2005; Wright et al., 2001) and has little effect on brain development, whereas a parent who talks to communicate with the child does promote language (and brain) development.

Many of these findings are underscored by concepts such as the "importance of the match," This important idea, suggested by Dr. Joseph McVicker Hunt (1961), is still important today to our understanding of optimizing learning. This concept suggests that children learn best when experiences are timed to match their developmental readiness. Hunt's studies are supported by the idea that a child learns language in the context of small phonemic (i.e., referring to sounds) and syntactic (i.e., referring to the structure of language) "bites" of information that sensitive parents adapt to their perception of the child's readiness. Discoveries about early brain development and the importance of the match underscore the value of an artfully applied curriculum. It is important to note that learning occurs in all areas of development, although the mechanisms may be different across areas.

Provide a Guide for Teachers, Providers, and Caregivers

A third purpose of the *Beautiful Beginnings* curriculum is to provide a guide for teachers, providers, home visitors, and parents as they think of ways to support development. Many adults who have had positive experiences in their own early development bring with them a repository of good responses and little games they learned in their own cradle of development. Many of the games we introduce are such experiences, drawn from the native games, chants, and play of adults and children through the ages. We don't pretend to have captured all of the types of social games peoples of all time have played with their babies, but we do reach across a number of them. In addition, some of the games and Experiences we introduce come from science, from the clever experiments scientists have used to learn more about how infants think and learn. *The Scientist in the Crib* by Gopnick, Meltzoff, and Kuhl (2001), makes the new knowledge about the infant's strategies for learning accessible to the lay reader. *Beautiful Beginnings* provides instructions for bringing some of the activities from scientific studies into the nursery and other child care settings so parents and teachers can see for themselves the wonderful things that babies can do when they know what to look for. That is, many of these Experiences seem to reveal skills that babies and toddlers have that we may not have been aware of.

A number of teachers and home visitors who have used *Beautiful Beginnings* in their classrooms and in working with parents have told us that *Beautiful Beginnings* helps them to better understand child development. Although some people who work with infants and toddlers have had academic preparation in early development, many others have told us that their courses did not probe deeply enough into infant–toddler development to guide them in how to respond with expanding experiences timed with new developments. Other early childhood teachers and home visitors do not have preparation in infant–toddler development. *Beautiful Beginnings* assists these emerging professionals in understanding both the nature and timing of appropriate developmental experiences for our youngest children. Some have found that using *Beautiful Beginnings* in conjunction with a screening system, such as the ASQ, is an excellent way to expand understanding of early development.

Adults who care for and love young children also use *Beautiful Beginnings* as a guide to equipping environments for early learning. The information provided in the curriculum pertains to teachers in center-based programs, home visitors equipping a lending library, and parents setting up their home to be a great learning environment.

The Experiences in the curriculum can be organized into an appropriately stimulating child development environment, a point we talk more about later. Teachers viewing *Beautiful Beginnings* in this way say that it guides them in providing a developmentally appropriate environment for the infants and toddlers they care for.

ABOUT BABIES AND CURRICULA

When using a curriculum with infants and toddlers, it is important to take extra care to keep the focus on the child, not just the activity or goal. Being flexible in following the child's interest is critical. Learning how to "read" young children is an essential skill when implementing the curriculum. A dance of observing and "tuning into" the infant or toddler provides the basis for selecting an experience. In *Infants Have Their Own Curriculum: A Responsive Approach to Curriculum Planning for Infants and Toddlers,* Dr. Ron Lally summed it up beautifully:

> Curriculum should be dynamic enough to move and flow on a daily basis with the infant's developing interests and changing needs…In this way, the curriculum is responsive and respectful of what the children bring to and want from these early experiences. (2000, p. 7)

According to Lally, a curriculum should also anticipate developmental stages while still allowing for individual variations in learning style. The curriculum also should be broad enough in scope to respond to all developmental domains simultaneously.

DEVELOPMENT OF *BEAUTIFUL BEGINNINGS*

Beautiful Beginnings: A Developmental Curriculum for Infants and Toddlers has been under development for many years. We, the authors, are experienced infant–toddler and early childhood educators. We were directors of an employer-sponsored child development center from 1982 through 1991, the SRI/Saint Elizabeth Child Development Center, Lincoln, Nebraska. That program today is known as the Donald O. Clifton Child Development Center, which serves employees of The Gallup Organization, and has since moved to Omaha, Nebraska.

In the early development of *Beautiful Beginnings,* we encouraged teachers to think about infants' development on a daily basis. We'd ask, "What's happening with Annie? When did Kumar start pointing to everything, asking, 'Dat?' How can we build on each of these exciting emerging new skills and interests? How can we respond to Ellie and what seems to be her passion for music? Did you notice Latrice's passion for responding to color and light? What are we doing to encourage Camilla to communicate with people around her and to help her engage socially?" It became apparent that teachers could use a formal guide, a menu of ideas from which to select. Together with the teachers, we experimented with many formats, and as other programs began to use the curriculum, new sections were added so it has evolved into what you see today.

Areas of Focus in *Beautiful Beginnings*

We selected a number of areas of development for *Beautiful Beginnings* to help teachers, home visitors, and parents focus on discovering engaging experiences for infants and toddlers. Yet, of course, the infant's development is holistic—development in one area affects development in others. Positive emotions free up the child's energy for learning. Language—having words— aids social development. However, it is still useful to think of areas of development, which we have organized into the following eight categories:

1. **Communication:** From her earliest moments, an infant is a communicator. *Beautiful Beginnings* provides first experiences for the young infant in back-and-forth communication, progresses to matching infants' coos and babbles, promotes gestures and first words, encourages reading to babies, and offers suggestions as language grows to promote and broaden an infant's understanding and increasingly complex expressions.

2. **Gross Motor:** The young infant explores the world through her body. Early intelligence is "sensorimotor." Thus, *Beautiful Beginnings* provides many activities that enable infants and toddlers to experience their own bodies in space as they develop increasing control over motor functions.

3. **Fine Motor:** Increasingly, a child gains the ability to use his hands to manipulate objects, from being able to get that rattle into his mouth to unbuttoning and buttoning. The growth in fine motor skills between the years birth to 3 years old is tremendous, and *Beautiful Beginnings* offers experiences that allow the baby to practice these skills as they emerge.

4. **Intellectual:** The baby's intellectual development begins with reliance on motor functions and makes a shift, later building on representations or symbols and using language to

process ideas. In this area, particularly, some Experiences in *Beautiful Beginnings* originate from the world of science, following on studies that demonstrate how truly "smart" babies are and providing babies with creative ways to solve problems (e.g., figuring out what happened to the toy that disappeared under the blanket).

5. **Discovery:** Because the world of infants and toddlers is so based on their senses—hearing, seeing, smelling, touching, tasting—and on movement—we provide many opportunities that simply allow the baby to experience the world sensorily. We are reminded of the wise words of the Greenspans in their wonderful book, *First Feelings: Milestones in the Emotional Development of Your Baby and Child* (1989). They noted that an early task for the infant is to become interested in the world through the use of her senses. Throughout the infant and toddler years, discovery tasks in *Beautiful Beginnings* enable the infant to tune in and heighten sensory awareness, thereby becoming more engaged within a wider world.

6. **Social:** The infant and toddler come to know the world through relationships. For them, their caregivers (teachers, parents) are central to all that they experience. Through sensitive, synchronous relationships, they gain skill in back-and-forth communication, come to trust that their needs will be met, learn to trust new people, and feel secure in new situations. *Beautiful Beginnings* Experiences help build on the infant's natural desire to relate by providing aids for building relationships with adults and peers.

7. **Self-Help:** Although toddlers are famous for their "me do it" approach to life, the quest for independence begins early and can be encouraged by "scaffolding" (e.g., providing appropriate support) so that the infant can do for herself what she is able to do. Thus, we provide early opportunities for the infant to help feed herself and to assist with dressing, and we provide for environmental aids so these opportunities for independence are natural and possible. For example, using easy pull-on pants is essential when the child is learning self-dressing; a simple step stool allows for independent hand washing, and shelves can be illustrated with pictures to show where objects should go to allow the child to put away toys independently.

8. **Pretend:** Some time between 12 and 24 months, the toddler makes an amazing discovery—that "things" can stand in for, or symbolize, other things. Of course, language is the best example of a symbol system the toddler begins to master at this time. For toddlers, we have included Experiences that help to build a child's skills in symbolization, which also allows the child to experience the joy of pretending that will later feed intellectual and social life and the wellsprings of creativity.

The Parts Add Up to a Whole

Having divided the areas of development, we now want to put them back together. *Beautiful Beginnings'* notion of development is consistent with current research on infant and toddler development that demonstrates how areas of development work together. The following are some premises on which our work is based:

- **Each area of development is important:** Thus, we encourage caregivers to offer Experiences in all areas. For example, we encourage Experiences that give equal weight to nurturing social-emotional and intellectual development.

- Closely related, **for infants and toddlers, learning is holistic:** We assume that learning in one area affects development in other areas. For example, music and movement experiences that engage the child's body and spirit are also likely to affect intellectual and emotional development, reminding us that children do not experience the domains separately.

- **Important milestones in language and communication development occur during this period:** Therefore, many opportunities to engage children in meaningful, expanding language Experiences are included; however, communication and thoughtful language should be a part of every Experience.

- Because development of infants and toddlers occurs in the context of their relationships, **it is important that relationships be smooth and synchronous, gentle and observant.** We assume Experiences will be offered in this vein and that Experiences will be fitted into calm, back-and-forth rhythms of security-promoting relationships, whether with parents, teachers, or home visitors.

- **Focusing on the individual, unique gifts and talents of each child is essential** to the success of any child development curriculum.

Components of *Beautiful Beginnings*

Here we provide an overview of the components contained within *Beautiful Beginnings.* Use of the curriculum components will be further detailed in Chapter 3.

- **Overview Goals Charts:** Overview Goals Charts provide a quick "map" of the curriculum for each of the following time periods: 0–6 months, 6–12 months, 12–18 months, 18–24 months, 24–30 months, and 30–36 months. Each Chart is organized according to areas of development: Communication, Gross Motor, Fine Motor, Intellectual, Discovery, Social, Self-Help (beginning with 6–12 months and beyond), and Pretend (beginning with 18 months and beyond). Each area of development for each time period contains eight Experiences (see next).

- **Experiences:** Each Experience is presented on a single page within the curriculum, grouped by age and area of development. Each Experience includes a goal for the Experience; a detailed explanation of how to carry out the Experience, often with alternative ways of doing things; and needed materials. As mentioned, Experiences are aligned with the Overview Goals Charts. We call these individual elements of the curriculum Experiences because we want to emphasize the infant/toddler's process (or experience) as they work toward mastery of a goal. We think if infants and toddlers are offered appropriate Experiences, mastery will follow in its own time. Some will want to call these curriculum elements Goals, and that substitution can easily be made with no other change to the curriculum.

- **Goals Sheets:** Goals Sheets (see pp. 26–27) may be used by the parent, teacher, home visitor, or parent educator to record the plans for the coming time period or to record what has been accomplished.

The Overview Goals Charts, Experiences, and Goals Sheet may be photocopied or printed from the accompanying CD-ROM. Follow copyright and licensing regulations located on the copyright page and on the CD-ROM.

- **Sticker Set:** A complete set of the Overview Goals Charts in the form of stickers that can be used in conjunction with the Goals Sheets for ongoing documentation is included. Additional stickers may be purchased from Paul H. Brookes Publishing Co. (see p. iv for ordering information).

- **List of Materials:** A complete list of needed materials for all Experiences is also included.

VALUE ADDED BY *BEAUTIFUL BEGINNINGS*

In summary, *Beautiful Beginnings* can enhance any infant–toddler program—whether the focus is home visiting, child care, or parenting more generally—in a number of ways. We identify a few of these benefits.

1. *Beautiful Beginnings* encourages parents and staff to observe children's development. It encourages them to watch more carefully for new developments.

2. *Beautiful Beginnings* leads the parent, teacher, or home visitor who does not have familiarity with all of the stages of child development through early development, providing the adult with hands-on opportunities to learn about development. One longtime user of the precursor of *Beautiful Beginnings* said, "It was my child development teacher."

3. *Beautiful Beginnings* provides a mechanism for infant/toddler child care programs to focus on development, rather than caregiving without an intentional developmental component.

4. *Beautiful Beginnings* provides a formalized way for parents, teachers, and home visitors to work together. Although it takes some planning and coordination for all to have input in regular goal setting and follow through on Experiences, the opportunities on behalf of the child are tremendous.

5. If the Portfolio option is adapted (see Chapter 3), *Beautiful Beginnings* can provide a record of a child's early development.

6. *Beautiful Beginnings* provides a way to create a safety net for children who may need more support and stimulation in a particular area of development (e.g., children who may not be developing optimally in some areas).

7. *Beautiful Beginnings* can assist teachers in both individual and group planning of Experiences for individuals and activities for groups. If used in a group setting, *Beautiful Beginnings* can guide the outfitting of a well-equipped infant/toddler setting. Materials for nearly all of the Experiences included in *Beautiful Beginnings* for children ages at least 18 months and older can be organized into learning centers and made continuously available in a toddler center.

8. Most important, *Beautiful Beginnings* can help teachers, home visitors, and parents provide children with Experiences that match their emerging developments, give them the joy of well-timed opportunities, and gently offer stimulation and engaging, fun activities in all areas of development. Successful matching by teachers, home visitors, and parents further rewards adults with children's positive energy, focus, and motivation.

CHAPTER 2

Infant and Toddler Development

Tony and Amalia are teen parents. They hadn't planned on having a baby, but now they have little Pedro and they want to do all they can to be good parents. It hasn't been easy, though—with both of them in school and working. Still, Pedro is the light of their lives. At first, Tony and Amalia thought that babies only ate and slept, but they were amazed to see that Pedro seemed to "converse" with them when they made little sounds that he could make as well, especially when they gave him plenty of time to respond. They found that such conversations seemed to cause him to brighten and be more alert. Now they want to know what comes next for their little communicator. How can they let him "begin" the conversations? He just makes a few sounds; when will he be able to make sounds like "mama" and "dada"? When will he know what they mean? It seemed a little silly at first, but they decided to show him some pictures in books, just for a few minutes, and to talk with him about them.

Tony and Amalia are discovering the wonders of infant development and early childhood educators can support their interest and caring by helping them learn more about Pedro's development and the possibilities for providing him enriching experiences at each stage of development.

Beautiful Beginnings draws on more than 50 years of strong research in the area of infant and toddler development. The example of Tony, Amalia, and Pedro illustrates real-world encounters with behaviors that have intrigued scientists, parents, and professionals alike.

As we have noted, the time span from birth to age 3 marks an amazing period of development. During this period, brain growth is faster than at any other time during the life span. This is when children acquire language and develop fundamental relationships with caregivers that contribute to lifetime patterns of trust, communication, and emotion regulation.

According to developmental psychologists and others, opportunities to have a positive effect on children's development are great during such periods of rapid growth and change. Even economists reflect on the principles of development. Nobel Laureate Dr. James Heckman espoused the importance of a child's earliest years. According to Heckman's (2000) principle of "dynamic complementarity," children who develop well at earlier ages will elicit interactions and experiences that support development thereafter, and that development so supported helps to foster more able individuals who support a better society.

DEVELOPMENTAL MILESTONES

This chapter briefly reviews some of the developmental milestones on which *Beautiful Beginnings* is built. These milestones are grouped according to the same age categories as in the curriculum: 0–6 months, 6–12 months, 12–18 months, 18–24 months, 24–30 months, and 30–36 months.

0–6 Months

The period from birth to approximately 6 months of age is an immensely rich period in an infant's life. During this period, an infant learns the rudiments of physiological regulation (e.g., to adapt to a schedule of eating and sleeping), to become attuned to important adults in her life, to produce sounds, and to develop expectations about caregiving and having her needs met. During this phase, much of what happens in infant development is a function of the sensitivity of the parent or other caregiving adult, who uses the child's rhythms as the basis for interaction. Contingent responsiveness (i.e., responding quickly to the baby's signals), face-to-face interactions and eye contact, sound sequences, and imitation in the relationship are all building blocks for the baby's development. Parents and teachers are often amazed at the baby's recognition of sounds (hearing), growing ability to focus and recognize color (vision), responses to being stroked and massaged (touch), enjoyment of movement (kinesthetic), and preferences for various tastes. *Beautiful Beginnings* promotes the Greenspans' theory (Greenspan & Greenspan, 1989, see Chapter 1) in that it encourages teachers, caregivers, and parents to help the baby gently "open" the senses, encounter the world through the senses, and experience moments of synchronous interactions using the senses (e.g., back-and-forth listening and cooing, looking at one another, looking away and looking back, sensitive touch). Most of the *Beautiful Beginnings* Experiences for the 0- to 6-month phase expand on the infant's sensory capabilities and depend on the rhythms of relationships to be the mechanism.

6–12 Months

During the latter half of the first year of life, the infant continues to depend on relationships for nourishment, love, responses, and information about the world. During this period, many changes occur—the baby increases intentional communication, begins to understand that things in the world exist in their own right, and, in accordance, demonstrates an idea of a relationship. The infant begins to demonstrate that he understands that there is a relationship between himself and the one communicating with him. Another major change during this phase is mobility. Now, the infant is physically exploring his environment, gaining new understandings of the world, and beginning to navigate his expanding world. The 6- to 12-month-old infant actively plays with sound, often babbling continuously (e.g., "ba-ba-ba-ba-ba-ba"). Interestingly, at the beginning of this phase, infants worldwide make all human language sounds, but by the end of the phase they only produce sounds of the language to which they are exposed (Jusczyk, 1997). This startling finding is testimony to how important language inputs are to infants and to their active work as language learners. Infants during this stage can also obtain the attention of caregivers and play astounding communication games. If you hide an object, somewhere during this period the baby will pull the cover off of the object, demonstrating a sense of object permanence, a major accomplishment. Object permanence coincides with the child's expression of attachment to the people who take care of him, which in turn allows the child to use the adult as a secure base if needed for exploration and comfort.

During this phase, *Beautiful Beginnings* Experiences continue to focus on back-and-forth interactions with babies (e.g., in which parent and baby exchange turns in communication)—expanding them into social and language games—and to many interactions with objects (e.g., manipulating them, hiding them, imitating with them). Whenever possible, the infant is guided to be an active participant in his own caregiving, such as helping to feed himself or participating in dressing.

12–18 Months

Babies make major strides toward independence during the toddler period. During this time, cognition, emotion, and expression change significantly. During the period from 12 to 18 months, children increasingly understand what objects are for, opening up a whole new world, and it becomes important to explore each object to see how it fits with another—how it works. Cognitively, children become problem solvers, such as when a child uses a stick to obtain an object, which indicates a beginning sense of the function of tools. Emotionally, at this age, children expand their ability to relate to others and begin to develop a sense of self as they identify their own body parts and self in a mirror. Enormous leaps in communication occur during this phase; first words or gestures may appear, but comprehension is far ahead of expression. The acquisition of these first words and gestures is a very important milestone—the beginning of understanding that a symbol (a word or gesture) can stand in for an object or action. Of course, walking is a major milestone of this period as well.

Because of the variety of skills inherent in each of these areas of development, *Beautiful Beginnings* emphasizes many different ways of playing with objects, such as putting things into and taking them out of containers. We assume that each new material and container offers a tiny way to expand on the emerging understandings of things and what can be done with them. *Beautiful Beginnings* emphasizes the importance of language, social, and self-help experiences during this period.

18–24 Months

During the period from 18 to 24 months, the toddler grows in communicative competence, expanding vocabulary and self-help skills. The child begins to join the symbols and make 2-word sentences. She uses symbols in pretend play. During this period, the child's play with objects takes on more and more purpose: putting things into containers; stacking and building; and learning what objects do, such as rolling, opening, or becoming a tower. The child also grows in the ability to do things by herself, including simple dressing routines and self-feeding. Children become increasingly competent at walking, and most children learn to run.

An 18- to 24-month-old child is a wonder of activity and learning. Typically, children of this age are voracious learners. *Beautiful Beginnings* Experiences during this phase build on the child's passion to learn. Children understand many things adults say to them and will typically try most new experiences offered to them that are within their ability level. Often, they surprise us with what they are able to do!

24–30 Months

Beautiful Beginnings offers many opportunities that match 2-year-olds' expanding abilities—stringing, painting, snapping, pounding, sorting, jumping, running, and so forth. The 2-year old, although sometimes turbulent, is an exciting person who wants to do it all. *Beautiful Beginnings* helps to structure her world so she is successful in her passion for independence. Between the ages of 24 and 30 months, young children in this age group seek to express their autonomy—"I do it" is a common intention of 2-year-olds. During this period a child's self-help abilities grow, and she may begin toilet learning. In terms of language and communication, the typical 2-year-old is full of curiosity and questions. She may have many words in her vocabulary by now. Socially, most children who are typically developing are interested in interaction with other children but often lack skills to interact well. Thus, although 2-year-olds benefit (and gain skills) by playing with other children, they find sharing and cooperative play difficult to sustain for very long periods of time. Most 2-year-olds hear parents and caregivers say "Use your words" at times in social interactions to avoid or stop children's negative behavior such as hitting and biting. Most 2-year-olds love physical activity—wheels, blocks, push-and-pull toys—and also can be quite purposeful in play and can engage in pretend play. A 2-year-old typically likes to scribble and may be able to imitate a simple line or circle stroke.

30–36 Months

At this age, children are able to complete many precise motions and love practicing with the objects they understand so well now (e.g., stringing, scooping, pasting, painting). Intellectually, a child may be able to focus on the properties of objects—color, size, and sequence. He understands cause and effect in new ways and can often talk about the past and the future. Language and symbolism continue to grow. This is a tremendous period for use of symbols in pretend play and in artistic expression (although adults may still not be able to recognize what it is that a child is drawing). The growth in pretend play leads to shared ideas in peer play; for example, children may establish together who will be the baby and who will be the mommy when playing "house." However, considerable guidance is often needed at this stage.

For 2-year-olds, *Beautiful Beginnings* Experiences emphasize practice with a myriad of household tools and objects, expansive and thought-provoking language, opportunities for artistic and pretend play, and gentle guidance in peer play and in personal responsibility for one's own bodily functions. Many children learn to control their toileting functions during this phase, although some may not be ready.

THE DEVELOPMENTAL NATURE OF *BEAUTIFUL BEGINNINGS*

Beautiful Beginnings offers Experiences appropriate to a child's age and development and then builds on them later. What follows next are examples of the spiraling nature of *Beautiful Beginnings* in which later opportunities add new elements of challenge or build on earlier development. The lists below do not illustrate all of the sequences in *Beautiful Beginnings*; they simply illustrate the sequential nature of the Experiences (and of children's development). Many other examples are in the curriculum. Below we list the name and number of the Experiences that you will learn more about later.

Learning to Categorize

Distinguishing differences and similarities is the basis for many later skills, such as being able to differentiate between a *b* or *d,* distinguishing between living and inanimate things, and so forth. Even young infants are able to distinguish some differences. Many people do not think this is possible, but young infants do perceive differences, the basis for a whole series of categorization tasks. The following are categorizing Experiences in the curriculum, beginning with those for children at the younger ages and progressing to those offered to older children. The general nature of the Experience is usually self-apparent from the title.

Categorizing (Intellectual #8, 0–6 months) invites the young infant to demonstrate that she sees differences in objects.

Distinguishing by Color and Size (Intellectual #7, 6–12 months)

Putting Round Shape in Sorter (Intellectual #2, 12–18 months)

Putting Square Shape in Sorter (Intellectual #6, 12–18 months)

Using a 3-Piece Shape Sorter (Intellectual #2, 18–24 months)

Matching by Color (Intellectual #7, 18–24 months)

Sorting by Color (Intellectual #1, 24–30 months)

Sorting by Shape and Identity (Intellectual #5, 24–30 months)

Identifying Colors (Intellectual #7, 24–30 months)

Identifying Opposites (Intellectual #8, 24–30 months)

Naming Colors and Shapes (Intellectual #1, 30–36 months)

Identifying Gender (Intellectual #2, 30–36 months)

Locating Objects by Color or Shape (Intellectual #5, 30–36 months)

Building a Concept of Containers

The container play Experiences listed below illustrate reciprocity in Experiences across areas of children's development. For example, in some cases, the child must learn a fine motor function before he is able to complete an intellectual task, or vice versa.

Playing with Things in Containers (Intellectual #1, 6–12 months)

Opening Containers (Fine Motor #3, 12–18 months)

Hand-Filling and Dumping (Fine Motor #4, 12–18 months)

Scooping and Dumping (Fine Motor #5, 12–18 months)

Putting Toys in Containers (Intellectual #3, 12–18 months)

Putting Small Objects in Container (Intellectual #1, 18–24 months)

Scooping Using Containers (Fine Motor #2, 30–36 months)

Connecting with Adults and Other Children

These Experiences help a child learn to relate to adults first, and later, other children. New skills build on earlier ones.

Developing Synchrony (Social #2, 0–6 months)

Waving "Bye-Bye" and Saying "Hi" (Social #4, 6–12 months)

Relating to Children and Adults (Social #1, 12–18 months)

Coming for Help (Social #6, 12–18 months)

Knowing Other Children (Social #7, 12–18 months)

Expressing Affection (Social #1, 18–24 months)

Giving Things Back (Social #5, 18–24 months)

Using Adults as Resources (Social #7, 18–24 months)

Naming Others (Social #1, 24–30 months)

Showing Items to Others When Asked (Social #2, 24–30 months)

Waiting for Turns (Social #3, 24–30 months)

Matching Pictures (Social #4, 24–30 months)

Sharing Show and Tell (Social #6, 24–30 months)

Talking About Friends at Home (Social #7, 24–30 months)

Responding to the Emotions of Others (Social #8, 24–30 months)

Talking and Listening in a Small Group (Social #5, 30–36 months)

Playing Jointly (Social #6, 30–36 months)

Matching Names and Pictures (Social #8, 30–36 months)

Learning Names for Things

Learning nouns (e.g., naming objects) begins with listening and watching, imitation, and understanding. From these early experiences, the remarkable ability to use a word to represent an object seems to simply appear. Of course, the process is more complicated than that, but these Experiences promote noun recognition.

Responding to Voices and Music (Communication #1, 0–6 months)

Experiencing Joint Attention (Communication #5, 6–12 months)

Listening to Words (Communication #6, 6–12 months)

Imitating Sounds or Expressions (Communication #1, 12–18 months)

Understanding Words (Communication #3, 12–18 months)

Pointing to Things in Books (Communication #5, 12–18 months)

Labeling Objects (Communication #6, 12–18 months)

Asking "What's That?" (Communication #3, 18–24 months)

Naming Things in a Basket (Communication #1, 24–30 months)

Naming Matching Cards (Communication #2, 24–30 months)

Labeling Areas of Room and Objects (Communication #6, 24–30 months)

SUMMARY

We have reflected on the nature of early development and we have identified how we have crafted Experiences for infants and toddlers that build on developmental events. In many cases, Experiences are sequential and build on skills the baby has acquired in earlier stages. In all cases, Experiences are designed to be fitted to the baby's interest and new developments. In Chapter 3, we describe how to implement *Beautiful Beginnings*.

Using *Beautiful Beginnings*
An Individualized Program

Barbara is 3-month-old Joshua's teacher. She and Joshua's mother and father together selected the following 0–6 Experiences for Joshua for the month: Sharing First Conversations (Communication #2); Lying on Tummy and Looking Up (Gross Motor #3), and Massaging (Discovery #2). Barbara made a Goals Sheet for herself to post in the child care setting. She made another one for Joshua's parents to post at home.

Sharing First Conversations was easy to offer as an Experience. Josh was very eager to communicate, so the teacher simply slowed down before feeding him, while diapering him, and when holding him so that she could make eye contact, listen for, and imitate his oooohs and coos. Because this had been chosen as one of Josh's Experiences for the month, however, she was sure to do this more than usual—several times a day. Josh seemed to coo more as a result of this focused attention.

At first, when Barbara and Josh's parents began working on Lying on Tummy and Looking Up, Josh didn't like lying on his tummy at all. Barbara and his parents both got down on the floor with him, providing face-to-face contact with him and playing with him, at least once a day. Barbara notes that Josh is now happy for a while when put on his tummy, and he seems to be holding his head higher.

For the last choice, Massaging, Barbara found that although she was able to have a couple of good massage experiences during the time period, she was not able to do this every day. Josh's parents, however, were able to give him a massage every night before his bath and they now say, "He loves it." Barbara keeps a record of Josh's responses for her developmental file for Josh. She will share this with the parents during their quarterly conference. Josh's parents have also been making notes about his responses, when time allows. They look forward to putting their notes together with those from Barbara. They've also taken a few pictures of their little fellow enjoying his massage.

Eloise is a home visitor for an early intervention program for children from low-income families. Her program staff has studied infant development, but recently they acquired an infant–toddler curriculum that offers more specific experiences to offer children in all areas of development. Now, she and the parents she visits in their homes concentrate on specifically identifying new developments of each child each week. The parents put a new Goals Sheet on their refrigerator every other week and use stickers to remind them of their plans for the child. She helps the parents identify new developments and works with the parents to be sure the child is ready for the Experience selected. She helps parents find ways to turn the Experiences into naturally occurring games, keeping the tone light and playful and respectful of the child's rhythms. Some of the parents she works with are reporting that they are enjoying parenting more than ever and are so excited about what they see their children doing.

USING *BEAUTIFUL BEGINNINGS*

Implementing *Beautiful Beginnings* can be a great adventure. In this chapter, we review how to use *Beautiful Beginnings* and how to expand on and enhance the development of individual children. *Beautiful Beginnings* was designed for this purpose—to help teachers, home visitors, and parents pause, reflect on, and build on the nuances of early development of children, one individual child at a time. However, our experiences have shown us that this curriculum also works well as a guide for group activities in an early childhood center; as a framework and philosophy for a home visiting program; and as a curriculum for a child development class for parents, such as in a school-based teen parent program with child care for infants and toddlers. Some 2- and 4-year teacher preparation programs have also found it helpful to include *Beautiful Beginnings* in course materials, as an orientation to an infant–toddler curriculum and development.

The *Beautiful Beginnings* Goals and Experiences for individual children are based on observations of each child's development, interests, and needs. People who interact with children in various roles (e.g., child care teacher, home visitor, parent) may use the curriculum in similar or different ways. We expand on the different ways people might use B*eautiful Beginnings* in a later part of this chapter.

The *Beautiful Beginnings* process includes 1) selecting Goals/Experiences, 2) getting organized, 3) offering Experiences, and 4) documenting the child's responses. We now expand on each of these steps.

Selecting Goals/Experiences

How does one go about selecting Goals/Experiences for babies and toddlers? Again, in the next section we will typically use our preferred term, *Experiences,* but we recognize some may call these *Goals.* Now, imagine it is the end of the month and your plan is to select two to three Goals/Experiences for the next month to offer to the child. But before selecting, it is important to follow these steps:

Observing the Child

The first step in planning effective Experiences for an infant or toddler is to tune in to that child's individuality. Every baby can teach you a great deal about her development—just watch. What seems to energize her? When does she shy away? What does she do when she is tired? How does she comfort herself? How does she communicate when she wants something? Even very young babies are continually sending signals related to these questions. Perhaps you notice that tiny things on the carpet fascinate the baby, and that she seems to want to try to pick them up. Or you notice that she lights up when a small animal is around. Many babies have passions. For example, some babies and toddlers seem to truly love listening to music. What new developments are emerging? Perhaps she is making new babbling sounds, something she wasn't even doing a week ago.

Taking Stock

It is often helpful for teachers, caregivers, and parents to review the Overview Goals Chart before selecting Goals/Experiences for an individual child. This exercise often suggests behaviors to observe. Many times the tiny buds of new developments may go unnoticed; however, by considering developments that may appear at a particular age or within a sequence, you may see better what is emerging. For more information on what to expect at each age, you can also consult the ASQ (Bricker & Squires, 1999) or other recognized guides on typical infant development milestones. Many people who do not have a background in child development find it helpful to regularly review the applicable chart to reflect on general developmental sequences. Although we do include the Goals/Experiences within age ranges, we are reluctant to assign them highly specific developmental ages. Children who lack resources may be delayed in emergence of some skills, and when it comes to selecting Goals/Experiences, we think what matters is finding the Goals/Experience that a child will resonate with given the abilities he does have. A developmental screener such as the ASQ used in conjunction with *Beautiful Beginnings* can provide the additional information about whether the child is developing typically for his or her age group and provide information as to whether an early intervention screening might be necessary.

Later in this section we discuss selecting other Goals/Experiences based on children's developmental needs or concerns. Now, with the *Beautiful Beginnings* framework in mind, come back and observe the child again, and really think about what he is telling you about the types of Experiences he would like to do and can benefit from.

Goals/Experiences can be selected in several ways, including 1) building on the child's interests and strengths, 2) expanding on new developments, and 3) filling gaps related to needs or concerns. Each of these is described next. From here on, for the most part, we use our preferred term, *Experiences,* instead of *Goals/Experiences.* The reader can substitute *Goals* for *Experiences* if using alternative "Goals language."

Selecting Experiences that Build on the Child's Interests and Strengths

Most babies have tremendous vitality and a love of life. Healthy babies are immensely curious. Like adults, some have more interests than others, but nearly all babies have some actions, objects, or people that they are interested in at any point in their development. As we have noted, babies often express what seems to be passion. Note how infants and toddlers repeat actions over and over. Have you seen the excitement that one baby expresses at the chance to go outside, or the way another brightens when music is played? Think of the child who expresses a strong love of new objects to manipulate. Even things that seem negative are sometimes just manifestations of this positive energy (e.g., when two 2-year-olds are fighting over the same toy because each wants it so much). *Beautiful Beginnings* builds on interest, strength, and passion. If a child is enthused about something, build on that energy by providing more Experiences of that kind. If he loves pull-toys, give him every opportunity to pull many different types of toys—heavy ones, light ones, ones with straight and curved handles. Then, perhaps give him the opportunity to push as well—so he learns about pulling and pushing exactly when his interest is the greatest. And on it goes.

Many people are familiar with strengths-based programs for adults. We believe that it also is important to build on the strengths and interests of young children. So, to reiterate, the best way to select a new Experience is to pick something that the child is telling you she likes to do. We think children have more fun and learn best when Experiences are built on interests, but we also think you will have more fun, too, because you will be rewarded by the child's enthusiasm for the Experiences selected just for her.

Selecting Experiences that Build on Development

So, most agree that development is an amazing wonder to behold. New abilities emerge daily among infants and toddlers. If adults select Experiences for children that allow them to practice new developments, children will grow and thrive. It is typical for children to like to practice new developments. As we noted in Chapter 1, babies so like to practice what they are developing that they have *function lust*—a love of functioning. Do you notice that when babies are learning to crawl, they want to crawl and crawl and crawl? It is the same with other developmental experiences. So, *Beautiful Beginnings* directs teachers', caregivers', and parents' attention to children's emerging developmental skills and suggests Experiences based on these strides. Again, adults who work with children may find the Overview Goals Charts helpful in suggesting things to look for and the sequence in which new developments typically appear among infants and toddlers. It is important to see the "buds" of a new development before deciding if it is appropriate for a planned *Beautiful Beginnings* Experience. If a baby has never babbled, it is not appropriate to select an Experience to teach words. Every new development depends on the building blocks being in place. This is one reason why the child's interest is a good basis for selecting an Experience. If interest is present, it often means the child is becoming developmentally ready.

Selecting Experiences Based on Needs or Concerns

For the most part, we recommend that teachers, caregivers, and parents select Experiences based on each child's interests and budding developments. However, there are some Experiences that children may not show interest in but that are good for them. For example, some young babies do not like to be positioned on their tummies for floor play. Yet, infants do increase back, shoulder, neck, and arm muscle strength when they have some play in this position. Thus, we do recommend sensitive selection of some Experiences in which infants may not show interest. In addition, some children who are vulnerable require more intensive stimulation in certain areas.

Selecting Experiences based on needs and concerns may not capitalize on a child's natural enthusiasm, so these Experiences must be approached with particular sensitivity and creativity and balanced with Experiences that build on positive interests.

In order to determine needs and concerns related to each child to guide Experience selection, teachers, caregivers, and home visitors may want to use an assessment or screener. An Experience could be selected following a "considered to be in need of follow-up" rating by the ASQ or *Ages & Stages Questionnaires®: Social Emotional* (ASQ:SE; Squires, Bricker, & Twombly, 2001) or another screener. It is possible that the reason the child scored in the low range is because critical experiences may be lacking. *Beautiful Beginnings* suggests Experiences be selected to enhance an area of concern. Selecting these Experiences should never replace referral to an appropriate early intervention program if this is deemed necessary, however.

Staff in many programs will select two or three new Goals/Experiences each time period for each child (whether monthly, bi-weekly, or weekly). For purposes of discussion, imagine that for one child, three Experiences are chosen for a 1-month period. If this is the plan, we recommend that at least one be based on the child's interests or strengths, one on new developments, and one on a concern. If the child is developing typically, select all of the Experiences based on interests, strengths, or new development. For children at-risk, such as children from very low-income families, one Experience should always be in the area of communication because of the tendency for such children to be delayed in this area (Hart & Risley, 1995). The Selecting Experiences checklist provided here is a helpful review when teachers, caregivers, and parents select goals.

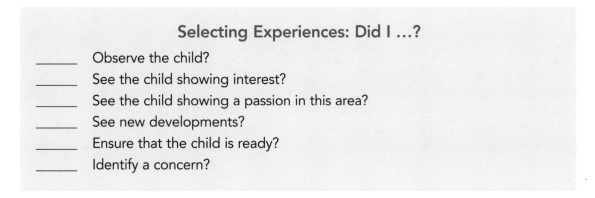

Selecting Experiences: Did I ...?

_____	Observe the child?
_____	See the child showing interest?
_____	See the child showing a passion in this area?
_____	See new developments?
_____	Ensure that the child is ready?
_____	Identify a concern?

Getting Organized

Imagine that three Goals/Experiences have now been selected for the coming month for a child. How do we get organized? Goals Sheets and stickers have been designed for *Beautiful Beginnings* to help teachers, caregivers, and parents stay organized and keep the plan for the coming period uppermost in a fun and gentle way. If you are planning for several children or have many other things competing for your attention, it can be challenging to remember all of the plans. These approaches may help you or the parents you work with to keep the plan in mind.

Using Goals Sheets

Goals Sheets are a reminder for teachers and parents of the plan for the month. They may be reduced and the smaller version put in a visible place, such as on a refrigerator. A master copy is on the *Beautiful Beginnings* CD-ROM and may be reproduced. In addition, Figure 3.1

Goals Sheet

Child's name: _Joey Smith_   Age: _25 months_

Goals: _____ Dates: (From) _4/1/06_ (To) _4/30/06_

1.
┌──────────────┐
│   │
│ Using Jars │
│ and Lids   │   _Fine Motor_____ # _6_
│   │
└──────────────┘
   (Activity)   (Area)   (Number)

2.
┌──────────────┐
│   │
│   │
│   │
│   │   _____ # _____
│   │
└──────────────┘
   (Activity)   (Area)   (Number)

3.
┌──────────────┐
│   │
│   │
│   │
│   │   _____ # _____
│   │
└──────────────┘
   (Activity)   (Area)   (Number)

Follow Up (Date, What happened?)

1. **4/12/06** Joey was not interested in this activity today.
   4/29/06 Today Joey loved helping me take the lid off the peanut
   butter jar at snacktime.

2.

3.

Comments:

Joey may need a little more practice before he is able to remove lids
consistently.

Parent /Caregiver Signature: _Jane Smith_   Date: _5/3/06_

Figure 3.1   A sample Goals Sheet completed for a child in the 24–30 months age group.

Goals Sheet

Child's name:_____ Age:_____

Goals: _____ Dates: (From) _____ (To)_____

1.
   [   ]
   (Activity)   _____ # _____
                              (Area)   (Number)

2.
   [   ]
   (Activity)   _____ # _____
                              (Area)   (Number)

3.
   [   ]
   (Activity)   _____ # _____
                              (Area)   (Number)

Follow Up (Date, What happened?)

1.

2.

3.

Comments:

Parent /Caregiver Signature: _____ Date: _____

provides an example of one that has been partially completed, and is followed by a blank Goals Sheet.

Using Stickers as Reminders

Many teachers, caregivers, and parents enjoy using stickers on their Goals Sheets to remind them of the plan for the designated time period. One set of six sticker sheets matching the Overview Goals Charts is included at the back of the book. Individual stickers may be peeled off and placed on printed copies of the Goals Sheets. Additional sets of stickers are available for purchase from Paul H. Brookes Publishing Co. (see p. iv for ordering information).

Using Materials

Preparing Materials

It is important to have all of the materials on hand before beginning. A list of materials to have on hand, grouped by age range, is provided on pages 43–48. Keep in mind that many of the same materials occur across age ranges and you may already have many of these things on hand. It is also critical to always use attractive, clean, and complete materials. For example, only give children complete puzzles with all of the pieces. This allows the child to experience a sense of completion and pride when putting the puzzle together. Have materials organized with everything in its own place. This provides a model of order in the environment with children and allows you to give the child your undivided attention.

Each of the processes of acquiring, storing, and presenting materials from the *Beautiful Beginnings* curriculum offers teachers opportunities for creative expression. Here, we offer suggestions for each of these uses of materials in a center-based or family child care setting.

Acquiring Materials

We strongly recommend acquiring at least one set of all of the materials suggested in the Materials List. Although this involves an initial investment, most recommended materials are fairly basic. We recommend programs' purchasing water tables for every room, solid cause-and-effect toys, and all of the other items in the materials list for the ages of children served in the program. It will be difficult for teachers to implement the curriculum if they cannot select freely from the full selection as seen on the Materials List.

Many of the materials will need to be created from found and individually purchased materials. For example, scooping activities require finding different types of divided dishes and buckets. Often, very beautiful containers that are safe for infants and toddlers can be found. Gorgeous stainless steel scoops used with warm-toned wooden bowls offer a lovely experience with color and texture as well as the opportunity to learn to scoop. Other materials can be made easily from ingredients on hand; for example, here is a simple playdough recipe:

Homemade Playdough Recipe

Ingredients	*Instructions*
4 cups flour	Cook over medium heat, stirring until stiff.
2 cups salt	Cool and knead. Store in a closed container.
2 tbsp. cream of tartar	
4 cups water (add food coloring if desired)	
2 tbsp. vegetable oil	

We have found that creative teachers continually are on the lookout for new fabrics, containers, trays, scoops, spoons, and pitchers from garage sales and auctions, and when traveling (materials acquired from other geographic areas can lend welcome diversity to the collection). Such exploration with materials pays off with infants and toddlers, for whom each new object offers a unique sensory experience! Certainly, materials used with infants and toddlers must always be inspected for parts that could break off or be considered unsanitary or unsafe for whatever reason. Paper and cardboard items should always be covered with lamination or contact paper and should be discarded or recovered when the coverage begins to come off.

Storing and Presenting *Beautiful Beginnings* Materials

The following are creative approaches we have observed providers using in storing and presenting *Beautiful Beginnings* materials.

- Create a storage closet for curriculum materials when not all materials will be placed on shelves in the classroom. Arrange materials for infants in baskets or see-through bags. Label each basket or bag. Some teachers create closet shelves that correspond to each area of the Overview Goals Charts and even color code materials for easy access.

- Create an orderly classroom environment. Set up learning centers emphasizing different areas of development (e.g., fine motor, gross motor, pretend). Select materials that correspond with planned Experiences. Give each material its own space and laminate a picture of the material on the shelf so that the child (and adult) remembers where materials belong. Always put materials in the same place each day.

- Do not mix a hodgepodge of toys and materials in toy boxes or bins. Do use bins for similar materials (e.g., for storing several round balls).

- When introducing toddlers to a new room or space, carefully select a few toys and materials and gradually add more materials as time goes on. This gives children the chance to learn about each material on the shelves and not become overstimulated.

- For toddlers, purchase one or several shelves that can be closed up or equip a shelf that can be turned to the wall, if materials have smaller parts that need to be secured. Then, you can open the shelves when you are able to give your undivided attention to the children and the use of the materials.

- Give children environmental cues for storing materials. Draw the shape of the material on the shelf or put a picture of what is to be hung on a hook beside the hook.

- Some programs provide carpet squares/rectangles or small tables to give children definition in doing their work/play.

- When presenting a new Experience to a child or group of children, plan time to demonstrate to the child how to locate the material in the classroom, and when finished, plan to show the child how to put the material back in its place in the orderly, predictable classroom environment. Some people are surprised to see how well toddlers are able to learn where to put and find objects in their environments. Of course, the quest for creating a predictable environment is an ongoing one, requiring gentle and relaxed support.

- Having a predictable environment allows a child to be in the lead in selecting materials throughout the day. Although some materials may have been put in the environment specifically for a particular child, others will enjoy them, too. The teacher can then observe if the focus child selects the targeted material and provide responsive guidance in a way that seems very natural within the context of the overall classroom experience.

Offering Experiences

Now for the most important part—presenting the Experience to the infant or toddler. Select a good time, when the setting is relatively free of distractions and the child is in a good mood, rested, fed, dry, and happy. One approach is to play with the child doing something you know he does often; then, when the moment seems right, introduce the new Experience. If you are working with a toddler, another approach is to show him what to do, slowly demonstrate what the Experience can be, and then let the child take over. In all cases, when playing with the baby or toddler, follow his lead and respond with warmth and support to sustain his interest. Watch carefully. Does he understand? Does he pick up on the Experience? (If not, put it up and try again in a few days or put the materials on an open play shelf and let the child approach them at his own pace.) Notice when you introduce the Experience if the child seems excited. (If so, you have selected well!)

Documenting the Child's Responses

The final step in the *Beautiful Beginnings* process is to document the child's response to the Experiences offered. Documentation will look different for organizations that have different purposes. Some intervention programs will probably want to document each specific encounter, noting the Goals/Experiences planned and documenting the follow-through for case files. Another early childhood program may choose to document by creating a portfolio or notebook. *Beautiful Beginnings* documentation can be adapted to fit within the documentation system that programs are already using or it can stand alone. We encourage people who are using *Beautiful Beginnings* to ask themselves: Do I need to keep a record of each Goal set, and if so, why? Do I need to document how the child responded when the Experience was introduced? Do I need to keep a record of how parents followed through? Do I need or want to keep a record of the child's growth and development related to the Experience? Answers to these questions will help you decide how to document progress.

Adapting *Beautiful Beginnings* to an Existing Record-Keeping System

We have found *Beautiful Beginnings* to complement and support most record-keeping systems easily; thus, teachers and caregivers can adapt *Beautiful Beginnings* documentation to their existing programs and record-keeping system. Most child development programs have documentation requirements. It is important to keep track of the wonderful story of each child's progress. Some write in a standard lesson plan book, and it works well to record weekly, biweekly, or monthly Goals/Experiences provided to children as well as other documentation. Other programs may adapt *Beautiful Beginnings* for a Management Information System entry, entering children's Goals/Experiences, follow-through, and responses into a computer that automatically combines the information with that from previous time periods and from other children.

Portfolios and Notebooks

If time allows, probably the most enjoyable, complete way to document is to create a portfolio or notebook. Using this system, teachers, home visitors, or parents enter Goals/Experiences on a Goals Sheet. They then record the child's responses to Experiences offered. The pages in the curriculum may also be printed from the *Beautiful Beginnings* CD-ROM and inserted into the portfolio.

Sometimes, adults administering the Experiences like to photograph the child during the Experience, to capture the unique responses of the child. Some teachers, home visitors, or parents who do not like to write often are able to write lovely narratives when they can describe what is in the picture. Thus, the curriculum can support adult literacy as well. A portfolio or notebook can be embellished; the possibilities are endless. Some teachers or parents like to add children's artwork, creating a memento of early development. When a child care teacher or home visitor is choosing to use a portfolio, it is important to include the parent in its creation. The teacher may take the lead in ensuring that the entries are made in the portfolio during each time period, but eventually both parent and caregiver can make entries. The portfolio, when complete (or too large to put anything else in), should be given to the parent to keep. Some parents regard a portfolio as a treasured baby book.

USING *BEAUTIFUL BEGINNINGS* IN VARIOUS SETTINGS

Beautiful Beginnings can be used in a variety of settings: in group child care such as center-based care; in homes, including home visiting programs or for parents' own use; in school-based teen parent programs; and in parenting education or group socialization programs. Even though we propose using *Beautiful Beginnings* in slightly different ways in each of these settings, the basic principles for using the curriculum do not change.

Using *Beautiful Beginnings* in Center-Based Settings

Beautiful Beginnings was designed as a guide for individualized experiences for children. In addition, *Beautiful Beginnings* can be adapted for planning group center-based experiences. Here's how:

1. Begin by thinking about the Goals/Experiences you have planned for an individual child.

2. Create a Group Goal/Experience for several children. This is an appropriate approach when children are of similar developmental levels and show similar interest in new experiences at about the same time.

3. Set up the Experience in a classroom with one or two children in mind, but make it available to all of the children at a similar developmental level.

4. Use *Beautiful Beginnings* to equip your classroom. Order the materials that support the curriculum. The Experiences in *Beautiful Beginnings* would best be set in a well-equipped classroom for children of these ages. Many of these materials—especially those for toddlers—could be set up on an ongoing or rotating basis in classroom learning centers. However, the magic is not in the material itself but in the encounter between the child,

teacher, caregiver or parent, and the material. Whether materials are made available in the classroom on an ongoing or rotating basis, these Experiences will "come alive" to a child when the materials and activities are discovered by or introduced to the child at a point well timed to match the emerging interest of the child.

Using *Beautiful Beginnings* in a Home Visiting Program

A number of home visiting programs, such as home-based Early Head Start programs, have adapted *Beautiful Beginnings* as their curriculum or in combination with other curricula (e.g., Parents as Teachers), which we describe later. They use *Beautiful Beginnings* by following the steps for selecting Experiences that we have outlined; however, an additional step is necessary when using the curriculum in home visiting programs. Home visitors not only choose Experiences with parents (as is often true in center programs) but they also demonstrate how to present the Experience. Often, home visitors will need to help the parent think about how to carry out the Experience during the week or period that follows. They will also need to help parents document their encounters with the child.

Home visitors may set Goals in conjunction with parents and introduce the Experience. They may leave a Goals Sheet to help the parent remember what has been selected. The checklist at the bottom of the page provides some additional suggestions of the types of information parents need to help continue the program.

As is true in classroom settings, Experiences used at home in the context of a home visiting program should flow naturally and easily, building on the child's natural energy. Some parents, if they are under high levels of stress or have some other vulnerability that affects their parenting, may find the Experiences neither natural nor easy, however. Thus, it will be important for the home visitor to model a relaxed approach, help parents select Experiences that are easy to do, and support parents in finding natural opportunities to make the Experiences fun. When implementing *Beautiful Beginnings* in a program for low-resource families, two additional processes require attention: blending *Beautiful Beginnings* with other purposes for home visiting and clarifying roles of multiple participants.

In early intervention home visiting programs for low-resource families, home visits often have multiple purposes. They may be used for family support as well as for enhancing child development. Early Head Start studies have shown that the more challenges and risks families have, the less home visitors are able to focus attention on child development and the more other needs of families may necessarily predominate (Raikes et al., under review). For example, it is

---

Checklist for Home Visitors

_____ Parent has input in selecting the new Experiences.

_____ Parent knows when to follow up.

_____ Parent knows how often to follow up.

_____ Parent has a written plan to follow.

_____ Plan is simple and easy to remember.

difficult to focus on introducing Experiences when the family is being evicted from housing. This tension may seem challenging when introducing a specific program such as *Beautiful Beginnings*. Yet, this study also shows that it is the children in these at-risk families who most lack stimulation and parenting support. In such programs, families often enjoy the specific reminders to focus on their child, such as using Goals Sheets with the stickers. It is important to keep the process as simple as possible and to keep a focus on the child while supporting parents more generally. The tensions are challenging to balance.

Second, it is important to keep in mind that in intervention programs, multiple people may be involved with a single family, and it is important to clarify roles in all areas and, specifically, around implementing the curriculum. For example, a program goal may be to support effective parenting among parents who themselves have not been well parented or who have multiple stressors that compete with parenting for their attention. One family may have a public health nurse, a social services provider, and a home visitor supporting them in reaching this goal. Because of the complexity of these issues and the relationships being established, it may take some time before all parties are able to carry out their roles to support a child's development, including potentially the successful use of the curriculum.

Materials for Using *Beautiful Beginnings* in Home Visiting Programs

Home visiting programs need a special approach to materials when using *Beautiful Beginnings*. Some home visiting programs may promote only using materials that parents can make in their homes. Although it is important to model using available materials, we believe that the materials that stimulate children's development are often not available to children from low-income families. It may be difficult for parents to acquire the materials, and some parents may not have the wherewithal to make toys and buy inexpensive materials. Thus, before embarking on *Beautiful Beginnings* in a home visiting program, the program should invest in the materials listed, as relevant to the ages of children served, in duplicate (one set for the home visitors and one set to use with parents or as a toy lending library). We believe that it is important that materials be left in the home for parents to use when implementing Experiences. In a weekly home visiting program, then, for the duration specified in a Goals Sheet, home visitors should bring materials the parent needs to carry out the Experiences and leave these materials in the home. If a program serves a large population, more sets of materials may need to be purchased, particularly of items needed for popular Experiences.

When Parents Use *Beautiful Beginnings* on Their Own

Many parents like to have a guide such as *Beautiful Beginnings* to keep their focus on their child's development and to give them ideas for fun things to do as their child grows and develops, not in the context of any home visiting or other program. Parents can use *Beautiful Beginnings* on their own successfully. We do not recommend *Beautiful Beginnings* as a way to accelerate children's natural development, but it is a very good way to stay in tune with children's development and to offer appropriately stimulating opportunities as development unfolds. If parents choose to follow a curriculum in the home, it is important for them to ask themselves these questions: Am I trying to make my child into a super baby, advanced in every way? Am I trying to avoid having to go to a pediatrician and other sources for developmental information?

These are not good reasons for adopting the *Beautiful Beginnings* curriculum. However, if parents can answer "yes" to the following questions, they are on the right track. Am I doing this because I want the baby to experience each stage of development fully? Am I doing it because it will help me become more aware of my baby's development? If so, these are good reasons for using *Beautiful Beginnings*, and we think these parents will enjoy it.

Many parents find joy and magic from looking for children's positive development and interests. This approach helps them keep a positive focus for parenting. Some busy parents find that *Beautiful Beginnings* helps them to create a special time with their infant or toddler or to individualize their activities if they have more than one young child.

We suggest that parents follow the steps for planning individual activities. Parents may also enjoy completing the Goals Sheets, or they may enjoy keeping a notebook or portfolio denoting the child's development and responses to Experiences.

Using *Beautiful Beginnings* in a School-Based Student-Parent Program

Some schools have used *Beautiful Beginnings* successfully as their curriculum in a child care program for teenage student-parents geared toward helping them learn more about child development. In addition to teaching these parents about development, *Beautiful Beginnings* also helps them achieve their required credits for graduation and gives them support in successfully drawing on the curriculum for their own child. Goals/Experiences are carried out in the same way as they are outlined on pages 22–25. Some school programs for teenage parents also assign an Experience to students to present to their baby or a group of babies in the classroom.

One program began creating "*Beautiful Beginnings* Take Home Bags" so that the student-parent could also do the Experiences at home with his or her infant or toddler. Each bag includes a copy of the Experience and all of the needed materials. The program encouraged observation and follow-through by adding a homework form that included questions such as, Did you observe any new developments in your child while doing this activity? What materials do you have around your house that you could use to create a similar activity to do with your child at home?

Using *Beautiful Beginnings* in Parenting Education or for Group Socializations

Beautiful Beginnings can be used as a curriculum for parenting education classes. It has also been used for parent–child sessions (in Early Head Start these are referred to as *Group Socializations*). When a number of children of similar ages and their parents attend parent–child sessions, a number of Experiences can be prepared in the form of learning centers. Parents can "rotate" with their babies through the learning centers, experiencing the materials and observing the children's reactions. This format has been particularly successful with parents of very young babies. It provides a form of support to these new parents and is a gentle way to help them discover the capabilities of their babies and to learn from other parents. The learning center approach also works very well with toddlers and their parents.

ADAPTING *BEAUTIFUL BEGINNINGS*

Beautiful Beginnings can be adapted to fit many different situations. When using the program, it is important to be sensitive to individual needs and concerns.

Using *Beautiful Beginnings* with Children with Special Needs

Almost all children can benefit from stimulating activities tailored to their developmental skills and needs. In most settings, *Beautiful Beginnings* can be used with children with and without disabilities. Here are some considerations to guide you in working with children with disabilities:

- If a child is functioning at a level less than his chronological age, begin with the child's functional age. For example, if a child is 2½ but is functioning at the developmental level of a child who is 11 months old, use the Experiences provided for the 6- to 12-month age range.

- If a parent is concerned about the chronological age difference, remind the parent that all children have relative strengths, but it is always most important to begin with the child and to find Experiences he can relate to.

- If the child has an individualized family service plan (IFSP), it is important to coordinate *Beautiful Beginnings* Experiences with the local Part C provider's plans. In some cases, it may be possible to use *Beautiful Beginnings* to help plan the child's IFSP.

- Some of the Experiences may not work exactly as they are described, depending on a child's disability. For example, in the Experience of naming the children in the room, for a child who has a visual impairment, you might encourage the other children to come and speak to the child one by one so that the child can learn to recognize their voices and then associate their voices with their names. You could also encourage the child to use her other senses, such as touch.

Taking Culture into Consideration

Children's backgrounds include a variety of experiences and traditions. Many of these are a result of important cultural variations that exist within our society. Because we know that even very young children absorb the lessons of cultural acceptability, these variations need to be honored and respected. In addition to generally valuing parental choices, this is important because children are absorbing lessons regarding cultural acceptability. For example, in some cultures, gazing in the mirror is not a valued or appropriate activity. It is important to make appropriate adaptations and respect the cultural differences in all children and families.

Cultural differences also exist in the extent to which parents of infants and toddlers see the value in intentional play. For example, some parents do not see the value of talking to their babies, or some parents may value storytelling but not reading books to a very small child. In a way that is respectful of a parent's wishes, you might introduce a wordless book that is more consistent with the parent's familiarity with storytelling. Consider books and objects within the child and family's cultural repertoire.

Integrating *Beautiful Beginnings* into Other Frameworks and Curricula

Many programs consider several guides or use multiple assessments and curricula. *Beautiful Beginnings* can fit very well with other systems. Because of its specificity, *Beautiful Beginnings* supplements many other curricula that are broader in focus. Here, we describe how *Beautiful Beginnings* fits in conjunction with the ASQ, the Early Head Start/Head Start Outcomes system, and other curricula.

ASQ

Many programs complete the ASQ with parents on a regular basis. The ASQ is the *Ages & Stages Questionnaires®: A Parent-Completed, Child-Monitoring System, Second Edition* (Bricker et al., 1999). The ASQ helps parents to learn what to expect at each age. Many children are developing typically, but in some cases a child receives a rating indicating that the child is functioning below expectations for the child's age. In such cases, the rating can lead to selecting a *Beautiful Beginnings* Goal/Experience that will ensure needed developmental opportunities. Some programs have also used the ASQ in selecting *Beautiful Beginnings* activities for a group of children. In reviewing the ASQ ratings for their entire group of children, some programs look for common areas children might benefit from, and then follow the *Beautiful Beginnings* steps as outlined previously for choosing a Group Goal/Experience.

Early Head Start Outcomes

Beautiful Beginnings is used in several Early Head Start programs. Outcomes for infants and toddlers as identified in Early Head Start Performance Measures (Administration for Children and Families, 2003) are coordinated with *Beautiful Beginnings* in Table 3.1. In addition, *Beautiful Beginnings* is conceptually consistent with the *Goals, Experiences, Roles, Modeling, and Sound Child Development Principles* (GERMS) model of curriculum required by the Head Start Performance Standards (U.S. Department of Health and Human Services, 1996). Similar to GERMS, a key component of *Beautiful Beginnings* is to ensure individualized goals for each child with clear parental input into the selection of the learning experience.

Other Curricula

Programs may already be using other fine curricula and approaches. *Beautiful Beginnings* can be and is being integrated very easily with curricula such as High/Scope (Post & Hohmann, 2000) and the Creative Curriculum (Dombro, Colker, & Dodge, 1997). Many curricula and approaches have fundamental child development principles in common with *Beautiful Beginnings* and can be readily integrated with one another. In correlating the High/Scope Key Child Observation Record (COR) with *Beautiful Beginnings*, one program found it very easy to align the two programs and welcomed the wide range of age-specific experiences *Beautiful Beginnings* added to their High/Scope based program (see Table 3.1).

Table 3.1. Comparison of developmental headings* used in various early childhood curricula

Ages & Stages Questionnaires® (ASQ)	Beautiful Beginnings	Early Head Start	High/Scope Key Child Observation Record (COR)
Communication	Communication	Communication, Language and Emergent Literacy Skills	Communication and Language
Gross Motor	Gross Motor	Physical Health and Development	Movement
Fine Motor	Fine Motor	Physical Health and Development	Movement Exploration and Early Logic
Problem Solving	Intellectual Discovery	General Cognitive Skills Positive Approaches Toward Learning Including Improved Attention Skills	Communication and Language Exploration and Early Logic
Personal/Social	Social	Social Behavior, Emotion Regulation and Emotional Well-Being Positive Approaches Toward Learning, Including Improved Attention Skills	Social Relations Sense of Self
	Self-Help	Positive Approaches Toward Learning, Including Improved Attention Skills	Sense of Self
	Pretend	Social Behavior, Emotion Regulation and Emotional Well-Being	Creative Expression Social Relations

*Some headings are listed more than once, if appropriate.

In Early Head Start home-based programs, *Beautiful Beginnings* has been successfully used in conjunction with the Parents as Teachers (PAT) approach as well as with the ASQ. In such cases, programs follow the general timeline and educational parenting materials from PAT, assess children periodically using ASQ, and set Goals and offer Experiences to children from *Beautiful Beginnings*. These programs have reported that the three approaches complement one another well.

You now have the framework for implementing *Beautiful Beginnings* in your particular setting with individual children, and it is time to put it into practice. The Goals/Experiences follow. We invite you to have fun with them and to experience the wonder of infant and toddler development.

Final Reminders for Using *Beautiful Beginnings*

Have fun!

Select Experiences that build on children's strengths and natural interests.

Introduce Experiences in synchronous, rhythmic ways.

Capitalize on caregiving routines and gentle play periods.

Experience the wonder of infant development.

Allow yourself to establish a rhythm of watching, noting strengths and interests, selecting experiences, and following through.

Find a system that helps you remember your plan.

Keep a record of the amazing events of the infant–toddler years.

Bibliography

REFERENCES

Administration for Children and Families. (2003). *Program performance measures for Head Start programs Serving Infants and Toddlers*. Washington, DC: U.S. Department of Health and Human Services.

Acredolo, L., & Goodwyn, S. (with Abrams, D.) (2002). *How to talk with your baby before your baby can talk*. New York: McGraw-Hill.

Bricker, D., & Squires, J. (with Mounts, L., Potter, L, Nickel, R. Twombly, E., & Farrell, J.) (1999). *Ages & Stages Questionnaires (ASQ)®: A Parent-Completed, Child Monitoring System (2nd ed.)*. Baltimore: Paul H. Brookes Publbishing Co.

Carey, W.B., & McDevitt (1978). Revision of the Infant Temperament Questionnaire. *Pediatrics, 61,* 735–739.

Dombro, A., Colker, L., & Dodge, D. (1997). *The creative curriculum for infants and toddlers*. Washington, DC: Teaching Strategies.

Gopnick, Meltzoff, & and Kuhl (2001). *The scientist in the crib: What early learning tells us about the mind*. New York: HarperCollins.

Greenspan, S., & Greenspan, N.T. (1989). *First feelings: Milestones in the emotional development of your baby and child*. New York: Penguin Books.

Hart, B. & Risley, T.R. (1995). *Meaningful differences in the everyday experience of young American children*. Baltimore: Paul H. Brookes Publishing Co.

Hunt, J.M. (1961). *Intelligence and experience*. New York: John Wiley & Sons.

Jusczyk, P.W. (1997). *The discovery of spoken language*. Cambridge, MA: MIT Press.

Lally, R. (2000, March). "Infants have their own curriculum: A responsive approach to curriculum planning for infants and toddlers." *Head Start Bulletin, 67.*

Post, J., & Hohmann, M., (2000). *Tender care and early learning*. Ypsilanti, MI: High/Scope Educational Research Foundation.

Raikes, H., Green, B., Atwater, J., Kisker, E., Constantine, J., & Chazan-Cohen, R. (Under review). *Involvement in Early Head Start home visiting services: Demographic predictors and relations to child and parent outcomes.*

Shonkoff, J., & Phillips, D. (2000). *Neurons to neighborhoods: The science of early development*. Washington, DC: The National Research Council.

Squires, J., Bricker, D., & Twombly, E. (with Yockelson, S., Schoen Davis, M., & Kim, Y). (2001). *Ages & Stages Questionnaires: Social-Emotional (ASQ:SE)*. Baltimore: Paul H. Brookes Publishing Co.

Thomas, A., Chess, S., & Birch, H. (1968). *Temperament and behavior disorders in children*. New York: New York University Press.

U.S. Department of Health and Human Services, Administration for Children and Families. (1996). Head Start program: Final rule. *Federal Register, 61,* 215.

Vandewater, E.A., Bickham, D.S., Lee, J.H., Cummings, H.M., Wartella, E.A., Rideout, V.J. (2005). When the television is always on: Heavy television exposure and young children's development. *American Behavioral Scientist, 48*(5), 562–577.

White, B.M (1975). *The first three years of life*. New York: Simon & Schuster.

Wright, B.F. (illus.) (1916). *The real Mother Goose*. Chicago: Rand McNally & Co.

Wright, J.C., Huston, A.C., Murphy, K.C., St. Peters, M., Piñon, M., Scantlin, R., & Kotler, J. (2001). The relations of early television viewing to school readiness and vocabulary of children from low-income families: The Early Window Project. *Child Development 72,* 1347–1366.

CHILDREN'S BOOKS

Acredolo, L., & Gentier, P. (2002). *Baby signs.* New York: McGraw-Hill.

Acredolo, L., & Gentier, P. (2002). *Baby signs for mealtime.* New York: Harper Festival.

Acredolo, L., & Gentier, P. (2002). *Los Gestos del Bebe* [Baby Signs in Spanish]. Barcelona: Ediciones Oniro.

Acredolo, L., & Gentier, P. (2002). *My first baby signs* (Baby Signs). New York: Harper Academic.

Acredolo, L., & Gentier, P. (2003). *Baby signs for animals.* New York: Harper Festival.

Acredolo, L., & Gentier, P. (2003). *Baby signs for bedtime.* New York: Harper Festival.

Brown, M.W. (1947). *Goodnight moon.* New York: Harper Collins Publishers.

Carle, E., & Martin, B., Jr. (1992). *Brown bear, brown bear, what do you see?* New York: Henry Holt & Co.

Dubov, C., & Schneider, J. (1986). *Aleksandra: Where are your toes?* Boston: St. Martin's Press.

Elhert, L. (1989). *Color zoo.* New York: Harper Collins.

Hill, E. (1980). *Where's Spot?* New York: Putnam Juvenile..

Hoban, T. (1986). *Panda panda.* New York: Greenwillow Books.

Hoban, T. (1993). *Black on white.* New York: Greenwillow Books.

Katz, K. (2003). *Where is baby's belly button?* New York: Simon and Schuster Children's Publishing Division.

Kunhardt, D. (2001). *Pat the bunny.* New York: Golden Books.

Miller, M. (1998). *Baby faces.* New York: Simon & Schuster.

Murphy, Chuck (2001). *Slide 'n' seek colors.* New York: Little Simon.

Murphy, Chuck (2001). *Slide 'n' seek shapes.* New York: Little Simon.

Oxenbury, H. (1995). *I can.* Cambridge, MA: Candlewick Press.

Oxenbury, H. (1998). *Baby faces.* New York: Little Simon.

Price, M. (1989). *My mommy.* New York: Knopf Books for Young Readers.

Roth, H. (1986). *Babies love a goodnight hug.* New York: Price Stern Sloan.

Scarry, R. (1979). *Richard Scarry's best first book ever.* New York: Random House Children's Books.

Scarry, R. (1980). *Richard Scarry's best word book ever.* Racine, WI: Golden Press.

CHILDREN'S MUSIC

Children's music is available in abundance from many sources. Libraries offer CDs and audiotapes of recorded songs and books that can be loaned out. Centers, child care providers, and parents may want to contact their local library to see if they have a bookmobile that can visit, and if so, a request can be made to include some of these recordings.

The following are some Internet sources:

Children's Music Web Sites

http://advancedbrain.com/
Advanced Brain Technologies; producers of products based on the most current research on the brain. Offers music products such as Music for Babies (1998–2004).

http://www.bestchildrensmusic.com
Offers parents a wide variety of musical selections for children—from orchestral to poetry set to music.

http://www.childrensmusic.org
Filled with links for parents and children alike to explore various types of music as well as music activities.

http://www.creatingmusic.com
Offers opportunities for children to play music games and puzzles and to compose their own music. This site offers a sample of what is include on the full CD-ROM package, available for purchase.

http://www.ellajenkins.com/
Features Ella Jenkins, Grammy-winning songwriter and producer of childrlen's songs featuring multicultural themes, including Ella's Favorite Singable Songs for Children.

http://www.happalmer.com/
Features Hap Palmer, an innovator in using music to teach children to use their imaginations.

http://www.jackiesilberg.com
Miss Jackie Music Company; dedicated to providing excellent children's music and early child-hood teaching tools.

http://www.kidsongs.com
An online store for the children's music series *Kidsongs.*

http://www.learningstationmusic.com
An online store for *The Learning Station* music and is geared toward children 6 years old and younger. Songs focus on dancing, physical education, and education.

http://www.mykidstunes.com
Sells a variety of music for children, including travel sing-along songs and foreign language music.

http://pbskids.org/rogers/songlist
A listing (with accompanying sound files and lyrics) of songs featured on the popular children's show *Mr. Rogers' Neighborhood.*

http://putamayokinds.com
Helps children explore and celebrate the cultures of the world through music.

http://www.raffisongs.com
The source for learning about Raffi, one of the most popular writers of children's songs, and his career, music, and products.

http://www.sesameworkshop.org/sesamestreet/music/
Music from *Sesame Street.*

http://www.songsforteaching.com
Invaluable for teachers who want to supplement their lessons with educational music.

http://store.musicforlittlepeople.com/aure.html
Sells a wide variety of genres, including lullabies and storytelling.

http://www.theteachersguide.com/ChildrensSongs.htm
Provides lyrics as well as midi files for popular children's songs.

http://www.wellbaskets.com/musicforbabies.html
Sells gift baskets with music CDs geared toward developing infants' brain development.

Materials and Equipment List

The following is a list of materials for each age group assembled from the materials listed in each Experience. Please note that although this list appears long, many items are repeated across age groups. Many of the materials are on hand already in most centers, and many materials such as playdough and beanbags can be made at little cost.

0–6 MONTHS	6–12 MONTHS	12–18 MONTHS	18–24 MONTHS	24–30 MONTHS	30–36 MONTHS
Audiotapes and/or CDs (classical, lullabies, heart sounds, nature sounds)	Activity rocker	Audiotapes and/or CDs (fun songs, nursery rhymes)	Adhesive tape	Adhesive tape	Adhesive tape
Audiotape and/or CD player	Adhesive tape	Audiotape and/or CD player	Audiotapes and/or CDs (songs, nursery rhymes and stories)	Aprons	Animal costumes and props
Balls (beach ball in contrasting colors)	Animals (stuffed)	Alarm clock	Audiotape and/or CD player	Art materials	Aprons
Bell (chime, or other noisemaker)	Audiotapes and/or CDs (fun songs)	Balance beam, low	Art aprons or smocks	Audiotapes and/or CDs	Art materials
Bells (attached to a wristband)	Audiotape and/or CD player	Balls, various sizes	Balance beam or old tires	Audiotape and/or CD player	Audiotapes and/or CDs
Blankets (large receiving)	Balls (all types and sizes, including beach balls)	Baskets	Balls (e.g., beach, puff, tennis)	Balls (various sizes and shapes)	Audiotape and/or CD player
Blocks (small)	Barrels (carpet-covered)	Bathtub	Barrels (carpet-covered)	Baskets and trays	Balls, various
Bolster	Beans or pebbles	Beanbags	Baskets and trays	Beads (large, wooden, colored)	Baskets
Books (chunky, fabric, vinyl, cloth, and plastic)	Beanbags (small, hand-sized)	Blankets of various types	Basin or water table (stable)	Beanbags	Baster
Bouncer	Bibs	Blocks (Duplo, small, medium)	Beads (large, with plastic-tipped strings)	Boxes (various)	Beads (small)
Containers of various sizes (e.g., empty diaper wipes container, margarine tubs, small boxes)	Blanket	Boards (2 feet by four feet wide)	Blankets	Bat (lightweight)	Beanbags
Cotton balls	Blocks (various sizes, some identical)	Books (board, including books and those that label nouns and verbs)	Blocks (alphabet, Duplo, small)	Blocks (foam, wooden)	Blindfold
Crawl-along (optional)	Body parts illustration (laminated)	Bowls (plastic, with lids)	Books (including those with nursery rhymes, with simple storylines)	Basin	Blocks (various)
Cups (at least 3 identical and 1 different)	Books (board, with simple illustrations those that introduce textures and early learning concepts)	Boxes (small and large, including huge refrigerator box)	Bottle paints	Boards (various)	Books
Diapers	Bouncer (stand-alone or doorway)	Broom	Boxes of various sizes	Books (including nursery rhymes)	Boxes (various)
Dolls	Boxes (large with small drawers, lined with textured fabrics)	Bubbles and bubble blower	Broom (child-sized)	Buckets	Broom and dustpan
Dowel rod	Bubbles and bubble blower	Cardboard (large enough to act as a barrier)	Buckets (divided)	Can	Brush (small)
Drinking straw	Clothes (easy to unsnap or pull off, e.g., hats or mittens)	Cars and trucks (small, for rolling down a tube, other small, plastic)	Cards (laminated with matching pictures or 2 of a kind pictures of objects toddler knows)	Cards (laminated, with pictures of object shapes outlined)	Chalk
Easy-to-grasp toys of different textures and types		Chalk (jumbo)	Cars and trucks (small, plastic)	Chair	Cheerios
Exercise roll, or pillow, or blanket/towel to roll up				Colored objects	Clothing (e.g., jackets, pants, socks, hats, socks)
				Containers with lids	Colored objects
				Cookie cutters	Containers (various, including divided)
				Crayons	Cotton balls
				Doll accessories	Crayons
				Doll (baby)	Cubbies for storing children's things

Column 1

Fabrics (different textures, large enough to lay baby on, swatches that baby can hold and/or beanbags)
Hand lotion or massage oil
Head set or earphones for tape or CD player (optional)
Highchair with tray
Jars (small)
Laundry basket or box
Nonfabric materials of different textures (e.g., sandpaper)
Mirrors (large and small)
Mobiles (including one that is black and white, wind-up)
Objects (manipulatives, two the same, small, safe items to pick up using thumb and finger)
Oils (massage, baby, vegetable, scented)
Outlines of common objects (for finger tracing)
Pad
Pans (baking)
Paper in different colors
Penlight

Column 2

Comb
Containers (things that toys can be put into with corresponding lids)
Contact paper (clear)
Cups (various types, including ones with easy-to-grasp handles, nesting cups)
Crayons (oversized)
Dish and spoon for self-feeding
Dowel rod
Fabrics (various textures and colors)
Finger foods (e.g., cooked peas, Cheerios, crackers)
Flowers
Foam-covered shapes or pillows (of all types for baby to crawl over)
Foil
Functional objects (simple, e.g., small hairbrush, bell, comb, spoon, telephone, steering wheel)
Hairbrush
Laundry basket
Magazine pages
Match box
Milk cartons (covered with contact paper, 4 in 2 different colors)
Muffin tin

Column 3

Chalkboard (large)
Clothing (e.g., socks and easy-to-pull-up pants, big shirts)
Contact paper (clear)
Containers of all kinds (e.g., for holding beans, macaroni, and sand)
Container lids
Cot
Cotton balls
Crayons (jumbo)
Cups (drinking, nesting, sippy)
Doll
Door bell
Eating utensils (child safe)
Flashlight
Functional objects (e.g., hairbrush and comb, broom and dustpan, purse, sponge, hat, telephone, pan and spoon)
Golf tees
Jars (with easy-to-remove lids, unbreakable, with scented materials
Hassocks
Ladder
Legos
Macaroni
Mat

Column 4

Cart, wagon, or stroller (optional)
Clothes and accessories (including hat, coat, sweater, socks, purses)
Clothespins
Colorforms (or Colorforms-type material in sticky plastic)
Containers of various types
Corn to shell
Cups or glasses (some that match)
Diapers
Dishes (unbreakable, divided with high sides, pet feeding)
Dishwashing materials
Doll (small) and rocker
Dress-up clothing (e.g., easy-to-take-off hats, coats, purses)
Fingerpaints
Foam shapes
Funnels
Glue (white, glue stick)
Hand- and face-washing set up
House (with a door such as a Little Tykes house or large box with door)
Inner tube or safety bouncer
Jars (unbreakable, with matching lids)

Column 5

Doll bed
Easel
Easel clips
Felt
Golf tees
Glue or paste
Hammer (plastic)
Hoops (Hula- and wooden)
Jars (with easy-to-screw-on lids)
Labels (for areas and objects in room)
Markers (various colors, including black)
Mirrors
Muffin tin
Nesting cups or barrels
Nursery rhymes
Objects (opposites, small)
Paints
Paintbrushes
Paper (various types, e.g., for easel, construction)
Pegboard (plastic)
Photographs (some in duplicate)
Pictures of toys and objects
Placemats
Plastic sheet

Column 6

Cups (plastic)
Envelopes
Eye dropper
Food coloring
Food items (e.g., bread, crackers, tortillas, peanut butter, bananas)
Functional objects
Handkerchiefs with sewn folding lines
Hairbrush
Jungle gym or hanging bar
Kite
Knife (butter)
Lotto boards (laminated)
Musical instruments
Napkins
Noise makers (i.e., variety of objects that make sounds)
Paints
Paintbrushes
Paint cups
Paper (various types)
Pencils
Pitcher
Plates
Puzzle rack
Puzzles (8-piece)
Pictures of children
Pitcher

0–6 MONTHS	6–12 MONTHS	12–18 MONTHS	18–24 MONTHS	24–30 MONTHS	30–36 MONTHS
Pictures (various, including 8-inch x 10-inch black-and-white illustrations of checkerboards, faces, triangles, heavy letters and numbers)	Music/Noisemakers (e.g., wind chimes, clocks, squeeze toys, sticks)	Materials to wrap objects (including fabric, fabric bags)	Jugs (milk or bleach)	Pretend toys (animal-related, e.g., fence, barn, zoo cages; dress-up clothes, e.g., hats, scarves, mittens, boots; tea party, e.g., tray, small cups, pitcher, small plates, table, chairs, plastic foods; transportation-related, e.g., cars, trucks, airplanes, boats)	Plate (utensils, place-mats, napkins)
Pillows (firm)	Objects (small enough to pick up such as uncooked oatmeal, punched paper holes, peas)	Mirror	Ladder (with wide spaces between rungs)		Pretend items (animals, e.g., masks, props; cash register, money; doctor's office; grocery store, e.g., food, cart; house, e.g., play household items; small people play, e.g., Fisher Price characters; post office, e.g., paper, mailbox, stamps)
Prints and pictures (black and white, laminated)		Muffin tin	Macaron (uncooked)		
Puppets	Paper (butcher, construction, contact)	Musical instruments (shakers including home-made ones using beans and rice sealed in containers)	Markers (permanent)	Puzzle rack	Puppets, such as hand puppets
Rattles of different types	Pegboard		Mats (flat, wedge)	Puzzles (5-piece)	Rice, beans
Ribbons	Photographs (of familiar persons)	Objects (small, safe, to fit in holes cut in container lids)	Mirror	Ramp	Scoops
Rings (e.g., curtain)	Pictures (of people with distinct faces)	Paper (various types)	Muffin tin or ice cube tray	Rolling pin	Sequencing materials (e.g., tower with rings, nesting cups; Montessori pink tower; Montessori brown stair)
Socks and mittens (with faces sewn on them)	Pillow	Pegs (jumbo, Discovery, Lakeshore)	Necklace (safe, long and beaded)	Scarves	
Sponges	Pop beads	Photographs (of children and people in their lives)	Nesting cups, boxes, or towers	Scissors (safety)	
Spoons (wooden and eating, at least 3 identical)	Pots and pans (including pie pans)	Photograph albums	Objects that divide into two parts	Scoops	Seeds
	Puppets	Pillows	Objects for problem-solving task	Scrub brush	Sink or basin
Toys (black-and-white bear, toy on a string, toys that make a noise when hit, wind-up toys)	Puzzles (simple, with knobs)	Pinwheel	Objects in primary colors (matching containers)	Shapes	Soil
Towel (large, absorbent)	Sheet of plastic or Plexiglas	Playdough	Paintbrushes and buckets	Slide (playground)	Soap
Tray for water play (such as high chair tray)	Socks, stretch	Pop beads and toys with simple connectors	Paper (clear contact, shiny fingerpaint or butcher, small pieces such as punched dots, large easel)	Snap frame	Songbooks of children's songs
Wash cloth	Spoons	Pots and pans, bowls, muffin pans and other household objects		Soap (bar, liquid, or flakes)	Sponges
	Steering wheel	Pounding bench and hammer	Playdough (purchased or homemade)	Sponges	Step stool
	Steps (low)	Puzzle (Lakeshore balloon with knobs)	Parachute	Spray bottle	String
	String or ribbon	Ribbons		Squeegee	Tape (heavy, for marking floor)
	Swimming pool (small, or dishpan)	Rug or carpet squares		Step stool	Targets for beanbags
	Telephone (rotary)			String	
				Swings (playground)	
				Telephones (toy)	
				Towels	

Toys (action toys, including pull-toys, noisemakers, shape fitters; small toys that can be put in containers, e.g., spindle toys, attractive toys that baby will obtain with a tool; cause-and-effect toys, e.g., pop-up toys, sound center; identical toys, such as blocks or coasters)

Tunnel

Wagon

Sand

Scarves

Scents (e.g., lemon juice, oil of banana, perfume, baby oil)

Scoops, spoons, plastic shovels (of all types)

Shape sorter (round shape in round hole, circle, square and triangle)

Shelves or cabinet (for exploring all types of objects)

Sippy cups

Sponges

Stacking bunnies

Stairs

Stick

Straws

String

Styrofoam (thick)

Tape (adhesive, masking or other heavy tape)

Tires

Towels

Toys, (action, cause-and-effect, e.g., buzzer box, toys with levers and gears, flashlight, pop up, sound center with leverls and gears)

Trays (small)

Tube (long, that a ball or car can be rolled down)

Tubs (plastic, with lids)

Pretend items (kitchen items, e.g., stove, utensils, toy dishes, pots, and pans; tiny people play toys, e.g., Fisher Price characters; transportation, e.g., bus, airplane)

Puppets

Puzzles (including 1 with 2 halves)

Riding toys

Rocker (child-sized)

Sand, oatmeal, or rice

Shape sorters (of different types, such as 3-shape)

Scoops of different types

Soap

Spoons (easy to hold, large and small)

Steering wheel

Step stool

Stickers

Stuffed or soft toys (e.g., bear, doll)

Telephone

Tent

Tissues

Toilet chair

Towels

Trampoline (mini)

Undergarments (extra children's)

Utensils

Washcloth

Water table

Zipper frame

Tic-Tac-Toe board or other board with squares

Toilet or potty chair

Toilet paper

Tongs

Toothbrush

Toothpaste

Towels

Tricycle

Tent (small)

Toothbrush, toothpaste, rack for toothbrushes

Utensils

Wading pool

Water table

0–6 MONTHS	6–12 MONTHS	12–18 MONTHS	18–24 MONTHS	24–30 MONTHS	30–36 MONTHS
		Stairs Wading pool (or bathtub, water table) Swing (with a safety strap)	Toys (push-and-pull, such as shopping cart, walker, wagon, corn popper or mower, toys with strings, riding toys such as car, fire engine, tricycle) Tube or stiff plastic string (for stringing beads) Tweezers Wagon Walking rope Washcloths Water table (optional) Zipper frame		

Beautiful Beginnings Experiences

0–6 Months

Beautiful Beginnings: A Developmental Curriculum for Infants and Toddlers   0–6 MONTHS

	1	2	3	4	5	6	7	8
Communication	Responding to Voices and Music	Sharing First Conversations	Dancing	Talking to Get Attention	Turning to Hear	Understanding Words	Chanting	Sharing First Books
Gross Motor	Checking Reflexes	Exercising	Lying on Tummy and Looking Up	Balancing on a Bolster	Placing Weight on Feet	Rolling Over	Sitting	Preparing to Crawl
Fine Motor	Holding Objects in Fisted Hand	Swiping	Mouthing	Grasping Objects in Two Hands	Playing with Toes and Fingers	Shaking and Banging	Using Thumb and Fingers	Using Two Hands Separately
Intellectual	Looking	Moving Mobiles	Tracking	Understanding Permanence Through Spatial Relations	Developing Visual Preferences	Introducing Color	Imitating	Categorizing
Discovery	Using All of the Senses	Massaging	Feeling Textures	Blowing Through a Straw	Smelling Differnt Scents	Riding on a Blanket	Playing with Water	Playing with Textured Containers
Social	Understanding Individual Differences	Developing Synchrony	Imitating Facial Expressions	Looking in a Mirror	Laughing	First Games: Playing Peekaboo	Falling in Love	Holding out Arms

Responding to Voices and Music

1

Goal: For baby to respond to voices and to music.

Experience:

1. Talk slowly and with animation to the baby. Give her time to respond. Does she seem to be listening? Does she stop her activity? Does she look at you? Does she try to "talk back" by cooing or gurgling? If she does, converse with her in this manner and answer her with her own sounds. When you talk to the baby, watch for a specific response that indicates that she is listening.

2. Turn on music and enjoy listening to music together. You may find it interesting that most babies prefer classical music. Babies respond to music in individual ways. Some stop moving, others move more, some coo, and others go to sleep. (Some may even respond by crying if the music or the timing are not right.)

The baby can also experience music through headphones. Some audiologists recommend placing earphones on the bone behind the baby's ear. (Putting the earphones directly on the ear could injure tiny hair cells in the ear.) Turn on the music at a low to mid-low level, carefully monitoring the volume.

Materials: CD or audiotape player; small earphones; audiotapes of music such as classical music, lullabies, natural rhythms

Sharing First Conversations

2

Goal:

For the baby to "converse" with you (or herself).

Experience:

1. When you have the baby's attention, wait for her to make a sound. Imitate her sound. Pause.

2. When she makes another sound, imitate that one. Do this at least 5–10 times throughout the day.

3. Work toward a conversation in which she speaks, you imitate, she speaks, you imitate, and so forth several times. Soon you will be able to experience the back-and-forth quality in communicating with the baby. Turn taking with a young baby while she begins to learn about the back-and-forth patterns of human communication can be quite magical!

The baby may move away during one of her turns. This may mean that she is finished, or it may mean that she just needs time to rest. Wait to see if she is going to "come back" before you end the conversation.

Another activity that helps a baby attune herself to her own sounds is tape recording her cooing, babbling, and even crying. When she is in a conversational mood, play her sounds back to her and watch her reactions.

Materials:

Audiotape recorder, audiotapes

Dancing

Goal:

Experience:

For the baby to experience rhythms and dance.

If you love music and movement, you will communicate the happiness they bring you to the baby.

Play music with an easy rhythm. Hold the baby closely and dance with him. Sway from side to side, moving forward and backward. Turn and twist in time to the music.

Your movements will stimulate the sense organs deep within the baby's ears. The sensations he experiences with this activity will help him develop position sense and balance for when he sits and stands. If you hum, your chest vibrations will also stimulate the baby.

The baby is likely to respond with pleasure when dancing with you.

Materials:

CD player or audiotape recorder, CD or audiotape music with an easy dancing rhythm

Talking to Get Attention

4

Goal:

For the baby to learn that she can get your attention by "talking."

Experience:

Stand with the baby and another person. Talk in back-and-forth conversation with the baby. Then gently, not abruptly, begin to bring the other person into the conversation. Begin to talk back and forth with the other adult for a while. See if the baby coughs or makes a sound to bring attention to herself. As soon as she does, focus your attention back on her and talk to her again. She will learn this mature way of getting your attention.

How does the baby react after doing this exercise? If the baby does not seem to notice the change in conversation partners, wait a few weeks and try again. Be sure to try several times.

Watch for times when the baby coughs or vocalizes. When she does, answer her immediately. Soon she will learn that she can "call" you in this way.

Materials:

None

Turning to Hear

5

Goal:

For the baby to turn toward a sound. This experience helps the baby learn to coordinate two senses—hearing and seeing.

Experience:

1. When the baby is on the floor, move several feet away and off to one side of her head. Softly call her name. If she turns to look at you, laugh and smile and talk to her. Do the same from another angle. If she makes no attempt to turn toward you, say her name a little louder and move closer to her. Let her see you as you talk to her. Then try again from one side or the other. Notice if she is searching for you with her eyes even though she may not be turning her head in your direction yet.

2. Softly ring a bell at the baby's side. Does she turn? If the baby does not seem to respond to sound after repeated tries on different days, then the parents should discuss the baby's hearing with a physician.

Materials:

Small bell or chime

Understanding Words

Goal:

For the baby to begin to understand the meaning of words, gestures, or signs.

Experience:

When presenting toys and materials to the infant, label them. When offering the baby a cup, say, "This is a cup. Would you like this cup?" When you pick it up for her, say, "May I get your cup?" When offering two toys, say, "This is a cup and this is a ball," gesturing to emphasize the object as you say its name. Within a few weeks, ask her, "Where is the cup?" If she looks at it, say, "There's the cup."

Present the baby with high-contrast black-and-white outlines of common objects such as a ball, spoon, cup, or dog. Draw her finger around the outside of the line while labeling the picture. Do the same with a book with high-contrast outlines.

When sitting with the baby and another person whom the baby frequently sees, ask where the person is. This person should say something to get her attention. When she looks at him or her, acknowledge the person.

Some parents and providers may want to teach their children to use signs. Some excellent guides are available on this topic (Acredolo & Goodwyn, 2002). As with words, the first step is for baby to understand your signs. Start by using simple, basic signs such as for EAT, MOTHER, and MILK. Say each word (e.g., "Eat") at the same time that you sign.

Materials:

Common objects such as cups and balls, outlines of common objects for finger tracing, books with high-contrast outlines

7

Chanting

Goal:

For the baby to learn to play a vocalizing game. This teaches the baby how to play games of imitation with you, a process you can use to teach many more sounds and skills as she grows.

Experience:

1. When the baby is facing you, make a little chanting noise as you perhaps did as a child, flapping your hand over your mouth repeatedly while making an "ah-ah-ah-ah" noise.

2. Now, to teach the baby to do it, just say "ah-ah-ah-ah" and try to get her to imitate you. When she does, wave your hand in front of her mouth to make the chanting sound. If she does her part to make this sound, reward her with a great response. This is wonderful fun when it works.

Materials:

None

Sharing First Books

8

Goal:

For the baby to begin to develop a love of books.

Experience:

The pleasurable feeling of reading can begin very early. This experience helps to familiarize the baby with books as objects as well as a source of pleasure during reading time.

1. Sit with the baby during a relaxed quiet time and look at a book with very simple pictures. Talk about the pictures. Encourage her in whatever responses she makes, such as patting or looking. If the baby wants to mouth the book (and if it is made of safe, durable material such as plastic or cloth), let her do so. When you look at books together, gently work toward looking at the book and talking about it. Do not worry about finishing a book with a young baby.

2. Point out different pictures and sounds if appropriate (e.g., animals, cars, airplanes).

Materials:

Books made of chunky cardboard, vinyl, or cloth, with one picture per page (high-contrast pictures are best), wordless books

Checking Reflexes

Goal:

To elicit the baby's reflexes (some of which are temporary).

Experience:

1. **Hand grasp** (clenched-fist reflex): Lay the baby on her stomach. The baby's hands should touch the surface she is lying on, and they will probably remain fisted. Typically, this reflex is present until about 3 months.

2. **Asymmetrical tonic neck reflex** (ATNR, fencing position): Lay the baby on her back. Place one hand on her chest to stabilize her. While you gently turn her head to one side, watch her arms. Note that when her head is turned to the right, the left arm will flex and the right arm will straighten, and vice versa. Typically, this reflex is present until the baby is about 4 months old.

3. **Moro reflex** (arms up, hands open): Cradle the baby in one arm to support her head, back, and bottom. Place your other hand on her chest. Still cradling the baby, slightly lower the baby's head and body and then quickly return to the beginning position. Note if the baby brings her arms up and extends them with her hands open. Typically, this reflex is present until about 4 months.

4. **Rooting reflex** (sucking): Stroke the corners of the baby's mouth and upper or lower lip. Note if the baby turns her head toward you and tries to suck your finger. (This may not occur just after feeding.) The rooting reflex ends a couple of months after birth when the baby begins to turn her head voluntarily.

Materials:

None

Exercising

0–6
Months

Goal:

For the baby to exercise muscles and to enjoy movement.

Experience:

With the baby lying on his back, do these exercises in a gentle, slow, and supportive way. Make eye contact and talk softly. Never force, and stop if the baby does not seem to be enjoying the experience.

1. **Knee bends.** Hold onto the baby's calves. Push his legs to his chest, then straighten his legs. Repeat 8 times.

2. **Alternating knee bends.** Hold onto the baby's calves. Bend the left leg while straightening the right. Alternate. Repeat 8 times.

3. **Arm crosses.** While holding the baby's hands, cross his arms over his chest. Straighten the baby's arms at shoulder level. Repeat 8 times.

4. **Arm raises.** Take the baby's hands and lower his arms to his side, then raise them over his head. Repeat 8 times. Do again, this time alternating arms.

5. **Foot-to-hand stretch.** Bring the baby's right calf to his left hand. Straighten his foot and raise his hand over his head so he is now stretched out. Change sides. Repeat 4 times. This exercise enables the baby to move in a reciprocal way across two sides of his body, motions he uses again in crawling.

6. **Sit-ups.** Hold the baby's hands and slowly pull him to a sitting position. If necessary, support his head with one hand while holding his hands with your other hand. Return the baby to his back. Repeat 2–4 times.

Materials:

None

Lying on Tummy and Looking Up

Goal:

For the baby's back and neck muscles to develop and become stronger.

Experience:

1. Lay the baby on his tummy on a comfortable pad. Place toys and puppets at his eye level. If he does not seem to like this position (and some babies have a definite preference), put yourself at his level. Talk to him. Hold a puppet or toy at his eye level and encourage him to look at it. Make this a "fun" position for the baby to be in. Gradually increase the "tummy time" from one session to the next.

2. Place a mirror in front of the baby and encourage him to look at himself in the mirror.

3. Lay the baby on his tummy with his arms draped over a small exercise roll. Many babies love this position. This will immediately give him a new vista. Encourage him to hold his head up high by holding or placing an interesting toy above him to attract him.

4. Lay the baby on his tummy over a partially deflated, large beach ball, while steadying his trunk with your hands.

Note: *Watch closely during exercises 3 and 4 so the baby does not slip off the roll or ball.*

Materials:

Comfortable pad; exercise roll such as a small pillow or a rolled up blanket or towel; interesting toys and puppets; mirror; beach ball

Balancing on a Bolster

0–6 Months

Goal:

Experience:

Materials:

For the baby's balancing skills to develop further.

1. Place the baby on her tummy, lengthwise on a bolster (long pillow or cushion). With one hand on her hip, slowly roll the bolster to the right and then to the left. When your baby is accustomed to the motions, roll the bolster farther toward each side. Help her extend her arms to feel the floor and pause so she has a chance to feel each hand firmly on the floor. Be sure not to roll the bolster so far that her hand gets caught.

2. Do the same thing with just the baby's legs.

3. Now do the same thing with both the arms and the legs touching the floor.

4. Now, with the baby leaning over the bolster in a crosswise position, place an attractive toy such as a puppet by the bolster, and encourage the baby to reach for the toy as the bolster rolls in that direction. Say, "Can you reach the toy?"

Note: *Use your hands to balance the baby carefully so that she does not slip off the bolster.*

Bolster, toy

Placing Weight on Feet

5

Goal: For the baby to place weight on his feet.

Experience: The baby should gradually be able to put more of his weight on his feet when held in a standing position.

Sit down and stand the baby in your lap. Support him with your hands but encourage him to put his weight on his feet.

Place the baby in a bouncer that allows his feet to touch the floor. Many infants seem to like this position.

Note: *Never leave a child unsupervised in a bouncer.*

Materials: Bouncer

Rolling Over

0–6
Months

Goal:

For the baby to experience rolling from front to back or back to front.

Experience:

Some babies roll over front to back first and others go back to front first. You can use leg crossover exercises with a baby to strengthen the torso muscles needed for rolling.

1. **Front to back:** Position the baby on her tummy. Slowly draw a toy across her field of vision from one side to the other. Then move the toy up and down so she has to look over her shoulder to follow it. In doing so, many babies will roll over to keep the toy in view.

    Place the baby on her tummy again. Now flex the baby's left knee and fold her right arm under her chest. A turn from front to back may follow automatically.

2. **Back to front:** Lay the baby on her back. Now flex the left hip and raise her left buttock, stretch her right arm out and upward, and then roll her toward the right and onto her tummy.

Rolling over is a skill that infants who are developing typically may master as early as 1 month or as late as 6 months. Don't become impatient and worry if a baby doesn't roll right away. Have fun with the exercises.

Materials:

None

7

Sitting

Goal: For the baby to progress toward sitting upright.

Experience: Sit on the floor for a short time with the baby sitting between your legs. Your presence gives the baby a safe feeling, and you can catch him if he begins to waver in this position.

After the baby can sit fairly well on his own but is still not totally ready for independent sitting, prop him up with firm pillows. Put some interesting toys around him to make sitting more fun.

Another way to support a baby is to line a firm box or laundry basket with pillows in such a manner that the baby is supported while sitting.

Note: *Be sure to stay close by with these activities.*

Materials: Firm pillows, box or laundry basket, toys

Preparing to Crawl

8

Goal:

For the baby to experience more freedom of movement in preparation for crawling.

Experience:

Put the baby on a firm pillow or bolster and encourage her to scoot over it. This will teach the baby how it feels to have her trunk lifted off of the floor.

Place the baby on a smooth floor (laying face down or on her hands and knees), and put your hand against her feet when she pulls them up under her. When she extends her legs, she will slide forward.

Let the baby crawl over your legs when you are sitting on the floor. Many infants can easily scoot this way.

Materials:

Pillow or bolster

Holding Objects in Fisted Hand

Goal:

For the baby to grasp an object in her hand.

Experience:

1. When the baby is alert, put a small, easy-to-grasp rattle in her hand. (If her hand is tightly fisted, relax her hand by inserting a finger or two and by gently massaging inward toward the palm.)

2. After you put the rattle in her hand, her natural reflex will cause her to grip it, but soon she will probably drop it. When she does, put the rattle back in her hand a few times.

Materials:

Small rattle

0–6
Months

Swiping

Goal:

For the baby to experience reaching for objects.

Experience:

Place a dowel rod across the baby's crib or play space, tying it securely at both ends. Suspend two items from the rod so that when the baby waves her hands she will hit the toys. If the baby does not try to hit the items, check the height of the toys. Are they at the best height for her to hit?

Change these items at least once a week; babies—even those who are very young—become bored easily. In a few weeks, you may want to hang objects the baby can mouth (e.g., wide strips of non-raveling fabric).

Materials:

Dowel rod, easy-to-move objects to hang from the dowel such as pieces of fabric, rattles, rings, and so forth.

Note: *Do not use any objects that the baby could choke on, and closely observe this activity.*

Mouthing

Goal: For the baby to explore toys by mouthing.

Experience: Babies mouth things because this is a major mode of exploration in the early months.

1. When the baby is alert and well fed, put a clean, easy-to-grasp toy in his hand. Many babies seem to enjoy mouthing toys before their hands are ready to guide the toys to their mouths, so you may want to gently guide the toy to the baby's mouth when you are working with him. Let him explore this new texture in his mouth. What does he do? Does this first exploration seem interesting to him?

2. At other times, when the baby is playing, gently guide a toy to his mouth so he can experience this new pleasure.

Materials: Clean, easy-to-grasp toys of different textures

Grasping Objects in Two Hands

0–6 Months

Goal: For the baby to hold objects with *both* hands.

Experience: When the baby is in a great mood, offer her a toy you know she can hold onto if it is put into her hand. Offer it in front of her to the center of her body (at her midline). She will probably bring both of her hands up because she has not yet learned how to use her hands separately. She may even make a little cage with her hands to grab the object. Wait for her to grab the object by herself.

Babies love to handle different types of fabric and toys. During the day, offer the baby a variety of these items to hold. You may need to pick them up for her frequently, but this is okay. Does this baby have a preference of toys or fabrics to hold?

Materials: Easy-to-grasp toys of different textures and shapes, fabric swatches

Note: *Be sure to avoid toys that could cause choking or allergies.*

Playing with Toes and Fingers

5

Goal:

For the baby to become more aware of fingers and toes.

Experience:

1. Put the baby in your lap so he faces you, or place him in an infant seat facing you.

2. Take the baby's hands and wiggle his fingers in front of him. Talk about each finger and then sing "Where Is Thumbkin?" Wiggle the appropriate finger during each part of the song.

3. Take off his shoes and socks and do the same with his toes, this time reciting "This Little Piggy."

Variations:
Put mittens with interesting designs or characteristics on the baby's hands and gently draw his hands in front of his face so he sees both of them at once. Let his natural arm-waving bring his hands to his attention. If he doesn't discover his hands, bring them to his attention again.

Gently tie a very securely fastened bell on the baby's wrist or ankle. This adds the element of sound to the activity. Watch the baby carefully so he does not remove the wristband or bell.

Draw the baby's hands together, and let him feel each hand with the other. Talk about what it feels like or what is happening (e.g., "You are touching your fingers").

Materials:

Action songs such as "Where Is Thumbkin?" or "This Little Piggy," mittens and brightly colored socks, small bell attached to a wristband

6

Shaking and Banging

Goal:
For the baby to experience banging and shaking toys.

Experience:
Offer the baby one of the suggested toys and hit the toy so that it makes a noise. See if the baby notices the effect. Help her achieve the same effect you did by hitting the toy. You may need to guide her hand to hit or shake the toy. However, when given a new toy, usually a baby will soon try to shake or bang it.

Materials:
Toys that make noise when shaken such as a chime ball; toys that make a noise when hit such as spoons and baking pans

Using Thumb and Fingers

7

Goal:

For the baby to begin to use her thumb as well as forefinger to pick up objects.

Experience:

Using the thumb and fingers when picking up objects is quite different from using the fingers and palm in a raking grasp.

1. To encourage the baby to use her thumb and fingers, offer a small, lightweight object, such as a block, which can be held between the baby's thumb and fingers.

2. Offer the block repeatedly over several days and watch to see if the baby increasingly uses the thumb and fingers to grasp the block. Each time, hold the block using your thumb and forefinger and offer it to the baby's fingertips rather than to her palm.

3. In a few months, when the baby is good at holding the block in this way, you can practice with small objects such as Cheerios. (See 6–12 months, Fine Motor #4.)

Materials:

Small, lightweight toy that is easily held, such as a small block

Using Two Hands Separately

Goal:

For the baby to learn to use his hands separately and to transfer objects between hands.

Experience:

Offer the baby an easy-to-grasp toy such as a block, placed slightly off to his side. After a few moments, offer him a second toy. What does he do? Does he drop the first toy to take the other one? Does he transfer the toy from one hand to the other? The idea behind this practice is for the baby to transfer a toy to another hand when offered a second toy and to take a toy in each hand.

To encourage the baby to use both hands, offer him a toy that is held most easily using two hands, such as a medium-sized doll. You will note that he may release and regrasp with one hand and then with the other. This exercise teaches him that his hands can work both together and separately.

Materials:

Easy-to-grasp toys such as blocks (you will need more than one of the same type of toy); medium-sized toy such as a doll

Looking

Goal: For the baby to discriminate visually.

Experience: At birth, an infant can see clearly 8–14 inches away and closer. At 2 months, he should be able to see objects held up to approximately 20 inches from his face. At this time he is ready to focus on mobiles hung low above his crib.

When lying on his back, an infant first looks to the side and then looks straight up. For this reason, place a mobile so that it is situated 12–20 inches above the baby's head to his left, right, or center. You should not place the mobile close enough that the baby could get tangled in the strings. Mobiles are not recommended for infants older than 6 months.

Several studies have shown that very young infants most prefer looking at things with high contrast, such as black-and-white simple designs, checkerboards, bull's eyes, and faces.

Many commercially available mobiles are inappropriate for young infants because the colors or designs are not distinguishable to their immature ability to see.

Materials: Mobiles of different types (including at least one that is black and white). Look at the mobile from the infant's point of view before purchasing it.

Moving Mobiles

2

Goal:

For the baby to develop a sense of herself as a "causal" agent in cause–effect sequences by moving a mobile through her own action.

Experience:

1. Tie a ribbon to a sturdy mobile. Make a loop and tie the other end to the baby's wrist, not too tightly, but snug enough to not slip off.

2. Wait for the baby's natural arm-waving to set the mobile moving. If the baby doesn't move much, move her arm for her to see what happens.

3. When the baby gets good at this, try tying the ribbon to the other arm. How long does it take her to figure out the difference? You might also want to try tying the ribbon to one of her feet.

Note: *Be sure to stay with the baby during this activity for safety reasons.*

Materials:

Sturdy, well-secured mobile; ribbon long enough to reach from the mobile to the baby's wrist or foot

3

Tracking

Goal:

For the baby to learn to follow a moving object with his eyes.

Experience:

Position the baby in your lap or on the floor. Bring a patterned design to the center of the infant's visual field, 10–13 inches from his eyes. Move the design in a small circle. Stop and count to five. Slowly move the design to the right. Rest for a count of five again. Move the design in circles again twice and stop for a count of five. Return the design to the center. Stop for a count of five and repeat, moving the design to the left.

Place the baby over a bolster and move a toy to the left and right as instructed above. (You will need to balance him on the bolster.)

Activate a mobile 10–25 inches above the infant. An infant can see as far away as 10–14 inches at 0–2 months and as far away as about 20 inches at 2 months, so position the mobile accordingly.

An infant can see 10 feet away at approximately 3 months. Observe to see if he watches you from across the room.

Interest an infant in a wind-up toy. Vary the distance of the toy from him to give him practice in following the movement of the toy with his eyes.

Materials:

A toy the baby likes to look at (possibly with a black and white face or patterned design), wind-up mobile, wind-up toy

0–6
Months

   81

Understanding Permanence Through Spatial Relations

Goal:

For the baby to begin to develop ideas about the permanence of objects.

Experience:

By approximately 5 months, a baby begins to understand that objects have permanence in space. Completely learning this lesson will take many more months. You can help her develop this ability by offering small, manageable challenges.

Present a favorite toy from different angles (frontward, backward, and sideways). Watch her expression to see if she seems curious, mystified, or happily familiar with the toy. When the baby is nursing or taking a bottle, let her move her head to find the nipple rather than bringing the nipple to her.

Position the baby in your lap. Attract her attention to a favorite toy. Place it on a table and make a one-quarter turn away from the toy so the baby has to turn her head to see it again. When she gets better at this, challenge her with a larger turn.

Hold the baby in your arms, facing out, and draw her attention to the toy again. This time, move her up and down and back and forth. Note whether she is keeping her attention focused on the toy. Sit the baby on the floor and place the toy near her. Partially hide it and ask, "Where is (the toy)?" Pull the cover hiding the toy and say, "Here it is!" After several months, she'll be ready for you to cover the entire toy.

Materials:

Favorite toy

Developing
Visual Preferences

5

Goal:

For the baby to develop her ability to choose (and for adults to become aware of and to honor the infant's preferences).

Experience:

1. Offer the baby two of the materials at a time and see which she seems to look at the longest.

2. Offer two familiar pictures and a third one, which is new. Does she prefer the new picture?

Infants become habituated to stimuli. That means they grow bored with looking at something after a while. But when something new and interesting is offered, an infant will often stare at the new material for a long time. You can see this by offering an infant one picture to look at and then adding something new. Does he seem to perk up when the new picture is offered and look at it for a longer period of time?

Materials:

Simple and complex 8-inch x 10-inch black-and-white pictures, including herringbone and newspaper print; 9-inch x 12-inch square checkerboards; faces with eyebrows and ears; picture of 3-inch x 3-inch ball in black-and-white stripes; black-and-white drawings of things in baby's environment; two triangles drawn tip to tip; heavy black letters and numbers

0–6
Months

Introducing Color

6

0–6 Months

Goal: For the baby to perceive differences in color.

Experience: Hold the baby on your lap. Name and point out the colors of toys as he explores them. Point out the different colors on a two-colored ball.

Cover a penlight with various colors of cellophane, first with one color and then another. Move the light past the baby in a 180-degree arc.

Hold paper, cellophane, and fabrics up for the infant to touch. Does he express a preference? Is there a blink of recognition or interest when you present different colors? This means the infant is noticing color differences.

Materials: Ball that is half one color and half another color, high-contrast colored toys, penlight, colored cellophane paper, papers and fabrics of different colors

7

Imitating

Goal:

For the baby to begin to play imitative games.

Experience:

Different babies imitate in different ways, so you will need to look for the type of imitation a baby prefers, whether visual, auditory, or motion-based. Not all babies imitate at this age, no matter how intelligent they are. Don't worry if the baby is not interested, but try again in a few weeks. Imitation is the basis for many skills the baby will learn in the future.

    To teach a baby about imitation, follow this sequence:

1. First, imitate the baby's simple actions (such as arm-waving, facial expressions, or head turns).

2. When the baby makes a motor response to your imitation, imitate that action even if it is a different motion from the original one.

3. Make another familiar motion and see if the baby will repeat that.

4. Play the game using a material such as a spoon to bang on a toy.

A baby may respond to each step of the imitation progression as you present it, but it may be several months before she can do the entire sequence.

Materials:

Toy to bang on, spoon

Categorizing

Goal:

For the baby to notice similarities and differences.

Experience:

Place one of the cups in front of the baby and say, "Here is a cup." Place the second cup in front of him and watch as he compares the two. Look for a blink of recognition. Next, offer a third cup and say, "That's one, two, three cups." Let him play with them. After he has lost interest in handling the cups, place all three out of his immediate reach and place the fourth and different cup in line with the others. Say, "Look. This one is different." The same game can also be played with spoons or other objects the baby may safely handle.

　　The infant should show a blink of recognition when you present the second and third items in a sequence. The infant should also show a look of interest when the different item is brought forward.

Materials:

Three identical cups and one that is different; three identical spoons plus one that is different (soup or wooden); any other objects that the infant may safely handle, with three of the same and one different

Using All of the Senses

1

Goal: For the baby to develop in all sensory modalities, (i.e., vision, hearing, touch, motion, smell, taste).

Experience: The sensory assessment worksheet on the next page will help you observe a baby to learn his preferences for different sensory modalities. In their book *First Feelings*, Stanley and Nancy Greenspan (1989) suggest that the first stage in the emotional development of infants centers around learning to open up the senses to achieve a calm, alert state.

Many infants prefer one sense to another. The first observations will be to identify the infant's preferred senses. If the infant is using a sensory modality he likes, he will brighten and show interest. He is not likely to ignore the activity or become upset when this sense is stimulated. Becoming calm is another way an infant demonstrates interest in a sensory modality.

After deciding the baby's strongest modalities, you can decide how to use these sensory modalities together with the less-preferred ones in order to develop these weaker areas. Thus, you will help the infant find more ways to respond to his world.

Materials: Discovery 1a, Sensory Assessment Worksheet (see next page)

0–6 Months

Using All of the Senses

1a

Sensory Assessment Worksheet

Instructions: In each category, circle the phrase that best describes the baby at this time.

0–6 Months

Vision	No brightening or quieting to faces or objects	Some brightening or quieting to faces or objects	Visible brightening to faces or objects	
Hearing	Becomes irritable with voices, new tones	Little response to voices, new sounds	Some brightening to voices, new sounds	Visible brightening or orienting to voices or sounds
Touch	Becomes irritable with touching or massage	Little response to touch or massage	Some response to touch or massage	Visible brightening or orienting to touch or massage

Motion

Movement tensing (response to rocking)	Little or no response	Some response	Responds well to rocking; may relax and go to sleep	Other
Position preference	Vertical	45 degrees	Horizontal	Other
Movement preference A	Calm	Medium	Brisk	Other
Movement preference B	Likes to be moved vertically	Likes to be moved horizontally		Other

Smell (What scents the baby seems to notice)	The mother	Clothing	Perfume	Other

Taste
Have you noticed the baby responding to taste in any way? Please describe.

_____

_____

The infant's strongest senses seem to be _____

The infant's weaker senses seem to be _____

I can use (stronger sense)_____ to strengthen _____(weaker sense) by

_____

Massaging

Goal:

Experience:

For the baby to respond to touch from loving hands.

Begin with the infant on her back, so you can look at one another. You will be "speaking" with your eyes and your hands. Then begin to massage the following areas:

Chest: Put some oil on your hands, and then rub a little on the infant's bare chest.

1. Starting at the middle of the chest, slowly rub out toward the sides. Next, lightly slide your fingertips back to the center. Move your hands out to the sides again, but go a littler higher with each repeated movement. The outward movement is firmer and deeper. The return-to-center stroke is light. Both of your hands are moving, but in opposite directions, as if you were smoothing the pages of a book.

2. Your hands will now move one after another. As your hands move up from the infant's hip, they should slide over the abdomen, then the chest, and over the opposite shoulder (i.e., left hip to right shoulder). Stroke in this manner repeatedly and rhythmically for a few minutes.

Arms: Now turn the infant on one side and massage her arms.

1. Hold her wrist with your left hand and extend her arm out to the side. Grasp her shoulder with your right hand and move slowly down the length of her arm. Encircle her arm with your hand and gently "milk" the limb downward. When your right hand reaches her wrist, release your left hand as your right hand holds her wrist. Start your left hand at the baby's shoulder, moving downward to her wrist, until your right hand is free once again. The movements should be rhythmical, flowing, and soothing.   *(Continued on next page.)*

Beautiful Beginnings: A Developmental Curriculum for Infants and Toddlers by H. Raikes and J. Whitmer. Copyright © 2006 Paul H. Brookes Publishing Co., Inc. All rights reserved.

0–6
Months

Massaging (cont.)

Experience: (cont.)

2. Your hands now begin together. Grasp the infant's shoulder and move downward, in a circular manner, but in opposite directions to the wrist. Slide your hands back to the shoulder and repeat several times.

Face: Beginning with the center of the baby's forehead, move your fingertips sideways along the eyebrows.

1. Press somewhat firmly as you move your hands to the sides of her face and lightly return to the center, repeating several times.

2. Slide down to the bridge of the nose, working gently and lightly, moving upward between the eyes and toward the forehead.

3. Lightly stroke the baby's eyelids, closing them carefully. Move your thumbs downward, along the sides of the nose, to the corner of the mouth. Gently stretch out the mouth, begin again at the eyelids.

The massage is over. Wrap the infant in the receiving blanket and hold her.

Materials:

Massage, baby, or vegetable oil or oil gel; a draft-free, warm room; 15 minutes of uninterrupted time; a large, absorbent towel; a receiving blanket

Feeling Textures

3

Goal:

For the baby to perceive differences in textures through the sense of touch.

Experience:

1. Lay the baby on her back on a blanket or towel, in just a diaper if possible. Talk about the object you have in your hand for the baby to feel. Name the object, describe what it feels like, and tell what you are going to do with it. Touch the baby's fingers, toes, arms, legs, and tummy with the various textures.

2. Experiment with the textures. Which does she like best? On which parts of her body does she like to feel the textures the most?

Not all babies will show a preference or immediately enjoy this activity, but they may in a couple of weeks.

Materials:

Objects of different textures: fabric swatches, sponges, cotton, and so forth

Discovery 0–6

Blowing Through a Straw

4

Goal:

For the baby to develop body awareness by experiencing a new sensation.

Experience:

1. Lay the baby on his back, preferably in just a diaper. Make sure you are both in a comfortable position.

2. Tell the baby what you are going to do and where you are going to blow on his body.

3. Stroke the area you have selected first to help the baby orient to the activity and enjoy it more.

4. Blow on the part of the body you have selected (e.g., arm, tummy, leg) through the drinking straw. Avoid blowing in the eyes and ears.

The baby's attention should be focused on the blowing and possibly on the body part being blown on.

Materials:

Drinking straw

0–6
Months

Smelling Different Scents

5

Goal: For the baby's sense of smell to develop further.

Experience: You can help make a baby aware of the many smells in her environment.

1. Gather a collection of small bottles or jars that contain scented sponges or cotton balls. These scents should be from the baby's environment, such as the mother's perfume, father's aftershave or shaving cream, baby oil, formula, or milk.

2. Show the baby the bottle and then smell the bottle yourself. Tell the baby what it smells like (e.g., sweet, sour) and what it is (e.g., orange oil, baby oil). Let the baby smell the sponge or cotton ball and note her reactions. Are there any preferences? Which smells are most interesting to her? Are they familiar? Sweet? Sour?

Materials: Small bottles or jars with scented sponges or cotton balls in them. Grocery stores sell many scented oils that represent the scents the baby is exposed to, such as oil of orange (found in the baking goods section).

Note: *Smells that are not too strong are better for younger babies.*

0–6
Months

Riding on a Blanket

Goal:

For the baby to orient to different types of movement.

Experience:

Two adults are needed for this experience. Put a blanket on the floor and place the baby in the middle of the blanket. Each adult takes two corners of the blanket.

1. As you lift the blanket very slightly off the floor to a height of only a few inches, rock the baby back and forth very gently. Do this activity in a carpeted area.

2. Making sure the baby is only a few inches off the floor at most. Turn around in circles, trying both directions.

3. Use a gentle, up-and-down motion when picking the blanket up off the floor.

4. Gently pull the baby around on the blanket.

5. Watch the baby's facial expressions and body movements. Does he prefer one movement over another? Talk to him and use joyful expressions.

Materials:

Large blanket, 2 adults

0–6 Months

Playing with Water

Goal:

For the baby to experience further sensation through water.

Experience:

By the time most babies are a few months old, they enjoy their baths. These experiences expand on the idea of fun and exploration with water.

Give the baby a dry washcloth to mouth, and then give her a wet one. Put one of each in the baby's hands and observe her preferences. You may have to manipulate the baby's hands so she can experience both the sensations of wet and dry. Babies often find this a soothing activity and enjoy the oral feeling of mouthing cloth. When playing with the cloth, babies may prefer wet to dry or vice versa.

Put a bib on the baby and take off her shirt. Put some lukewarm water in her highchair tray. Let the baby experience playing with the water. Be ready for and expect spills, so choose the place for this play accordingly.

Materials:

Two washcloths or other suitable fabric for baby to mouth, highchair with tray, bib, and warm water

0–6 Months

95

Playing with Textured Containers

Goal:

For the baby to refine his sense of touch.

Experience:

1. Line the inside and outside of different containers with different types of textured materials listed below.

2. Talk with the baby about the materials and what they feel like. Help the baby explore the containers.

3. Put the baby's favorite toy in a container and let him feel for it.

Materials:

Containers of different sizes (e.g., baby wipe container, small boxes, margarine tubs); different fabrics and textures for covering them (e.g., satin, felt, corduroy, sandpaper); favorite toy

0–6 Months

Understanding Individual Differences 1

Goal:

For the baby's unique temperament to be understood.

Experience:

This activity involves observing nine different temperament categories.

1. Observe the baby's behavior in each of these areas and put check marks under the degree to which the baby displays each. There are no right ways for a baby to be—just differences. By observing and noting naturally occurring individual differences in babies, caregivers can fine-tune their responses.

Characteristic	Low	Medium	High
Activity level			
Rhymicity (regularity)			
Intensity			
Mood (fussy to positive)			
Adaptability			
Attention			
Distractibility			
Approach (withdrawing to sociable)			
Threshold of response			

Source: Carey & McDevitt, 1978.

Researchers Thomas, Chess, and Birch (1968) developed these categories to help caregivers achieve a realistic view of what to expect from children. Parents and caregivers shouldn't blame a child or themselves if a child has more difficult temperamental characteristics. Instead, they should adjust caregiving in accordance with the child's temperament.

2. Pick two of the previous characteristics and think about how you might use this knowledge to care for this child. For example, if the baby is low in adaptability, adults may need to explain what is coming next, allow more wind-down time, transition the baby gradually, and so forth.

Materials:

None

0–6 Months

97

Developing Synchrony

Goal:

For the baby and adult to feel "in tune."

Experience:

Synchrony is experienced when parents (or other caregivers) and infants seem to be "in tune" with one another—when adult and infant actions and responses mesh. For example, this is demonstrated when good eye contact is established between a baby who is more than 3 months old and an adult. Or when the infant coos, the adult responds, and vice versa. The interactions are characterized by a conversational and harmonious quality.

1. To establish synchrony with a baby, try to learn her rhythm. When you are with her, watch her closely. If she talks, match her sound. If she makes a facial expression, do the same. Let yourself become completely involved in conversation with this incredible baby.

2. When she tires, give her a chance to look away and rest. She may not be done, and you might try again after a short while to recapture her attention. If not, respect her need to end the conversation.

3. In general, feel her energy and rhythm. Ask yourself: Do I feel a synchrony with this baby? When? Can I feel this baby's rhythm? Is there something with my own moods that makes synchrony more likely at some times rather than others? Do I feel synchrony when I rock the baby? Feed her? Talk to her? Look at her? Can I tell when the baby is tired of interacting and wants to rest? If I don't feel in synchrony with this baby, what might be the barrier? How can we achieve synchrony many times during the day?

Materials:

None

0–6 Months

Imitating Facial Expressions

3

Goal:

For the baby to imitate adult facial expressions.

Experience:

1. When you have the baby's attention focused on your face, protrude your tongue v-e-r-y slowly toward the baby. Wait a long while for the baby to respond. You may be amazed when a little tongue begins to appear in response.

2. If you don't get a response, try again, and wait again. (Remember that even some alert babies won't want to play this game.) It may take several tries, but if the baby likes this game, the reward will be worth it.

Variation: You may also try this game by opening your mouth into a big O.

Materials:

None

0–6
Months

Looking in a Mirror

4

Goal:

For the baby to link her motions and expressions with images in the mirror, which builds awareness of self and cause–effect relationships.

Experience:

A mirror teaches social cause and effect because the baby can feel her own movements or expressions at the same time that she sees movement or expression. The rewards for her actions are immediate.

1. Sit the baby in front of a large mirror or hold one in front of her.

2. Draw her attention to the mirror and let her look at herself. Many babies don't need much encouragement in this game because the mirror has such strong drawing power. In fact, most babies love looking into a mirror and may even laugh and coo at the baby in the mirror.

3. Talk to her about what the two of you are seeing in the mirror (e.g., "See the baby? See Emma? What a nice baby").

Materials:

Large or small mirror (a hand mirror will work, but a large mirror is particularly effective)

0–6 Months

Laughing

Goal:

Experience:

For the baby to experience the joy of laughter.

Babies laugh for different reasons. Laughter can be stimulated in a number of different ways in babies who are ready to laugh. Be sure to be sensitive to your baby's cues when she has had enough.

Here are some ideas. Most rely on the element of surprise, which can bring great joy and laughter to an infant. But things that are a little surprising are sometimes scary to some babies, so it is important to find the line between what's scary and what's surprisingly fun for each child.

Hold the baby on his chest and very gently swoop him toward another person he likes, or gently swoop him toward the mirror so he meets a familiar face (himself).

Walk your fingers around the baby's tummy saying, "All around the mulberry bush, the monkey chased the weasel." When you get to the part that says "Pop! goes the weasel," exaggerate your voice and bring your fingers under his chin.

Jiggle your head or a toy.

Materials:

None

0–6
Months

First Games: Playing Peekaboo 6

Goal:

For the baby to be *introduced* to game playing, imitating, and object permanence.

Experience:

Make sure that you and the baby are in a comfortable position where you can see each other. Tell the baby which game you're going to be playing (e.g., Peekaboo, So Big, Mousie, Bumblebee). Go through the game once, doing the actions yourself; then do the actions with the baby, guiding him through the actions. Repeat the game several times so the baby becomes familiar with the actions. Peekaboo is a great first game:

Put the baby in your lap face up or in an infant seat. Make sure the baby can see you and that his head is slightly raised. Tell the baby what you are going to do ("Play Peekaboo?"). Then gently cover his eyes with the blanket, clean diaper, or your hands for a few seconds. Take away the cover or your hands, and say, "Peekaboo!" Repeat this several times. Reassure the baby and make sure this is a fun game for him.

Variations:
Cover your own face instead of the baby's.

Use a mirror and either cover the mirror or move the baby out of the reflection.

Play Peekaboo anywhere—such as at a doctor's office or in the grocery store line.

Encourage older siblings to play this with the baby.

Materials:

Words and actions for songs/poems such as "So Big," "Pat-a-Cake," "Mousie," or "Bumblebee"; clean diaper or lightweight blanket

0–6
Months

7 Falling in Love

Goal: For the baby and adult to fall in love.

Experience:

In their book *First Feelings*, Stanley and Nancy Greenspan (1989) proposed that the second stage in an infant's emotional development is falling in love. This is fostered in the infant when she feels love expressed toward her. Every infant needs someone who thinks she is the most wonderful person ever. Every parent or caregiver needs to "woo," or reach out to, his or her baby.

Watch the infant for signs that relationship building is taking place for her.

- Does the baby respond emotionally? When you look at her, do you feel a spark or liveliness?

- Is the baby starting to show a preference for you and familiar people?

- When you smile warmly at the baby, do you feel warmth, need, and interest?

- Does the baby focus on you when you interact?

- Do you feel a connection in talking to the baby?

- When you and the baby are interacting and the baby is distracted, is distraction easily overcome?

If your answer to some of the questions in the list above is "no," then perhaps you should spend more relaxed time focusing on wooing the baby by touching and making sounds, or involving only one sense (e.g., only touch). Some babies require a great deal of stimulation before giving a response; others respond quickly. It's important to find the level of stimulation each infant needs.

Materials: None

0–6
Months

Holding out Arms

8

Goal:

For the baby to learn to reach out to another.

Experience:

Teach the baby to reach out for you in several ways.

Before picking up the baby, wait a second. Give him time to reach out for you. Many babies do this on their own if you give them the opportunity.

Wear a bright scarf around your neck. Let the ends hang loose. When you reach down to pick up the baby, lean in closely so that the baby will reach out for the ends of the scarf. Let the baby play with the scarf before you pick him up. Soon he will reach out for you without the scarf.

Materials:

Bright scarf

0–6
Months

6–12 Months

Beautiful Beginnings: A Developmental Curriculum for Infants and Toddlers   6–12 MONTHS

	1	2	3	4	5	6	7	8
Communication	Imitating Verbal Cues	Repeating Events	Playing with Animals and Puppets	Recognizing Names	Experiencing Joint Attention	Listening to Words	Listening to Music	Reading Books
Gross Motor	Bouncing and Rocking	Turning and Stretching	Pulling Up	Playing Crawling Games	Exercising	Crawling Up and Down Stairs	Ball Rolling	Walking with Support
Fine Motor	Releasing on Purpose	Holding and Playing with Objects	Poking Holes	Developing Pincer Grasp	Scribbling	Activating Cause-and-Effect Toys	Throwing and Dropping	Putting Spoon into Cup
Intellectual	Playing with Things in Containers	Learning Object Permanence	Taking Rings off a Spindle	Using String as a Tool	Imitating	Learning Object Functions	Distinguishing by Color and Size	Finding Things
Discovery	Listening to Sounds	Crumpling and Uncrumpling	Exploring a Texture Box	Blowing Bubbles	Throwing a Tasting Party	Discovering Animals and Flowers	Experiencing Water Play	Finger Painting with Pudding
Social	Sharing Time	Expressing Feelings	Playing Back-and-Forth Games	Waving "Bye-Bye" and Saying "Hi"	Blowing a Kiss	Experiencing New Situations	Exploring Body Parts	Pretending
Self-Help	Playing on the Floor	Eating Finger Foods	Holding a Cup and a Spoon	Completing Activities	Getting Interested in Undressing	Playing in an Arranged Room	Using a Spoon	Using a Cup

Imitating Verbal Cues

1

Goal:

For the baby to better discriminate between and mimic sounds.

Experience:

1. Imitate the baby, making babbling sounds (e.g., "ba-ba" or "ga-ga"). Make your sounds as close as possible to the baby's babbling sounds.

2. Listen for baby to repeat the sound, at first approximating it with any babble, then later making close to the exact one. Reinforce the efforts.

3. Now make a new sound and wait for baby to babble in return. Work toward baby imitating the sound more closely.

Materials:

None

Repeating Events

Goal: For the baby to communicate through action and sound that she wants an action repeated.

Experience: In this activity, you are watching the baby for signs that she wants to continue playing. Get involved by playing a game with baby using one of her favorite toys, such as a silly or dancing clown, then stop. Watch to see if she kicks, bats at the toy, vocalizes, or moves all over. If she gives you a cue she wants you to resume activity (e.g., bats the toy), resume activity on her cue.

Play this game when you are bouncing her on your knee or moving her legs. Play vigorously, then stop. What is baby's response? Wait for her to give you a signal that she wants you to resume, and then do so.

Repeat an action with a toy and then stop. Has her response changed? Note if baby talks or touches, looks at, or smiles at the object. Repeat the action again, then stop. Does baby do one or two things to keep your attention? As she progresses, she may actively try to start the action again to get you to participate. For example, she may pat her hands on yours to play Pat-a-Cake.

Materials: Baby's favorite action toys

Playing with Animals and Puppets

3

Goal:

For the baby to begin to play games with puppets and toy animals, which helps expand her range of communication modes.

Experience:

Hold a puppet and play games such as I'm Going to Give You a Kiss. Pretend to have the puppet kiss the baby. Make the puppet dance and be animated. Wait for the baby to communicate with you in response by making a gesture to continue the game.

With a toy animal or animal puppet, make accompanying animal sounds. For example, "What does this cow say? 'Mooooo?'" Make the cow puppet approach the baby as you say this.

These experiences expand the baby's communicative competence by laying the groundwork for the baby to later "talk through" a puppet or toy animal.

Materials:

Bright, colorful puppets with distinct faces; stuffed animals

Recognizing Names

4

Goal:

For the baby to learn his name and associate names with people.

Experience:

1. While baby is playing, call his name. If he turns, smile and say, "Hi, Omar!"

2. Ask the baby, "Where's your mom (or the name of someone in the family who is in the room)?" Have that person try to get baby's attention. When baby turns to the person, show excitement and say, "There's Omar!"

3. Repeat, asking about other people the baby knows who are actually there or in photographs.

Materials:

Family member, photographs of people familiar to baby

Experiencing Joint Attention

5

Goal:

For the baby to look at something at the same time the adult does (to share attention), and to begin to develop his ability to communicate about what he is looking at jointly with another person.

Experience:

When looking at something with the baby, point to what you are looking at and say the name of the object or person.

Carry the baby around the room and touch things you see in a way that captures the baby's attention. Talk about each object. (This is also a good way to calm or orient a child in a new environment.)

Note if the baby looks at you to share pleasure and then returns his gaze to the object of his attention. When he does, you can respond to what you think he is looking at, such as "Yes, that is a truck." Or the baby may share pleasure with you by looking at an object and then back at you, seeming to ask for comment or some other response.

Some babies near 1 year of age may point at objects themselves. Often this pointing means, "What's that?" or "Look at that." Supply a label when baby does this.

If you touch an object when playing with baby, see if he looks at the object and then goes to play with it. Later (12–18 months), he may bring an object to you for shared pleasure or for you to comment on it.

If you are teaching baby signs, take note of things around him that he is interested in and research baby signs that cold be added. For example, if the baby shows interest in airplanes, look up the sign for *airplane* and use that when he looks at an airplane. Use the word *airplane*, too, so that he associates the object, sign, and word with one another.

Materials:

Whatever is of interest to the baby in your environment

Listening to Words

Goal:

For the baby to have her vocalizations reinforced and associated with word meanings.

Experience:

By 10 months, some babies have meaningful words in their language repertoires. It is important to listen for them.

1. Listen for sounds resembling words, such as "hi," "mama," "dada," and "ba" (which can mean *baby, bottle, blanket, ball*), and any others that are used consistently.

2. When you hear what resembles a word, give the baby a positive response and elaborate on the meaning. For example, say, "Here's Dad" while pointing to the child's father. That will help her want to repeat the vocalization and to associate vocalizations with their meanings.

Materials:

None

Listening to Music

Goal:

For the baby to use music for fun and relaxation.

Experience:

Play audiotapes and/or CDs with the baby and sing along. Model an appreciation and love of music.

Play music during baby's naptime for her to listen to as she drifts off to sleep.

Sing songs with infants individually and in groups. Children this age love songs such as the following:

"Itsy Bitsy Spider"

"Rock a Bye Baby"

"Twinkle, Twinkle, Little Star"

"Baby Bumblebee"

"Open, Shut Them"

Materials:

CDs or audiotapes and CD or audiotape player

Reading Books

8

Goal:

For the baby's love of books to grow, and for the baby to learn to point to pictures.

Experience:

1. Begin by intentionally creating a positive, warm atmosphere for reading time. It is good to set up a time each day for reading. Sit with baby on your lap while you read. In some cases, it is good to sit in the same chair so that the baby comes to expect reading when you sit there, but it is not necessary.

2. Point to the pictures as you read. Then encourage baby to answer your question, "Where's the ____?" by pointing. You can also ask the baby to put his finger on the ____.

Remember, it is hard for some children this age to sit longer than a few seconds or minutes, initially. Stay with the activity as long as the child is able to enjoy it and the reading time will eventually grow longer and longer. Pay careful attention to what he shows interest in and build on those interests as much as possible. Do not worry about reading the "story" or about looking at a complete book with a child this age.

Materials:

Chunky infant/toddler books with one picture on a page (e.g., *First Books* by Discovery Toys, board books, wordless books)

Bouncing and Rocking

Goal:

For the baby to experience self-bouncing and self-rocking. Self-bouncing and rocking give baby a sense of motor effectiveness (i.e., a sense that "I can make this happen!") and they reward motion.

Experience:

Babies find bouncing and rocking great fun, especially when they can make these actions themselves.

Put baby in a bouncer or activity rocker. Such an apparatus allows the baby to initiate the motion of rocking. Stay close as she bounces. Help her make the motion if she doesn't seem to do it spontaneously.

Play bouncing games with baby on your knee, such as, "Ride a cock-horse, to Banbury Cross, to see an old lady upon a white horse. Rings on her fingers, and bells on her toes, she shall have music wherever she goes." Later, move baby to your ankle and bounce more vigorously.

Some children take to bouncing activities and others don't seem to like them. If your child isn't excited about the bouncing, try it later.

Note: *Carefully observe pound restrictions on bouncer chairs and rockers. These are typically not appropriate for babies older than 1 year of age.*

Materials:

Bouncer, baby activity rocker

Turning and Stretching

2

6–12
Months

Goal: For the baby to build torso muscles and confidence in moving.

Experience: Begin with baby in a sitting or crawling position. Put toys slightly out of her reach and encourage her to reach and stretch for them. You may use an apparatus on which the toy is hung slightly out of reach so baby needs to stretch a little to grasp the toy.

When she is sitting, dangle a toy on a short ribbon and encourage her to reach and stretch.

Invite her to grasp the end of a stretchy piece of material. An old sock works well. Pull on the other end and encourage her to pull her end. This tugging will help her to use her arm and shoulder muscles. Don't let go of the fabric too quickly or it will snap her.

For a child who is not yet crawling, put an attractive toy just out of her reach. Encourage her to scoot and stretch to get the toy.

Materials: Toys on short ribbons, stretchy material such as a sock, apparatus for sitting where toy is hung above baby's eye level to encourage reaching

3

Pulling Up

Goal:

For the baby to learn to pull herself up.

Experience:

Help the baby get the feeling of being on her feet by pulling herself up during play.

Give the baby the opportunity to pull herself to her feet by grasping a dowel rod.

Put her near low furniture when sitting so she can pull herself up when she is ready to try it on her own.

Note: *Protect her so that she does not slip.*

Materials:

Dowel rod

Playing Crawling Games

4

6–12 Months

Goal:

For the baby to sit and crawl in different ways.

Experience:

Let baby crawl in (or sit in, if not crawling yet) boxes and laundry baskets.

Let baby crawl in a carpet-covered barrel or play tunnel. If you don't have one, make one with blankets and furniture.

Make an obstacle course with foam shapes or boxes and pillows. Create ways for baby to go high, low, in, out, over, and under spaces.

Roll a toy under a table and encourage baby to get it. Or, move an attractive toy around so baby needs to move to find it. Laugh when she finds the toy and have fun with this.

Grab baby by her legs. When she pulls to get away, tug a little and then let her go. Make her work a little to get away (as long as it is fun for her).

Sit by baby and when she leans on you, act like you are falling over. Laugh and tell her she pushed you over. Sit up and let her do it again.

Play crawling Peekaboo. Move around the room, playing Peekaboo from each new place. Encourage the baby to look for you, play Peekaboo, and crawl to join you in each new place.

Materials:

Boxes, laundry basket, tunnel, foam-covered shapes and materials, pillows, blankets, balls, interesting toys

Exercising

Goal:

For the baby to develop strength, flexibility, and balance.

Experience:

The following exercises build strength and gross motor skills.

Partially deflate a large beach ball. While helping the baby balance, lay him on his back on the ball. Gently roll the ball back and forth, which encourages baby to lift his head and torso to maintain his balance. Do the same with the baby on his tummy.

Using a smaller beach ball, roll baby face forward until he catches himself with his hands. Somersault him over or let him walk over on his hands.

Put the baby on an appropriate surface (e.g., safe table, carpeted floor) with his hands on the surface and encourage him to walk on his hands wheelbarrow fashion while you support his torso. When he can do this, move your hands to his hips, knees, and then ankles.

Lay the baby lengthwise on a large bolster. Roll the bolster to the left and right as baby reaches out to correct imbalances.

Note: *Always make sure the baby is able to breathe properly.*

Materials:

Oversized beach ball, regular beach ball, bolster

Crawling Up and Down Stairs

Goal:

Experience:

For the baby to learn to crawl up stairs and to come down the stairs.

1. **Crawling up stairs:** Put the baby on the steps and stay with him while he learns to climb. Watch to see that he doesn't turn around or lose concentration as he goes. Later, you might put a gate on the third step so that the baby cannot go too high. The baby can then practice climbing on his own fairly safely.

   You can also purchase or make a set of small steps. Many of the various rocking boats available commercially flip over to a stair side that is low, safe, and great for practice. Low footstools and boxes can also be used for climbing practice.

2. **Crawling down stairs backwards:** Position baby on the stairs in a crawling position. Turn him so his feet come down the steps first, the safest way for a baby to navigate stairs independently. Only allow him to come down the stairs in this fashion. Whenever he starts to come down any other way, turn him around so he understands this is the way to come down stairs.

Help the baby turn himself around to get off a bed, hassock, small box, or imitation stairs. Soon he will learn to always turn himself around, and you will feel more comfortable that he knows how to lower himself.

Note: *Always supervise an infant on elevated furniture or stairs.*

Materials:

Steps, low objects to climb on

7

Ball Rolling

Goal:

For the baby to learn to push a ball and to play another give-and-take game.

Experience:

Encourage baby to sit with her legs spread apart. Sit facing her in the same position. Roll a small ball to her, saying "ball," and encourage her to roll it back to you. You may need to guide her hands to push the ball the first several times. Experiment with what is the best-sized ball for your baby.

Sing a song about rolling the ball to the baby, whether you make it up yourself or know another one. "I roll the ball to ___, she rolls it back to me." Repeat the song until the baby becomes familiar with it.

Materials:

Small, medium, and large balls

Walking with Support

6–12 Months

Goal:

For the baby to experience standing and walking in a natural way.

Experience:

Arrange some boxes and chairs so that they are a few inches apart. (Spread the chairs farther apart as baby gets older.) Play a game in which you put a toy on one of the chairs or boxes and then let baby throw the toy off. Then pick up the toy and move it to another chair or box. Encourage him to go get the toy and throw it off again.

Get a wagon or activity walker. Let the baby push it to walk, if she is interested.

Materials:

Boxes and chairs arranged in a trail, small and interesting toys, toy such as a wagon or activity walker that supports child while he walks

Releasing on Purpose

1

Goal:

For the baby to learn voluntary release.

Experience:

Babies of this age find taking hold of something easier than voluntarily releasing it. This exercise teaches important release skills.

1. Sit facing baby with a pie pan in front of each of you.

2. When you have his attention, grasp a block and draw his attention to it. Drop it in the pie pan. Make the release exaggerated so that baby sees the action and the block hits the pan with some noise.

3. Do this several times and then let baby try to drop the block in the pan.

You may need to play this game on and off for a few weeks before baby can join in.

Materials:

Pie pans, blocks

Holding and Playing with Objects

6–12
Months

Goal:

For the baby to hold and play with 2 (or 3) things at the same time.

Experience:

1. Offer a toy to one of baby's hands and then to the other. Encourage him to hold on to the first when you offer the second. Initially, most babies will drop the first toy when offered the second. Later the baby will begin to hang on to one when given the other. Still later he will play with the two together.

2. When the baby has mastered holding two objects, try the following: Hand baby one block, then give him a second. If he has one in each hand, give him a third block. Watch him carefully to see how he handles the problem. Where can he put it? Does he put two blocks in one hand? Does he appear to think about it, then lay one down, pick up the new one, and then pick up the one he just put down? Does he put one block in his mouth so he can hold the other two?

Materials:

Any kind of material, such as blocks, in pairs or in threes. Materials should be fairly small (but of course, not small enough to swallow) so they can fit in the baby's hand at the same time.

3

Poking Holes

Goal:

For the baby to exercise her increasing visual acuity and deftness of forefingers by exploratory poking.

Experience:

Place toys with small holes in front of the baby. Let her experiment with putting her fingers in the holes to practice poking.

Materials:

A pegboard, other things with holes such as a rotary telephone

6–12
Months

Developing Pincer Grasp

4

6–12 Months

Goal:

Experience:

Materials:

For the baby to develop thumb and forefinger (pincer) grasp.

Put baby in a highchair or walker and put the small things in the tray. Let her work to use her thumb and forefinger to pick up the items.

Finger foods such as crackers, cooked peas, Cheerios or other small cereal

5

Scribbling

Goal:

For the baby to begin the writing process.

Experience:

1. Tape paper to a highchair tray or table.

2. Place the baby in the highchair or booster seat that safely attaches to a table.

3. Sit beside him and scribble with a crayon on the paper. He may want to watch you for the first several times.

4. Hand him the crayon. If he puts it in his mouth, gently redirect the crayon to the paper. If he does not try to make a mark on the paper, take his hand and make the scribbling motion.

Don't worry if he doesn't scribble. He may watch you for several weeks before he is ready to try. If he only wants to put the crayon in his mouth, put the crayon away and bring it out again in a few weeks.

Materials:

Large, oversized crayons; big pieces of paper; adhesive tape

Activating Cause-and-Effect Toys

Goal:

For the baby to make a motion that activates a toy.

Experience:

Many cause-and-effect toys are very popular with children this age. They begin as fine motor experiences but also provide important intellectual value (an action leads to an effect) and emotional value ("I can make things happen").

Show the baby how to activate some of the levers, dials, or buttons on one of her cause-and-effect toys and watch to see what she is able to do. Make a mental note of the motions she does today so you can introduce others later.

Materials:

A cause-and-effect toy is one in which the child's action causes a subsequent action in the toy, such as a sound or light turning on.

Throwing and Dropping

7

Goal:

For the baby to learn more about releasing objects and throwing.

Experience:

Many babies like to throw things over the edge of a highchair or play yard. You may think that the baby is trying to tease you, but actually he is exercising his newfound ability to drop and throw. Play throwing games with the baby, although you are likely to tire of this game before the infant does.

If the baby is unable to throw, put the beanbags on a low table that he can stand up next to and let him push them off.

Try tying a string or ribbon on a toy that he likes to drop and attach the other end to the railing of the play yard. Show him how to drop the object, then how to pull the toy back after he drops it. Now he can play the game by himself.

Materials:

Beanbags, ribbon, or string; favorite toys

Putting
Spoon into Cup

Goal: For the baby to put an object into a container.

Experience: Show the baby how to put a spoon into a cup. It may
take several aims before she is successful. Give her
plenty of time to make attempts.

Materials: Spoon, cup

Playing with Things in Containers

Goal:

For the baby to learn about taking things out of containers and putting things in containers.

Experience:

Fill a muffin tin with small toys. Encourage baby to take the toys out.

Do the same thing with a tote, sack, or other container.

Show baby how to take pieces out of a simple knobbed puzzle.

Later you can show baby how to put things into containers. Drop in one object and then encourage her to drop the next. Take turns until she understands.

Using a coffee can or other can that is safe around the edges, cut an opening in the plastic lid large enough for baby's hand to fit through. Encourage baby to drop toys through the hole. This is good preparation for shape and puzzle work.

Materials:

Interesting containers of all kinds, including pots and pans, plastic containers, totes, boxes, container lids in which you can cut out a hole; small toys in quantity; knobbed puzzles

6–12
Months

Learning Object Permanence

2

6–12
Months

Goal:

For the baby to learn that things exist even when out of sight.

Experience:

1. Engage the baby's interest in a toy. While she is watching, lay the toy down and drape a small blanket over part of it. Ask her, "Can you find the ____?"

2. If she finds the toy, clap and show excitement.

3. When she has successfully found the partially covered toy, hide more and more of it with each new game…finally covering the toy completely.

Another version is to put the toy in a box and encourage her to find it. Next, put the toy back in the box. While baby is watching, move the toy from the box to under the blanket. Can she find it now?

Materials:

Blanket, interesting toy, small box

Taking Rings off a Spindle

3

Goal: For the baby to learn that some things come apart.

Experience:

1. Sit with baby on the floor facing you.

2. With great animation, pull a ring off of the spindle. Show baby the ring.

3. Pull others off. Let baby pull the rings off. Share delight in the surprise of pulling the rings off one by one.

Variation: Show baby how to pull large pop beads apart. Encourage her to try.

Materials: Spindle toys such as those made by Fisher Price or Lakeshore, large pop beads

Beautiful Beginnings: A Developmental Curriculum for Infants and Toddlers by H. Raikes and J. Whitmer. Copyright © 2006 Paul H. Brookes Publishing Co., Inc. All rights reserved.

Using String as a Tool

6–12 Months

Goal:

For the baby to begin to understand how a tool (such as a string) can help to solve a problem.

Experience:

Tie a string or ribbon to a favorite toy or use a commercial pull toy. Attract baby's attention to the toy and encourage her to get the toy. Watch to see if she pulls the string to retrieve the toy. If she doesn't, show her (with excitement) how pulling the string will allow her to obtain the toy. (When baby is a little older, lay a second string beside the first one but don't attach the second string to a toy. Encourage baby to pull the string that is attached to the toy.)

If the baby does not seem to respond to this task, try something related but simpler. Draw her attention to one of her favorite toys. Place the toy on a pillow that is a little out of baby's reach. Encourage her to get the toy. Watch to see if she pulls the pillow closer to her to get the toy. If she goes for the toy rather than pulling the pillow, pull the pillow to show her how to bring the toy closer to her.

Note: Always watch baby when playing with strings; they can be a strangulation risk.

Materials:

Pillow, attractive toy, string or ribbon, pull toy

Imitating

Goal: For the baby to learn to imitate motions.

Experience:

1. When baby is shaking a toy, imitate his actions. Watch for him to repeat the action.

2. Imitate the baby shaking a toy again, but this time, add a second motion after you repeat his. This motion should be one you have seen him do before. Wait for him to repeat this action.

3. Make a motion that relates to the first but is an altogether new action for baby. For example, after baby bangs his hand on the table, slide your hand along the table. Encourage him to repeat this familiar and new action.

4. Another time, initiate one of the baby's familiar motions but not when he is doing it. Encourage him to repeat.

5. Even more complex, make a motion that you know is new to this baby, and wait for him to imitate. Watch to see how closely he approximates the motion. After several trials he may imitate the motion exactly.

Materials: Some of baby's favorite toys, including some to shake and bang

Learning Object Functions

Goal:

For the baby to learn that things have a purpose including some common household objects.

Experience:

1. Offer baby a bell. See if she rings it. If not, show her what to do with it. Later, offer her the bell by the base. See if she changes her grip to grasp it by the handle.

2. Next, offer baby the telephone and the other objects listed below. Offer them one at a time, slowly, and observe to see if she seems to know their purpose.

3. Say the name of the objects and the sounds associated with them, if appropriate. Show her what to do with each of the objects.

4. Make up games to play with her using the objects.

Materials:

Bell, telephone, hairbrush, comb, cup, spoon, steering wheel

Distinguishing by Color and Size

7

Goal:

Experience:

For the baby to perceive differences in color and size.

1. Show the baby two containers—a red one containing pebbles and a blue one that is empty (see Materials).

2. Shake the red one; then give baby the red one to shake.

3. Bring out the second set of red and blue containers and see if he shakes the red one. If he does, it will tell you he is remembering color and has learned the cue—this color has the shaking sound.

4. Bring out a third set of red and blue containers and see again if he picks the one that shakes—red. Introduce the words *red* and *blue* (e.g., "See the red can? The red can shakes").

Variation: Use large and small cylinders (e.g., orange juice cans). Introduce the words *big* and *little*.

Note: *Watch carefully to make sure the baby does not swallow the small materials.*

Materials:

Containers such as milk cartons (small) covered with sticky shelf-lining paper or colored, heavy tape. For color discrimination, make a set of four. Cover two of the containers with red shelf-lining paper and two with blue.

Put pebbles in the red ones so they make a noise when shaken and be sure to seal tightly with tape. Leave the blue ones empty and be sure to seal tightly.

For size discrimination, have two cylinders of one size and two that are larger. Fill the larger containers with pebbles to make a noise and leave smaller ones empty. Again, seal tightly with sticking shelf-lining paper.

Finding Things

8

Goal:

For the baby to develop intellectually through exploring the environment.

Experience:

Young children love to explore. Think about how they think, and plan interesting discoveries.

1. Set up a corner in your classroom or home that you can call the "discovery corner."

2. Each day or once a week, set out a new toy or object in this corner for baby to explore and discover. Make it even more exciting by hiding the toy in a small drawer or special box for baby to open. The baby will naturally explore. Be sure to allow her to explore many parts of the home or school most of the day when you can watch her to ensure her safety. Don't confine her to a play yard. Make every room the baby explores fun and safe.

3. When baby finds a treasure, think of something fun and interesting to tell or show her about what she has found. Be excited about her discoveries. Expand on these discoveries and interests.

Materials:

Interesting containers of all kinds including pots and pans, plastic containers, totes, boxes, and containers from which you can cut out different kinds of lid openings; small toys in quantity; knobbed puzzles

Listening to Sounds

1

Goal: For the baby to enjoy listening.

Experience: Explore the wide variety of sounds in baby's environment. Make the wind chimes ring, the sticks click, and so forth. Name the sound and its source as baby listens. Make a point of introducing as many new, enjoyable sounds as possible.

Materials: Noise makers such as wind chimes, clocks, squeeze toys, sticks

Crumpling and Uncrumpling

2

6–12 Months

Goal:

For the baby to experience textures of paper and their changing shapes when crumpled.

Experience:

Give baby the paper and let her experiment with touching and crumpling it. If she doesn't crumple it entirely, then you do the crumpling, and show her how the crumpled paper can be opened up to change its shape. Many of the paper materials listed below can be crumpled for a long time before they tear off.

Variation: Try making a ball of tape and let baby play with it, experiencing the stickiness.

Note: Watch to make sure baby doesn't get little pieces of paper in her mouth.

Materials:

Tape, butcher paper, construction paper, magazines

Exploring a Texture Box

3

Goal:

For the baby to explore and discover many fabric textures.

Experience:

Put the fabrics in a box and let baby pull them out one by one. Rub them over baby's arms and put them on his head. Laugh and play games with the various fabrics.

Tell the baby about the fabrics using a lot of descriptive words (e.g., "This cloth is smooth," "This one is rough," "Is this bumpy?").

Materials:

Box full of all kinds of fabrics such as satin, fur, wool, chiffon; board books that introduce textures

6–12
Months

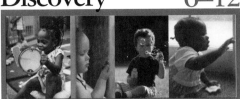

Blowing Bubbles

4

Goal:

For the baby to have fun with bubbles, which stimulates his beginning sense of object permanence (bubbles are "here" and then they are gone).

Experience:

Babies love watching the bubbles; it's something you both can have fun with.

Show the baby how you blow bubbles. Some babies may be able to imitate blowing and produce bubbles. Be careful not to let the baby taste the bubble soap; it's not toxic but it doesn't taste good, which may discourage him from doing the activity!

Materials:

Bubbles and bubble blower

Throwing a Tasting Party

5

Goal:

For the baby to experiment with taste.

Experience:

When the baby is eating solid foods, put the food she can eat in front of her and encourage her to try some new flavors. You might try different kinds of melons on one occasion and vegetables on another.

Take small cups or a muffin tin and put pieces of an interesting, new, and safe (small, easy to eat) food in each section of the muffin tin. Tell the baby you are having a "tasting party."

Take note of which kinds of foods the baby likes.

Note: *Make sure you follow guidelines from experts or the child's physician on which foods to introduce and when.*

Materials:

Small cups or muffin tin; foods such as melons or vegetables that can be broken up easily or small foods

6–12
Months

Discovering Animals and Flowers

Goal:

For the baby to touch, feel, and smell animals and flowers. Instilling in young children a love of living things is an important sensory and values experience.

Experience:

Find opportunities for baby to experience nature in many ways. For example, let her play with animals that have been around children and have very gentle natures. Make sure you or someone else holds the animal while the infant pets and touches it. Don't allow the baby to pull the animal's fur or poke its eyes. Make sure you use the word *gentle* frequently.

Invite him to touch and smell flowers.

Materials:

Gentle animals; growing flowers if in season, or cut flowers

Experiencing Water Play

7

Goal: For the baby to experience further the wondrous feel and soothing nature of water.

Experience: Water play is soothing to babies of all ages.

1. Fill a pool or large dishpan with a small amount of water.

2. Let the baby sit in or sit beside the water and splash, experiencing the fun of water.

3. If you have a group of children, you may offer water play to all of the children, provided that they are wearing swim diapers or other protective covering.

Sometimes babies this age do not like the bath, so work to make baby's bath relaxing, unrushed, pleasurable, and fun.

Note: *Always supervise children carefully when working with water.*

Materials: Small swimming pool or dishpan

6–12
Months

Finger Painting with Pudding

8

Goal: For the baby to experience the freedom to smear.

Experience: This experience gives babies the opportunity to let go and explore the natural desire to smear.

1. Place an infant in the highchair or on the floor. Tell her she is going to finger paint.

2. Put a small amount of pudding on the highchair tray or a piece of paper. Some babies may need a demonstration to get started.

3. Be prepared to follow this experience with a bath.

Some people do not want to use food as an art material. If you do not want to use food or if the prospect of pudding everywhere is overwhelming, let baby smear some water with food coloring on a tray.

6–12 Months

Materials: Highchair, pudding that is nonstaining (such as butterscotch or vanilla), bib (Optional: paper, food coloring, water)

Sharing Time

1

Goal:

For the baby to learn about give and take in sharing information and experiences.

Experience:

Babies can learn so much just by hearing you talk about daily tasks. When you are going about your regular routines, show baby the tools you are using and tell her the names of the objects and what you are doing. For example, "See, Annie, this is cookie dough. We make it into little balls, bake it, and then we have cookies to eat." If you (or baby) aren't having a good day, walk around showing her many things in your home or classroom. It is amazing how many times this technique will turn a child's mood around. This experience helps the baby re-engage in the world around her.

As the child gets older, encourage her to reciprocate by showing you things. When she does show you something, talk about what she is showing you. This is a fabulous opportunity for language development.

Materials:

Anything interesting that you or baby find or are working with

6–12
Months

Expressing Feelings

2

Goal:

For the baby to express a full range of feelings.

Experience:

By 7 months old, your infant will be expressing many emotions: disappointment, surprise, joy, anger, anticipation, fear, and boredom. It is important for him to be free to express all of these feelings. Doing so will make him a richer, healthier, and more energized person. You can help him to be aware of his feelings and can help him learn how to express them by labeling them when you see them. Here are some examples of phrases you can say that will help label the baby's feelings:

- "You are angry."

- "Are you afraid?"

- "That makes you really happy, doesn't it?"

It is important when working with children this age to notice their facial expressions. Look at baby's face more often to learn more about his more subtle emotions. Watch for all of the possible emotions your baby is expressing and take note of the situation that caused them and his reaction.

Talk with baby about his feelings and you will be laying the framework that he can draw from to label his own feelings.

Materials:

None

6–12
Months

Playing Back-and-Forth Games

3

Goal: For the baby to have fun and to learn to play a variety of games.

Experience: Any back-and-forth play between you and baby can become a game. You may pull a sock in tug-of-war, bounce her on your knee, approach her and say, "Boo," and so forth. It is important to know that baby is learning a great deal from these games—how to anticipate, how to hold someone's attention, how to keep her attention focused, and how to take turns. Try one of the following:

So Big: Ask your baby, "How big is Ellie?" Take her hands, raise them over her head, and say, "Ellie is so big." Work toward doing this game with a verbal cue, such as when you say, "How big is Ellie?" to get her to put her own hands in the air. Around 9 months, she may be able to lift her hands on your cue.

Pat-a-Cake: Take baby's hands and pat them to this rhyme:
"Pat-a-cake, pat-a-cake, baker's man,
Bake me a cake as fast as you can.
Roll it, and toss it, and mark it with a ___
(Fill in with baby's first initial, mark on tummy)
And throw it in the oven for baby and me."

As with So Big, try to teach your baby to do Pat-a-Cake by responding to verbal cues, but be patient. It may take many repetitions of Pat-a-Cake before she claps on cue.

Peekaboo: Play Peekaboo by putting a blanket over your head and asking, "Where's [fill in with your name]?" Put a blanket over baby's head and ask, "Where's [fill in with baby's name]?" Encourage her to hide herself (or you) on the verbal cue of "Peekaboo."

Materials: None

6–12
Months

Waving "Bye-Bye" and Saying "Hi"

4

Goal:

For the baby to learn the conventions for greeting and departures.

Experience:

Bye-bye: When you leave baby, wave good-bye and say, "Bye-bye." Next, when someone else is saying good-bye to her, wave baby's hand and say, "Bye-bye." Later, wave and say, "Bye-bye" and wait for her to do the same.

Hi: Say "Hi" to baby whenever you greet her. If she says "Hi" (and many babies seem to do this at a very young age), respond to her in kind. With your reinforcement, she will greet you more and more with a "Hi." Some infants even hold up one hand in a kind of salute when they say "Hi."

Materials:

None

6–12
Months

5

Blowing a Kiss

Goal:

For the baby to learn to show affection by blowing a kiss.

Experience:

1. When you leave the room, blow baby a kiss. For several days, do this each time you leave the room.

2. When you leave, ask her to blow you a kiss. Hold her hand by her mouth and turn her hand the way she would if she were doing it independently. Model blowing the kiss again for her each time.

3. After she learns to blow a kiss, ask her to blow kisses in response to your kisses.

4. Later, encourage her to blow you a kiss after a verbal cue.

Materials:

None

6–12 Months

Experiencing New Situations

6

Goal:

For the baby to develop positive feelings about new places, situations, and people.

Experience:

Many infants are leery of new people and situations at this age. You can help baby adjust by thinking of the experience from his point of view.

Remember, you represent security to the baby. By staying with him for a while, you show him that you approve of people and situations and you give him time to get used to them. Allow extra "getting-used-to time" for new places and people, especially if you will be leaving him.

Some babies have a small blanket or toy they like to take into new situations. Research shows that children explore more when they have a security item in a new situation. The blanket or toy stands in for you in your absence.

When in a new place, walk around with baby and show him things on the wall and in the room. Introduce him to the people and objects in the room by talking about each thing or person as if it were an exciting discovery. With your positive, relaxed introduction, the baby will become interested and may lose the apprehensive feelings. The information may also help him engage.

Materials:

None

6–12
Months

Exploring Body Parts

7

Goal:

For the baby to begin to identify parts of her body.

Experience:

A great way to introduce baby to her body is through massage. When you are massaging baby, label and describe each body part.

When looking in the mirror, touch and talk about what you are seeing. "Here's your nose. Here's Mommy's nose."

Baby will naturally explore you and other members of the family. As she does, tell her what she is exploring. "Hair. This is Abbey's hair. Where is Maria's hair?" When she is able to show you, share your excitement with her.

After you have played this game for a while, ask baby to find different parts of her body, such as her eyes, hand, and mouth. When baby is comfortable doing this, get out a puppet or picture and ask her to find body parts she knows on the puppet or picture.

A next level of learning is to connect pieces of clothing with the appropriate body part. Hold up a hat and say, "Here's your hat. Your hat goes on your head. Where's your head?" Do the same with other clothing items.

Many wonderful finger plays and songs involve body discovery. Examples include the finger plays Open, Shut Them or This Little Piggy Went to Market. An example of a song is "Head and Shoulders, Knees and Toes."

Materials:

Puppet, large pictures of people with distinct features

6–12 Months

Pretending

Goal: For the baby to begin pretend play.

Experience: By around age 1, most babies are engaging in first pretending, which is not quite real pretending but is actually imitating. By encouraging baby to imitate you now, you will be helping him toward real pretending, which will come soon.

At this point, the goal is for the baby to watch you and try to match your activities.

When talking on the telephone, offer the baby a few moments after you are finished (or use a play telephone). When you are dusting furniture, offer him a cloth. When stirring, give him a bowl and a spoon and show him your motion.

Think about all of the various activities you do and see if there is a way for baby to imitate some of your activities.

Materials: Materials used in household activities

6–12 Months

Playing on the Floor

1

Goal:

For the baby to learn to amuse herself on the floor. It is important by 6–7 months of age for infants to be spending at least some time each day learning to amuse themselves for short periods.

Experience:

If you are working with a baby who doesn't seem to want to play independently, you can help through these experiences:

1. First spend time on the floor with her. If you usually hold her, sit beside her but put her on the floor. Keep her engaged and excited about your play so her first association with floor play is positive.

2. Put her on the floor with a few interesting toys, maybe even a new toy. After she has played by herself for awhile, join her by sitting beside her but not necessarily holding her. Leave her again but come back frequently for her to share with you. It is important that you not just put her down and disappear. (This will give her the idea that playing by herself means that she has to give you up, and she may not choose that.) By frequently coming back to her you are telling her that you are interested in what she is doing and that you like her discoveries.

3. Set up a time each day for the baby to engage in independent play—perhaps right after a meal or in the late afternoon. Soon she will learn her routine and gladly go to her independent play.

Materials:

Interesting toys

Eating
Finger Foods

2

Goal:

For the baby to begin to feed himself.

Experience:

1. Place a few bites of finger food on the tray in front of baby when he is sitting in a highchair.

2. Show him how you put food in your mouth using your fingers and encourage him to do the same.

3. Talk to him about what he is eating.

Materials:

Simple finger foods such as peas, crackers, or soft fruits that the child is able to eat, cut into fine, easy-to-pick-up pieces

Note: *Watch that foods are not a choking hazard.*

6–12
Months

Holding a Cup and a Spoon

Goal:

Experience:

For the baby to **begin** to use a cup and spoon.

Cup:

1. Put a small amount of liquid in the cup. It should be a liquid that baby is familiar with and enjoys. Offer her a little drink. If she takes some, offer a little more. Throughout the day, offer her a few sips from a cup, especially when you think she may be thirsty but not hungry.

2. Encourage her to hold the cup on her own. You may want to gradually replace one of the infant's bottle feedings with a cup, but only do so if you are sure she is getting adequate nourishment.

Spoon:

1. When baby is being fed with a spoon, give her another spoon of her own to hold. This will keep her hands busy so she doesn't grab for the feeding spoon or put her hands in her mouth. This also helps her to associate the spoon with eating.

2. When she is holding her spoon, guide it toward the dish and up toward her mouth.

Congratulate her on her success in self-feeding.

Materials:

Cup with an easy-to-grasp handle, such as a sippy cup; dish; small, infant-sized spoon

6–12
Months

Completing Activities

4

Goal:

For the baby to stay with an activity until it is completed. This helps baby to develop an approach to tasks that will help him later in many intellectual, social, and self-help tasks.

Experience:

1. Show the baby how to put several pieces in a container, which he probably already knows how to do.

2. Offer him some of the pieces and let him put in the next ones. Ask if there are any more pieces, and look around for the missing ones. If there are more, pick them up and put them in the container with great animation. "Look, let's put all of the pieces in the container."

3. Whenever you are working with toys, ask him if there are more. Reach around and pick up the missing pieces.

4. Put lids on the containers when all of the pieces are in and say, "All done."

Materials:

Any toy or set of toys that have several steps toward completion, such as a container with small pieces

6–12
Months

Getting Interested in Undressing

5

Goal:

For the baby to begin to be an active participant in undressing.

Experience:

Think of the baby as a participant in the undressing process. Unfasten his shirt, but let him try to take it off. Untie or unbuckle his shoe, but let him try to take it off. Pull his sock halfway off, and let him finish.

Talk about the undressing process when you are undressing him. "Now, we will take off your shoes. Pop. Here comes your other shoe." Help your baby to understand and be interested in undressing.

Play undressing games such as Peekaboo with scarves and hats.

Materials:

Clothes with easy-to-unfasten fasteners, hat, shoes, socks

6–12
Months

Playing in an Arranged Room

6

Goal:

For the baby to learn to "make the rounds" in a pre-arranged environment. This will help develop baby's curiosity.

Experience:

1. Lay out the toys in the home or classroom in learning center fashion so that there are distinct areas of play.

2. Encourage the baby to explore first one and then another of the areas until all have been explored. Some babies, when they begin such an adventure, may only go to one area. Quickly, however, a baby will learn to look for interesting things if you teach him that environments can be interesting.

Materials:

Toys and materials of different types

6–12
Months

Using a Spoon

7

Goal:
For the baby to use a spoon to feed himself.

Experience:
You may have already done previous spoon-use activities with this baby. If so, this familiarity will make it easier for him to use the spoon for self-feeding now.

Offer the baby a spoon with every meal. Put it in his hand as he begins self-feeding. Be sure to use soft, easy-to-navigate foods, and don't worry about the mess. Use a good bib and possibly plan for baths to follow for a while.

He is now on the road to independence. If he is hesitating in his spoon use, pretend to eat with a little spoon yourself. Let him see your utensil when you eat and be sure to let him eat when you do. Soon he will want to eat just like you.

Materials:
Small, easy-to-use spoon; soft foods; a dish from which to easily scoop food

6–12
Months

8

Using a Cup

Goal:

For the baby to use a cup for nourishment.

Experience:

If you introduced baby to the cup earlier, by now she should be ready to use one more frequently and successfully. During each meal, put out her cup with a little milk or juice. Refill as needed.

Whether you use a cup with a lid is up to you. A lid does prevent spills and pouring; however, some infants never use a lid and learn readily to drink from the cup. If you don't use a lid, you will need to teach baby not to dump the liquid out. Simply put the cup away whenever she dumps it and show her what to do with it. Continue to explain to her that cups are for drinking.

Materials:

Easy-to-handle cup, such as sippy cup, with or without the lid

6–12
Months

12–18 Months

	1	2	3	4	5	6	7	8
Communication	Imitating Sounds or Expressions	Indicating Wants	Understanding Words	Responding to Commands	Pointing to Things in Books	Labeling Objects	Appreciating Music	Reading Books
Gross Motor	Walking Fun	Moving In and Out	Throwing	Carrying Objects While Walking	Walking Variations	Turning to Go Down Stairs	Sweeping	Jumping Off
Fine Motor	Pulling Apart Toys	Turning Pages	Opening Containers	Hand-Filling and Dumping	Scooping and Dumping	Pounding	Connecting Toys	Scribbling
Intellectual	Stacking	Putting Round Shape in Sorter	Putting Toys in Container	Experimenting with Cause and Effect	Understanding Object Functions	Putting Square Shape in Sorter	Predicting	Problem Solving
Discovery	Discovering Household Objects	Smelling Different Scents	Experiencing Water Play	Swinging	Wrapping and Unwrapping	Blowing and Sucking	Dancing with Musical Instruments	Playing Hide and Seek
Social	Relating to Children and Adults	Expressing Range of Emotions	Pointing to 3 Body Parts	Identifying Own Image	Playing Ring Around the Rosie	Coming for Help	Knowing Other Children	Being Helpful to Others
Self-Help	Cooperating with Dressing	Feeding Self	Giving Up the Bottle	Finding One's Place at the Table	Sleeping on a Mat, Cot, or Bed	Putting Only Edibles in Mouth	Sitting in a Small Group	Putting away Objects When Asked

Imitating Sounds or Expressions

1

Goal:

For the toddler to become skilled at imitating sounds and words.

Experience:

If you have been working with this toddler for some time, you have probably been imitating his vocalizations and he has begun to learn to imitate yours. He is probably ready to imitate words that you say.

When you talk to him now, slow your speech way down and, as you did before or as you would with a younger child, wait for a response from him. Place the emphasis on the last word of the sentence when you are talking to him. For example, say, "This is the *ball.*" Listen for his attempts to imitate the word. If he tries to imitate the word *ball,* repeat it back to him so he can hear it one more time. "Yes, this is the *ball.*"

Sing familiar songs such as "Twinkle, Twinkle, Little Star" several times a day, and then wait before singing the last word of every line. Soon the toddler will be filling in the blanks.

Ring a bell or other sound maker and encourage the toddler to create a word for the sound it makes (e.g., "What does this sound like? Can you say, 'ding dong?'").

Materials:

Audiotapes and CDs with nursery rhymes and songs, sound-making toys

Indicating Wants

2

Goal:

For the toddler to learn to use more sophisticated means of communicating with gestures or words.

Experience:

As soon as the toddler indicates by pointing or vocalizing that he wants something, such as his bottle, a drink, or a cracker, be sure to respond. (Sometimes we do the opposite and wait until the child cries before responding.) Responding immediately teaches him that vocalizing brings results.

When he is crying and seems to be asking for something, such as a cracker, say, "Tell me what you want." Or, use language for him: "You want a cracker? Next time, tell me with your words or show me." Some parents and teachers help children to use gestures or signs to communicate their wants at this stage, before or while using words.

Materials:

Suggested: Books describing signs (e.g., those by L. Acredolo and associates)

Understanding Words

3

Goal:

For the toddler to recognize words that are names for objects and actions.

Experience:

Whenever you and the toddler are together, talk about what you see and about the objects that you are playing with. This teaches him that things have names, and it may lead him to use an information-seeking question, such as "What's that?"

Another kind of word for the toddler to learn is an action word. Some toddlers learn to say "go" and "do" before they learn nouns. When your toddler brings you a toy to wind, say, "Wind?" When he takes your hand to go outside, say, "Go" and so forth. Use action words to describe other things that he does (e.g., *lift, rock, run*).

Assess whether you are labeling things in his environment at every opportunity.

Materials:

Books that label nouns and verbs such as *Panda, Panda* by Tana Hoban

Responding to Commands

4

Goal:

For the toddler to understand and comply with requests.

Experience:

The ideal time to begin this activity is when a child is between 6 and 12 months old. Now it is time to increase the number and complexity of requests. Be sure to get the toddler's attention before you initiate the request and, of course, be respectful of his play (by not interrupting). Some parents use signs with words to make requests.

1. First, see if the toddler can respond to the following requests:

   "Come here, please."
   "Give it to me."
   "Want a cracker?"
   "Bring me the…"
   "Do you want to go bye-bye?"
   "Do you want to go outside?"
   "Do you want a drink?"
   "Where's_____?"

2. Now, see how if he can respond to more complex requests, such as

   "Take the ball [object he knows] to Annie (in same room)."
   "Go get the ball [in another room]."

3. Continue to expose him to more complex requests and celebrate his success with each.

Materials:

Toys that toddler can identify, books describing signs (e.g., by L. Accredolo and associates)

Pointing to Things in Books

5

Goal:

For the toddler to recognize objects and identify them in books.

Experience:

1. When looking at a picture book, point to objects the toddler is familiar with. Point and say, *"Ball,"* "Here is a *ball*," "I'm putting my finger on a *ball*," and so forth.

2. Ask her to put her finger on the ball and praise her for doing so.

3. Another time, without showing her first, ask her to use her finger to point to the ball.

Materials:

Word books, such as Richard Scarry's *Best Word Book Ever* or *Best First Book Ever*

Labeling Objects

6

Goal: For the toddler to name objects.

Experience:

1. **Working with familiar objects:** Get three objects that you think the toddler can name. Ask her, "Where's the…[select one]?" Ask her to point to each of them in turn. As she does, praise her and say the name of the object again. Next, point to the objects and ask her, "What's this?" for each item and help her pronounce each object's name.

2. **Introducing new objects:** Next, do the same as above, but when you are introducing a new item say, "This is a…[name the new object] and this is a…[name another object she already knows]." Then, ask her to point to the new object when you name it. Later, point to the object and ask her to name it. Finish by asking the names of objects lined up on the floor or on a table.

Variation: Walk around your house or classroom with your toddler and ask her to label things as you point. "What's this?" "What's that?"

Materials: Toys and materials the toddler is familiar with and is learning about

Appreciating Music

7

Goal:

For the toddler to further develop appreciation for and participate in music, an important mechanism for toddler language and cognitive development.

Experience:

Encourage the toddler to sing along and try motions associated with songs. Some recommended songs for children this age are:

"The Wheels on the Bus"

"The Popcorn Song"

"Five Little Monkeys"

"Put Your Hands on Your Head"

"The Name Game"

Some recommended audiotapes or CDs are:

Music for Ones and Twos by Tom Glazer

Songs to Sing with Babies by Miss Jackie Wiesman

Materials:

Audiotape or CD player, audiotapes, or CDs with nursery rhymes and songs

Reading Books

8

Goal:

For the toddler to further develop a love of books and language.

Experience:

Daily book reading is one of the best things a parent or teacher and a child can do together. Previously, your purpose in reading books to the toddler was to help him sit still and point to things or name objects in pictures when you pointed to them. Now his pointing and labeling give you an opening. Each time he points or vocalizes, add a new concept.

Here's an example. When he comments or labels a picture, expand or tell him a little about the picture. If he says, *"ball,"* you might say, "Yes, it's a *round, blue* ball." You have expanded his idea of *ball!* You can use this approach to other vocalizations and gestures he offers.

Materials:

Here are some recommended books:

Where's Spot? by Eric Hill

Aleksandra, Where Are Your Toes? by Christine Dubov & Joseph Schnieder

Richard Scarry's Best First Book Ever by Richard Scarry

Richard Scarry's Best Word Book Ever by Richard Scarry

Babies Love a Goodnight Hug by Harold Roth

My Mommy by Mathew Price

Slide 'N Seek Shapes by Chuck Murphy

Black on White by Tana Hoban

I Can by Helen Oxenbury

Baby Faces by Margaret Miller

Pat the Bunny by Dorothy Kunhardt

Where Is Baby's Belly Button? by Karen Katz

Brown Bear, Brown Bear, What Do You See? by Bill Martin, Jr., & Eric Carle

Walking Fun

1

Goal:

For the toddler to gain skill and confidence in walking after she has begun to walk on her own.

Experience:

Place a wide board on the floor and encourage the toddler to walk on it. If you have a very low balance beam, you can also let her experience that with your support.

You may also try laying a ladder on the floor and invite the toddler to walk between the ladder rungs. She may need you to place your hands under her arms for support and encouragement.

Go to a wide-open space (such as a shopping mall) and let her walk ALL around. It is fun for the toddler to experience walking in large, open spaces.

Materials:

Ladder, wide board, low balance beam

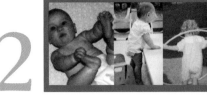

Moving In and Out

2

12–18
Months

Goal:

For the toddler to gain agility to climb in and out of boxes and to move through obstacles.

Experience:

Place favorite toys in boxes of different types and encourage the child to step or climb in and out of the boxes. You'll probably observe that he repeats this activity many times. You may find it fun to chant, "In and out. In and out. You are climbing in and out."

Obtain a large box, such as a refrigerator box. Cut a door and encourage your toddler to step or crawl into the box.

Place three small tires together and encourage him to move in and out of the openings.

Materials:

Boxes of different types, large enough for toddlers to move in and out of; large box such as a refrigerator box; tires

3 Throwing

Goal:

For the toddler to develop skill in throwing balls and beanbags.

Experience:

Stand a few inches from the toddler and gently toss (i.e., almost a hand-off) a medium-sized ball to her. Congratulate her on catching it, and encourage her to toss (or give) it back to you.

Get an oversized ball, such as a beach ball, and roll it around the room. Have the toddler join you. You may want to make up a ball-rolling chant: "Roll, roll, roll the ball, all around the room." Now, encourage her to roll the big ball back and forth with you. Another ball-rolling song-chant, "I roll the ball to Daddy, he rolls it back to me," is fun to do in accompaniment.

With a beanbag, demonstrate an overhand throw. Give the toddler a beanbag and ask her to throw the bag using an overhand motion. When toddlers are learning throwing, they enjoy practicing this skill over and over. You can make it clear to her now that beanbags are good for throwing but that blocks, trucks, and similar things are not. It is important to give children acceptable outlets for practicing new skills such as throwing.

Materials:

Balls of every size, small beanbags

Carrying Objects While Walking

Goal:

Experience:

For the toddler to learn to carry things while walking.

As the toddler is gaining confidence in walking, give him things to carry to someone else or to another place.

1. Put an object in a shallow pan or muffin tin and show the toddler how to hold it with two hands without dumping it. Encourage him to carry it across the room.

2. When he has mastered this skill, let him try to carry an object on a tray. Add to the number of objects on the tray as his skill progresses.

Materials:

Toys, small tray, muffin tin, small toys that don't roll

Walking Variations

Goal:

For the toddler to expand walking skills—to walk up and down inclines and backwards, after the toddler has mastered walking on her own and is ready for variation.

Experience:

Using a wide board, make a very gradual "hill" and encourage the toddler to walk up and down it.

Take a walk to a nearby hill and either with or without supporting her, let her experience her own balance and skill on an incline.

Explore other new ways of walking with her:

- Show her how to walk backwards. Walk backwards together. Then try walking sideways.

- You can also try taping a line on the floor and walk normally on the line. Then try tiptoes, backwards, and sideways on the line.

Materials:

Wide board, something to use to create an incline, adhesive tape

Turning to Go Down Stairs

6

Goal:

For the toddler to consistently choose the safest way to go down stairs.

Experience:

At this age, many toddlers can step down stairs with someone holding their hands. However, this method is not safe if there is no one to hold hands with.

Whenever you are on the stairs, be sure the toddler turns herself to come down feet first on her tummy. Stand several steps away from her when you become somewhat able to trust her. If you have doubts, you may need to teach her to turn around and come down on her tummy.

Later, when you feel sure she can come down safely by herself, you may stand at the bottom of the stairs, but still exercise caution.

Note: *Always watch the toddler on any raised surface to make sure she can choose the safe way off.*

Materials:

Stairs

182

Sweeping

Goal:

Experience:

Materials:

For the toddler to learn how to use a broom.

1. Give child a small broom and lightweight balls. Show her how to sweep the balls to make them go in the direction she wants.

2. Now, show her how to sweep the balls into a box, helping her direct the balls where she wants them to go.

Broom, box, lightweight balls

Jumping Off

8

Goal:

For the toddler to learn how to jump off low objects.

Experience:

1.   Begin with a low box, pillow, or step and show the toddler how to jump off of it. Take his hands and help him to jump off and then encourage him to try it himself.

2.   Increase the height of the box or step, giving him lots of praise for taking the leap.

Note: *Heights must be low enough that the child does not hurt himself.*

Materials:

Various boxes, pillows, steps, and hassocks

Pulling Apart Toys

Goal:

For the toddler to pull apart objects (disconnect connecting toys).

Experience:

Put together two or three toy pieces and show the toddler how to pull them apart. Model this several times and then let the toddler do it. This ability precedes the ability to put together the blocks or beads.

This experience also teaches the child about part–whole relationships.

Materials:

Duplo blocks, stacking bunnies or other stacking toys, large pop beads or any other connecting toys

12–18 Months

Turning Pages

12–18 Months

Goal: For the toddler to be able to turn pages in books—first cardboard (board books), then paper.

Experience: Sit and turn book pages with the toddler using a cardboard book. Invite him to do it by himself. When he has mastered pages with a cardboard book, give him ones with paper pages.

The attraction of hinged objects is very strong at this age. If you have toys or a board with hinged doors, bring these out for additional "hinge practice."

Materials: Stiff board books, paper books, hinged toys

Note: *Avoid books with plastic hinges because pieces of plastic could be bitten or broken off.*

Opening Containers

Goal:

For the toddler to learn to remove lids from containers.

Experience:

Show your toddler how to take off the lid of a safe container. Invite her to try it by herself. Let her practice frequently.

Materials:

Easy-to-remove lids and jars or other containers. The best is a commercial set of three plastic jars with lids. Pop-off lids also work well.

Hand-Filling and Dumping

4

Goal:

For the toddler to be able to fill a container with her hands and then dump the contents.

Experience:

1. Begin with a large container. Show the toddler how to use her hand to scoop and fill the container. Not much instruction will be needed to teach her how to dump the container.

2. Let her repeat the process while you talk about filling and dumping.

3. Repeat this exercise with smaller containers, such as cups.

Remind the toddler, if necessary, that the filler material (e.g., sand) is for scooping and filling, not eating. If the toddler is more interested in mouthing the materials than scooping and filling, try the experience again in a few weeks.

Materials:

A series of containers from cups to wash tubs; various kinds of materials to fill the containers, such as sand or uncooked macaroni (This Experience works well using a water or sand table.)

Scooping and Dumping

5

12-18
Months

Goal:

For the toddler to use a tool for scooping.

Experience:

1. Show the toddler how to scoop into the sand, macaroni, and so forth using a tool and how to turn her wrist so the material doesn't fall out of the scoop.

2. Show her how to empty the scoop to make a new pile.

3. Continue to encourage her to practice until she can scoop without spilling all of the contents.

Materials:

Shovel, flour scoop, spoon, sand, uncooked macaroni or other substances, each providing a fun, new scooping experience (This Experience works well using a water or sand table.)

Pounding

12–18 Months

Goal:

For the toddler to develop wrist and eye–hand coordination by pounding pegs.

Experience:

Obtain a simple pounding bench. Push up all of the pegs and show the toddler how to hit one repeatedly until it is flat with the surface of the bench. Invite her to take a turn.

Materials:

Simple pounding bench and broad-based hammer

Connecting Toys

7

Goal:

For the toddler to acquire hand strength and accuracy through joining connecting toys.

Experience:

In an earlier activity, the toddler pulled apart connecting toys. Now he is ready to join them.

1. Show him the two ends of the connecting toys. Point to one and then to the other end. Slowly join and pull apart the two pieces.

2. Now, invite the toddler to try. When he is finished, remember to show him how to put the materials back in their container and where they belong.

Materials:

Connecting toys such as Duplo Legos, stacking bunnies, or large pop beads

Scribbling

Goal:

For the toddler to learn to make marks and motions on paper.

Experience:

1. Begin by doing a back-and-forth scribble on paper, and then ask the toddler to imitate this. He may have been doing this for a while, so let him just practice starting with what he has done previously.

2. Now, tell him you will show him a new way to mark, making a circular or round mark. Show him how to do this and invite him to try.

3. Do the same with up and down and then diagonal strokes.

4. If he has been doing mostly continuous scribbling, ask him to try to make just one mark following your demonstration. This variation helps the toddler develop impulse control.

5. Provide a variety of materials to encourage his continued exploration, and continue to model and invite him to make circular, back-and-forth, up-and-down, and single marks, while mostly encouraging him to scribble in his own way.

Materials:

Jumbo crayons, large pieces of paper, adhesive tape, jumbo chalk, a large chalkboard mounted upright (optional)

Stacking

1

Goal:

For the toddler to begin to learn to stack with blocks and other objects.

Experience:

While your toddler is watching, build a two-block tower. Give her two blocks and encourage her to make a tower also. You may find that some blocks work better for the toddler than others. Empty yogurt cartons work well for first stacking. Label all of your actions: "I'm building a tower. Now, I'm knocking the tower down."

Place two blocks side by side, and use one to push the other in a train-like fashion. Again, remember to label all of your actions.

Encourage her to stack other things as well as basic building blocks.

Materials:

Blocks of all different kinds

12–18
Months

Putting Round Shape in Sorter

2

Goal: For the toddler to fit a round shape in a round hole.

Experience: A circle is the easiest shape for the toddler to recognize and fit into a hole. Later, she will learn to discriminate between many shapes, and still later, will learn to discriminate the many shapes in letters and words.

Cut a round hole in a lid of a plastic tub (e.g., margarine tub). Draw your finger around the hole to emphasize its roundness. Label it "round." Trace the circumference of a ball or cylinder that fits in the hole. Show the toddler how to drop the ball through the hole.

Purchase a commercial balloon puzzle (or other puzzles with round shapes), and show your toddler how to fit the circular shapes into the circle holes. Trace the shapes and label as before. Many toy companies make a simple puzzle with knobs and circle shapes.

When using a commercial shape sorter, tape closed all but the circle hole. Now the toddler can concentrate on fitting the round objects into their place. Later, take the tape off and let part of the learning task be finding the circle hole.

Materials: Small balls, plastic tubs with lids, balloon puzzle or other puzzle with round shapes, shape sorter with cylindrical holes, adhesive tape

Putting Toys in Container

3

Goal:

For the toddler to learn the entire container play sequence: putting objects into a container, taking the lid off, emptying the container, and putting the lid back on.

Experience:

Show your toddler the container and objects. Show him the opening and how each object fits through it. He will have wonderful repetitive hours (cumulative) of fun. He may need some help getting lids on and off occasionally.

This experience helps the toddler learn to focus his attention, and it also helps him learn about sequencing his actions (First, I..., then, I).

Materials:

Containers of all kinds with objects of all kinds; slots and holes in lids that fit objects (e.g., wooden clothespins, dominoes, formica chips)

12–18
Months

Experimenting with Cause and Effect

Goal:

For the toddler to experiment with an action that creates an event.

Experience:

Show your toddler how to pull a lever, turn on a light switch, ring a doorbell, and so forth. As always, label your actions and hers: "You made the bell ring." Teach her the power of her actions to make things happen.

Look around the toddler's environment. Are there other ways that you can provide even more cause-and-effect opportunities? An example would be to tie a string to the light switch so that the toddler can turn the lights on and off by herself.

Materials:

Buzzer box; toys with levers and gears that create action; other things in the home or child care program such as easy-to-turn-on flashlight, alarm clock, light switch, and doorbell

Understanding Object Functions

5

Goal:

For the toddler to learn more about the uses of objects.

Experience:

Show the toddler what to do with an object and let her play with it. When she uses it correctly, praise her and show her other uses (e.g., give her a mirror and after she looks in it, show her how to brush her hair in front of it). You can help her incorporate these objects into her routines, using the same object in the same ways each day. As she explores your home or classroom, help her find meaning in the objects in her environment.

As always, use these experiences to expand her vocabulary, describing the objects and their uses.

Materials:

Household objects that have a specific use: mirror, hairbrush and comb, broom and dustpan, purse, toothpaste and toothbrush, pans and spoons, tools, and so forth

Putting Square Shape in Sorter

Goal:

For the toddler to correctly fit a second shape in a shape sorter.

Experience:

1. If you have already introduced the circle shape, trace around the square opening and a square or cube piece that will be going through the opening. Show the toddler how to fit the piece through the hole, and invite him to try it.

2. The second part of the activity is to let him fit two shapes. Give him a shape sorter to fit both circle and square pieces. You may do this by having one lid that has both shapes cut out or two separate containers with a circle hole cut in the lid of one and a square hole cut in the lid of the other.

Materials:

Simple puzzle or shape sorter requiring toddler to fit square or cube shape into a hole. Tape shut shapes that are too difficult for your toddler (such as triangle or rectangle that may also be on shape sorter). You can use homemade versions using cans with plastic lids and a block for the square shape.

7

Predicting

Goal:

For the toddler to anticipate outcomes.

Experience:

Attach a tube to a railing or something stationary so that the tube is at an angle. Drop a ball or toy car through the top end. Watch the child's eyes to see if she anticipates the ball or car coming out the other end.

Drive a toy car down a decline. Let go of it so that it rolls on its own momentum. Place a block in its path. See if the toddler anticipates the car stopping.

Using a ball machine, drop the ball and encourage the child to anticipate the ball's path. Put a small basket under the machine to catch the ball. Move it away and note if the child anticipates the ball rolling away when it comes to the end.

Materials:

A long tube with a small object such as a toy car that will go through the tube, toy such as an oversized marble machine with a small ball, a decline with a small car

Problem Solving

Goal:

For the toddler to solve problems and overcome obstacles.

Experience:

When playing with the toddler, roll a ball under a shelf or other low piece of furniture. Encourage her to get the ball. Talk her through the process. Now repeat the process, but let the ball roll farther so she can't reach it on her own. Place a stick nearby that would enable her to retrieve the ball by swiping. Let her struggle somewhat to solve the problem independently. Talk to her about how to solve the problem, but try not to solve it for her.

When you and the toddler are playing with an object, create a barrier for her to work around to get the object. Again, slowly talk to her and encourage her toward a solution.

Make a homemade string and object toy as described below. Let the toddler work with this problem.

Throughout the day, situations will occur that will require your toddler to use problem solving. Don't rush to solve the problems for her; let her work with them. She is developing flexibility of thinking by struggling. When she runs into difficulty, your encouragement will keep her working for a solution.

Materials:

Stick, small ball, anything that can act as a barrier but can easily be gotten around, box rigged with a string on the lid so child has to pull string to get lid off, piece of cardboard with a round hole in the middle and string that goes through the hole attached to a cylinder

Discovering Household Objects

1

Goal:

For the toddler to learn by exploring a *new* group of objects.

Experience:

Designate drawers or cupboards in your home or child care setting that the child can explore freely, and fill these with safe objects.

At home, let the toddler "help" clean out the sock drawer or put canned goods in the cupboard. A brush, comb, washcloth, and empty shampoo bottle are fun and safe things to play with in a bathroom cupboard.

Provide word labels for objects.

Note: *Be sure to complete a safety check for all items in cupboards and drawers that the child can reach!*

Materials:

Things found around the house: plastic bowls with lids, spoons, muffin pans, pots, pans, sock drawer, any safe items

12–18
Months

Smelling Different Scents

2

Goal:

For the toddler to expand his sense of smell.

Experience:

This is a repeat of an experience that can be done with much younger children. You may have done this with the child you are working with now. Like you would with a younger child, sit with the toddler and open a jar or bottle that contains scented cotton balls or sponges. Try several different containers. Your child will probably try to taste the scent, so be sure that the scents are nontoxic and that he is carefully supervised.

As he responds to the differences in the scents, take note of his preferences.

As always, provide word labels for the different types of scents if you can.

Materials:

Small jars or bottles with cotton balls or sponges in them that have various scents (e.g., lemon juice, oil of banana, cloves, perfume, baby oil)

Experiencing Water Play

3

Goal:

For the toddler to further experience being in the water.

Experience:

Put the toddler in 2–3 inches of water. Let her splash, play, and enjoy being in the water. You can choose whether to have the toddler in a swim diaper or a swimsuit. Floating toys are optional. Some toys are hollow and take in water, which toddlers may drink, so solid ducks, balls, and other solid objects are better choices.

When doing water play, make sure that towels are readily available to dry off the child and to clean up around the pool so indoor floors or non-grassy areas outside won't be dangerously slippery.

Note: *With water play, always make sure the toddler is supervised.*

Materials:

Bathtub, wading pool, towels, water toys

12–18
Months

Swinging

4

Goal:

For the toddler to experience motion, rhythm, and the feeling of moving back and forth.

Experience:

Swinging is a very enjoyable activity for most children because they generally love the feeling of motion and breeze. Swinging tends to calm children who are unhappy or who just need some personal space, and it can also be helpful to children with sensory integration issues.

Start out slowly and tell the child about going back and forth. As the toddler becomes more comfortable and confident, you can push her higher, but watch body language carefully to learn about her preferences and tolerance.

Materials:

A swing with a safety strap

12–18
Months

Wrapping and Unwrapping

5

Goal:

For the toddler's curiosity and sense of touch to be stimulated.

Experience:

1. Wrap a toy and then unwrap it in front of the toddler. Exaggerate your movements and expression to add to the fun.

2. Next, give the child a wrapped toy and let him try to unwrap it. Adhesive tape doesn't need to be used for the wrapping until the child has become proficient at unwrapping without it. Use different textures of wrapping materials to provide sensory stimulation.

You can also experiment using other wrapping materials, such as cloth, aluminum foil, or towels.

Materials:

Any interesting object to wrap; different wrapping materials such as paper, fabric, foil, bags, adehsive tape, and ribbon

12-18 Months

6

Blowing and Sucking

12–18 Months

Goal: For the toddler to experience blowing and sucking to discover new body sensations.

Experience: Blow bubbles toward the toddler. Use big, animated expressions. Hold the bubble wand near the toddler's mouth and invite her to blow.

Show her how to blow on a pinwheel. Encourage her to try.

Put colored water in a glass and show your toddler how to blow bubbles using a straw. Another time, talk about sucking and show her how to suck to get liquid out of a glass using a straw.

Materials: Bubbles, pinwheel, straw, candle, colored water, sturdy plastic straws

Dancing with Musical Instruments

Goal:

For the toddler to experience rhythm and different types of music.

Experience:

Play different types of music for the child. Invite him to dance and/or play an instrument to the music. You may want to pick him up and dance with him in your arms to give him the feel of the beat.

You can also get on your knees and hold his hands, showing him the joy that movement offers as you model moving various parts of your body.

Marching around the room with the instruments is also a good way to share the fun and learning that music offers.

Materials:

Audiotape or CD player, various types of music (e.g., folk, classical, jazz, Disney, children's artists such as Hap Palmer and Raffi), simple musical instruments, rattles, bells

12–18
Months

Playing Hide and Seek

8

Goal:

For the toddler to develop the concept of *in and out* and to experience the fun of Hide and Seek.

Experience:

Children love small nooks and openings. Create hiding places by providing boxes or by making a tent with a blanket over a table.

Playing "Where is...?" makes the game one of great suspense and delight.

1. Take turns hiding and seeking with your toddler. You may need to recruit a third player so you can hide with the child at first to convey the purpose of the game.

2. While waiting with the toddler, say things like, "Now be very quiet. We're hiding. He can't see us. Do you think he will find us?"

Materials:

Boxes, blanket, hiding places such as behind curtains or chairs or in closets

Relating to Children and Adults

Goal:

For the toddler to relate to other children and adults.

Experience:

Teaching young children how to be friends is an important skill. Help the toddler meet and feel comfortable with other children and adults who come into her space by introducing them and having them offer her interesting things. Encourage her to be friendly with and to spontaneously greet people she knows. Talk about what other children are doing with her and encourage her to say hello and good-bye, which are good beginning social skills. Look through a photo album with the child to review names and faces of familiar people.

Helping the child to develop a good relationship with you also is a critical foundation for her social development. In the child care setting, if you have a child who seems to be slow to relate or who is still adjusting, spend individual time with her as often as you can. The child's relationship with you is very important, and it helps to form the basis for how she will relate to other adults and children.

Materials:

Photo album of adults and other children in the toddler's life

12–18
Months

Expressing Range of Emotions

2

Goal:

For the toddler to learn to express a range of emotions and to express affection toward others.

Experience:

Observe your toddler at play. Determine if she is expressing surprise, interest, excitement, anticipation, fear, jealousy, anger, and/or joy. It is healthy to express all of these emotions. Name her feelings. "You seem *happy* to see the puppy."

    Note particularly if the toddler is reaching out with positive emotions to others. Expressions of affection should be fairly consistent at this point. Is she giving hugs and kisses? Model positive expression of affection to the toddler, as appropriate and whenever possible.

Materials:

None

12–18
Months

Pointing to 3 Body Parts

3

Goal:

For the toddler to learn more about who she is by identifying parts of her body.

Experience:

With your toddler, play, "Find your ____ (e.g., toes, tongue)" games. Begin with 1 part on the face and/or limbs and then work up to including 3 or more body parts. Often, the accomplishment sends the family and toddler into peals of delight.

Ask the toddler to wash her arms, hands, and other body parts.

Using a mirror, help the toddler find her nose, tongue, and other body parts. You can do the same using a doll.

Read board books that help children learn about body parts.

Materials:

Mirror, pictures, doll, board books such as *Aleksandra, Where Are Your Toes?* by Christine Dubov

12–18
Months

Identifying Own Image

Goal:

For the toddler to identify his image in a photo or mirror.

Experience:

Look at photos of the toddler together. At the same time, look at photos of various members of his family. Encourage him to pick out the ones of himself. In a child care setting, you can also do this with class photos.

Look in the mirror with the toddler. Talk about who he sees.

Put a photo of the toddler at his place at the table. See if he can find his place by identifying his own photo.

Materials:

Photos of toddler, a mirror

12–18
Months

Playing Ring Around the Rosie

5

Goal:

Experience:

For the toddler to continue to learn social games.

1. Gather two or three children and ask them to hold hands with each other. You may only be able to play with two others at a time until the children learn how to hold hands.

2. Sing "Ring around the rosie, a pocket full of posies. Ashes, ashes, we all fall down."

3. Fall down at the end.

Materials:

Other children

6 Coming for Help

Goal:

For the toddler to recognize when she needs help and how to ask for it.

Experience:

When the toddler comes to ask you for help, be sure to respond quickly and appropriately. Do not wait for her to cry before helping her. When she does come for help for a task that is truly too hard for her, tell her that you are proud of her for asking for help.

When the toddler does cry out of frustration, tell her to ask for help when it is too hard. Say, "Help. You need help. I'll help you."

When the toddler asks you for help and you think she really can do the task herself, offer support and give just the minimum amount of help while she does most of the task herself. Or you can say, "I'll watch you try."

Materials:

Whatever the toddler is working with

12–18
Months

Knowing Other Children

7

Goal:

For the toddler to identify children he plays with and to create a sense of community in a group of toddlers.

Experience:

Look at photo of children in a child care group or in the toddler's life. Name the children. Ask the toddler to point to each child as you name him or her in the photo.

Later, ask the toddler to name the children in the pictures himself.

Play name games and sing songs of hello and good-bye using children's names. Also sing "Where is Alia?"

Materials:

Photos of children the child knows, possibly in an album

12–18
Months

Being Helpful to Others

Goal: For the toddler to learn how to be helpful.

Experience: When you are working in the home or in the child care setting, give the toddler the opportunity to help you. For example, say to her, "Will you please take the towel to the bathroom?"

Running these errands will help the toddler to feel useful and will expand her understanding of the environment and her ability to follow directions. When she is successful, compliment her on being such a good helper and thank her for all of her completions and attempts.

As you go through your day, think of all of the ways the toddler could help you with simple tasks. Show her how to fold clothes, how to stir, and how you put dishes on the table. Her efforts will not be perfect, of course, but the value to her esteem and learning will be great. Compliment her on being a helper.

Materials: Materials you are working with in the home or center that the toddler can identify

12–18 Months

Cooperating with Dressing

1

Goal:

For the toddler to be an active participant in the dressing process, and to learn to do some tasks involved in dressing/undressing.

Experience:

Most toddlers will learn to undress before they learn to dress themselves.

1. To begin, pull the toddler's socks part of the way off and let her finish pulling them off. It is important to talk her through it, explaining what you are doing and asking her to do.

2. Think of undressing and dressing as a partnership from here on. Let toddler do what she can do and work together to do what she can't do. For example, let her reach for her shirt armholes. You may need to guide her arms, but don't do it until she has worked at it herself to some extent. Make her pants into "holes" and let her step into them, and then help her pull them up.

3. Keep encouraging her until she is an active participant in every aspect of dressing and undressing. This can be a joyful learning process!

Materials:

Socks, pull-up pants, big shirts

Feeding Self

Goal:

For the toddler to become independent in feeding himself.

Experience:

1. Cut up the toddler's lunch and present his food and utensils together with those for the rest of the family or child care group.

2. As you eat together, treat the toddler's self-feeding as a matter of fact. Assume he will meet his food needs. Every so often you may want to turn his cup or remind him to use his spoon.

3. Let your toddler feed himself without worrying about how he does it. Reinforce his attempts by telling him what a big boy he is.

Materials:

Easy-to-eat foods, cup that toddler can maneuver, child-safe eating utensils such as a sippy cup

12–18
Months

Giving Up the Bottle

3

Goal:

For the toddler to be independent of his bottle when his family has determined that he is ready.

Experience:

A note before beginning: Make sure the toddler is getting adequate amounts of food at meals and liquids throughout the day. Offer a regular mid-morning and mid-afternoon snack with opportunities to drink out of a sippy or other cup as well.

Bottle independence is best achieved through a process in which you help the toddler give up the bottle in steps.

Note for child care teachers: It is clearly the parents' decision when weaning should occur. However, pediatricians often recommend that this process begins at 12–15 months. In centers, discourage toddlers from carrying bottles around, use a cup or sippy cup at mealtimes, and work out an arrangement with the parents as to when the bottle is given at the center.

1. Begin by helping the toddler become free of his bottle during play times, and discourage him at other times from walking around sipping on his bottle. Throughout the play periods, offer him frequent drinks out of a cup. (For many, a sippy cup works best.)

2. Tell him you will be putting the bottle up but that he may drink out of the cup as many times as he likes.

3. Be sure his play day is well planned and interesting. If his playtime is full, he is less likely to turn to the bottle when he is bored.

It is important to help the child find other outlets than the bottle in times of distress. Offer a soft toy and yourself as comfort when he is upset.

If you decide to let him continue to use his bottle at specified times, tell him when he can have it. "We'll get your bottle at _____." Some children with strong sucking needs may need to have a bottle of water available into their second and third years.

Materials:

Sippy and regular cups and drinks the toddler likes, interesting toys

12-18 Months

Finding One's Place at the Table

4

Goal:

For the toddler to find her place at the table at mealtime.

Experience:

Attach the toddler's picture at her place at the table. Show her and say, "This is your place." When she is seated, talk to her again about it being her place. When she is away from the table, ask her to show you her place.

At another mealtime, call her and see if she can find her place without help.

Materials:

Picture of toddler, clear adhesive shelf paper that can be used to affix the picture to the table

12–18
Months

Sleeping on a Mat, Cot, or Bed

5

Goal:

In a child care setting, for the toddler to "graduate" to the next stage of sleeping arrangements such as going from a crib to a mat.

Experience:

1. Show the toddler her own mat, cot, or bed, and tell her she will now be sleeping on that. (Make sure you lay out the sleeping arrangements for the toddlers in the same place every day.)

2. Tell her that her blanket will still be with her and that she will be like the other (older) children.

3. Stay nearby to offer her back rubbing the first few days.

4. If she gets up after lying down, remind her that it is naptime and ask her to lie down. If she cooperates, congratulate her on her success in staying and sleeping on her mat or bed.

Materials:

Mat, cot, toddler's blanket

12–18
Months

Putting Only Edibles in Mouth

Goal:

For the toddler to only put edibles in his mouth and to know the difference between what does and what does not go in his mouth.

Experience:

Watch the toddler carefully as he plays with small but inedible materials. If he puts something in his mouth that he should not, make a face and indicate to him to spit the material out. Tell him, "Good job…we don't eat playdough," when he spits it out. He will probably try again, but he'll probably look at you as he puts it in his mouth. Shake your head "no" to indicate disapproval.

If he persists in putting small things in his mouth after you have indicated several times not to do so, remove the materials. Bring them out later in the day or another time and try again.

Note: This experience should be closely observed. Do not try it if you don't think you can give the baby your undivided attention. Do not allow the toddler to play with small materials such as beads until you are sure he will not put them in his mouth.

Materials:

Small toys and materials such as playdough, uncooked macaroni, crayons, and other materials that could be tempting to taste

12–18
Months

Sitting in a Small Group

7

Goal:

For the toddler to learn to sit in a group for songs, finger plays, and language games.

Experience:

In child care programs, determine where in the room you will have small-group time. Mark this spot and be consistent in having your group time there every day. Work with a small group of children at a time. Have a very interesting activity, such as bubbles or Guess the Surprise items in a bag. Make your group time very short and interesting. Positively reinforce all of the children who sit for the entire time. Keep group time very short.

If you are having trouble maintaining the children's attention, try closing off your group area and be sure that nothing else is going on in the room at the same time. You can also designate the space by putting tape on the floor or rug and putting carpet squares out for each child to sit on.

Materials:

Bubbles, small objects to put in a bag, bag, tape, rug or individual carpet squares

12–18
Months

Putting away Objects When Asked

Goal:

Experience:

For the toddler to put toys away when asked.

1. Begin by asking the toddler to help you pick up his toys.

2. Bring him the basket or box that the pieces go into. Hold the basket for him.

3. Put in one piece and ask him where the next one goes. Compliment him for putting away the pieces.

4. Next, show him where the containers go. Walk the basket to the appropriate place with him. Point to where the containers go on the shelves. Help him put the containers away.

5. Later on, invite him to take the container back to its appropriate place. You may need to remind him where things go.

6. Finally, ask the toddler to put the containers on the shelves without your pointing to where they go.

Be totally consistent in putting the toys away each day in the same place. You may help the toddler (and yourself) remember by putting a picture of the toy on the shelf where it goes, affixing the picture with clear adhesive shelf paper.

Materials:

Toys, shelves, baskets

12–18
Months

18–24 Months

Beautiful Beginnings: A Developmental Curriculum for Infants and Toddlers   18–24 MONTHS

	1	2	3	4	5	6	7	8
Communication	Expressing Basic Needs with Words	Combining 2 Words	Asking "What's That?"	Matching Objects to Pictures	Repeating Nursery Rhymes	Anticipating Lines in a Familiar Story	Singing Songs	Continuing a Love of Books
Gross Motor	Pushing and Pulling	Running	Learning First Somersaults	Walking on a Balance Beam	Understanding *In, Out, and Through*	Kicking a Ball	Playing Independently on Riding Toys	Following the Leader
Fine Motor	Practicing First Scooping	Playing with Sticky Shapes	Matching Lids and Jars	Transferring with Large and Small Spoons	Stringing Large Beads	Using Funnels	Shelling Corn	Cup-to-Cup Pouring
Intellectual	Putting Small Objects in a Container	Using a 3-Piece Shape Sorter	Understanding *Part and Whole*	Problem Solving	Nesting 3 Cups or Boxes	Stacking Many Blocks	Matching by Color	Telling Immediate Experience
Discovery	Bottle Painting	Playing at the Sand Table	Playing with Playdough	Finger Painting	Playing Parachute	Taking a 5-Senses Nature Walk	Painting with Water	Cooking
Social	Expressing Affection	Expressing Emotional Control	Dealing with Fears	Understanding *Mine*	Giving Things Back	Putting Stickers on Body Parts	Using Adults as Resources	Knowing Self from Mirror Image
Self-Help	Bringing Things for Nap	Using a Spoon to Eat	Washing Hands and Face with Help	Zipping and Unzipping	Undressing	Learning First Outdoor Safety Rules	Blowing Nose	Indicating When Wet and Dry
Pretend	Holding Telephone to Ear	Rocking a "Baby"	Sweeping/Washing Dishes	Trying on Hats and Purses	Pretending to Drive	Pretending to Cook	Using Objects for People	Using Objects for Objects

Expressing Basic Needs with Words 1

Goal: For the toddler to continue "using her words."

Experience: When a toddler cries to have a need met, such as asking for a drink, ask her to use words to tell you what she wants.

Don't get into power struggles or make an issue, but simply remind her by modeling the words she would need, such as, "Need a drink."

When she uses the appropriate words, compliment her and meet the need right away.

Materials: None

Combining 2 Words

2

Goal:

For the toddler to combine 2 words to add meaning.

Experience:

If a toddler is using single words regularly, you may help the child add a second word to add meaning to his communications. For example, he may say "drink," and you may add "want" or "Bobby" to create "want drink" or "Bobby drink."

You can help a toddler who uses signs to put 2 signs together by adding a second sign to the toddler's sign or word. Remember to say the words at the same time that you use the signs.

Materials:

None

Asking "What's That?"

3

Goal: For the toddler to develop the ability to ask questions.

Experience: If you have been working with a toddler for some time, you've probably been asking him, "What's that?" as you did your labeling walks. Now give him the opportunity to be the questioner as he realizes that everything has a name. He may do this by asking, "What's that?" or he may ask, "That?" or he may just point. You may make a game out of it.

Encourage this type of questioning, and whichever method he uses, supply the label, expanding his language at every opportunity.

Materials: Objects in the room

Matching Objects to Pictures

Goal:

For the toddler to expand his use of nouns.

Experience:

1. Select one basket of objects or a tray of cards. Take the objects or cards out one at a time and line them up in front of the toddler. Together name each item.

2. Put away the cards or objects.

3. Now invite the toddler to take out the cards or objects, naming the objects or what is pictured on the cards.

Materials:

Baskets of 3–7 objects such as different kinds of animals, plastic fruits and vegetables, and so forth; cards with pictures of objects

Repeating Nursery Rhymes

5

Goal:

For the toddler to expand her memory for words and enjoyment of rhyme.

Experience:

1. Recite nursery rhymes and/or listen to audiotapes or CDs. These may be played during naptimes as well. (Be sure the wording in all of your versions of the rhyme is the same.)

2. Then recite the nursery rhymes with the toddler and leave off the last part of every line. See if she fills in the missing words.

3. Gradually work backwards until the toddler can recite the entire rhyme.

Materials:

Nursery rhyme books, audiotapes or CDs

Anticipating Lines in a Familiar Story

Goal:

For the toddler to improve her memory for following and remembering a story.

Experience:

Read and tell one or two stories over and over. *The Three Bears* is a good choice, but be sure all versions of the story are consistent. Vary your voice with the characters as you read their lines. Work with the toddler to stay with you through the story.

At first, her attention may wander, but over time she will anticipate familiar lines. Encourage her to fill in the lines with you. For example, "But Daddy Bear's porridge was too…?"

The goal here is for the toddler to become so familiar with the story that she helps to tell it.

Materials:

Stories or storybooks with simple storylines such as The Three Bears or *The Baby's Lap Book,* by Kay Chorao, accompanying puppets and videos (optional)

Singing Songs

7

Goal:

For the toddler to further develop a love of and familiarity with music.

Experience:

Encourage the toddler to sing and pantomime along with the lyrics in these and other songs:

"Johnny"

"Johnny works with one hammer, one hammer, one hammer. Johnny works with one, then he works with two." [Repeat with *two* and *three*. Final verse: "Then he goes to sleep. Goodnight, Johnny."]

"If You're Happy and You Know It"

"If you're happy and you know it, clap your hands." [Repeat.] "If you're happy and you know it, then your hands will surely show it. If you're happy and you know it, clap your hands." [Repeat, substituting "stomp your feet," "pat your tummy," "wiggle your fingers," and so forth for "clap your hands."]

"Row Your Boat"

"Row, row, row your boat, gently down the stream. Merrily, merrily, merrily, merrily, life is but a dream." [Repeat several times.]

Materials:

The following audiotapes and CDs are recommended for the toddler's collection (see also websites for children's music in Bibliography):

Learning Basic Skills Through Music by Hap Palmer

Sounds from Sesame Street Records

Continuing a Love of Books

8

Goal:

Experience:

Materials:

For the toddler to continue to develop enjoyment of books.

Read to the toddler every day and encourage her caregivers to read to her at night before bedtime.

Many wonderful books are available for children of this age. Just a few are listed below. Your local library can supply lists of books great for this age.
　Recommended books for this age include the following:

Where's Spot? by Eric Hill

Aleksandra, Where Is Your Nose? by Christine Dubov and J. Schneider

Lily Goes to the Playground by Jill Krementz

Pushing and Pulling

1

Goal:

For the toddler to move objects by pushing and pulling.

Experience:

Provide the toddler with toys to *push*. For variety, offer boxes, small chairs, or a wagon. Put something in the box or wagon and show the toddler he is transporting the toys he is pushing.

Offer a variety of toys to *pull.* Encourage him to walk and pull toys in various ways (e.g., without watching the toy, by looking back at it, by walking backwards, by going fast, by turning corners).

Materials:

Pushing toys such as a shopping cart, activity walker, wagon, corn popper; pull toys with strings attached to them

18–24 Months

Running

Goal:

For the toddler to learn the joy of running.

Experience:

After he has mastered walking, chase after the toddler and tell him to run quickly or you'll catch him. When he does run, tell him what a great runner he is.

Throw a ball or small toy and encourage the toddler to run after it.

Stand by the toddler and prepare for a race. Say, "On your mark, get set, go!" Run alongside him.

Materials:

Small, attractive toy or ball

Learning First Somersaults

3

Goal:

For the toddler to experience doing a somersault with help.

Experience:

Is she is interested, help the toddler get down on her hands and knees with her hands at the bottom of a wedge's "slide" and her knees at the top of the slide. Ask her to put her head down on the mat and to tuck her chin. Then slowly lift her legs over her head to help her complete the somersault.

Another method is to put a medium-sized ball on a mat. Have the toddler lie down on the ball, face down, with her head hanging down. Encourage her to walk her hands along the mat so that she begins to roll forward off the ball. Remind her to tuck her chin, and help lift her legs to complete the somersault.

A toddler will often relax into a somersault when you assist her through the roll.

Materials:

Foam wedge mat approximately 12 inches high x 18 inches wide x 24 inches long, beach ball, flat mat

4

Walking on a Balance Beam

18–24 Months

Goal:

For the toddler to walk on a low balance beam independently.

Experience:

If your toddler hasn't walked on a balance beam before, help her get used to it by providing support at first. You may have already encouraged your toddler to try walking across a balance beam this way. In either case, gradually withdraw your support. Play a game to encourage her to cross independently. Give her much praise for trying to walk (no matter how far) on her own.

Encourage the toddler to walk around the outside of a tire or along a garden wall.

Note: *Hold on to the toddler's hand if she is unsteady on her feet.*

Materials:

Balance beam about 4–6 inches off the floor, old tires, or a low garden wall

Understanding *In, Out,* and *Through*

5

Goal:

For the toddler to learn new ways to move in, out, and through large containers.

Experience:

Create a series of boxes, tunnels, tires, and/or forms for the toddler to crawl in, through, and on top of. Let the toddler explore these spaces freely, and, as he moves, describe his position. For example, when the toddler is inside a box, say, "I see you're *in* the box."

Set a ladder with wide spaces between rungs on its side on the floor and encourage the toddler to crawl back and forth through its rungs. If the toddler doesn't understand, you might demonstrate the concept by moving a stuffed animal through the rungs the way you want the toddler to move. For variation on this activity, set the ladder on its side against the entrance to a tent or a box.

Set up a tent. After the toddler is familiar with the tent, construct a tunnel to the tent's entrance and invite him to crawl in and out of the tent.

Materials:

Foam shapes, large boxes (refrigerator and dishwasher boxes are great), old tires, carpet-covered barrels, wooden ladder, tent, fabric for constructing a tunnel

Kicking a Ball

Goal:

For the toddler to kick a ball that is not in motion.

Experience:

1. Begin with a large beach ball. Show the toddler how to kick the ball.

2. When the toddler is proficient in kicking the large ball, introduce a smaller ball to her. Practice kicking this ball with her.

3. The next step is to show the toddler a broad target, such as a large box turned on its end. Encourage the toddler to be a soccer player and to kick the smaller ball into the box.

4. The toddler may now be ready to kick a moving ball. Roll the large beach ball very slowly toward her and encourage her to kick it as it comes to her. This skill is not to be expected from many toddlers.

Applaud all efforts.

Materials:

Large and small beach balls, large box

Playing Independently on Riding Toys

Goal: For the toddler to get on, ride, and get off riding toys independently.

Experience: Offer the toddler a riding toy. Observe and support his ability to get on and off and to navigate the moving toy.

As his skill develops, offer different kinds of riding toys.

When some proficiency has been achieved, find a *gentle* hill and encourage the toddler to ride up and down the hill.

Materials: Different kinds of riding toys, including types to sit *in*, such as a small car or fire engine, and types to sit *on*, such as a small tyke bike or tricycle

18–24 Months

Following the Leader

8

Goal: For the toddler to imitate large motions.

Experience: Invite the toddler to imitate you while you model a range of physical movements. The following are different games to play:

Reach for the sky and then reach for the ground. Repeat 4 times.

Sit on the floor with your legs outstretched. Reach high and make yourself "big." Then tuck your arms in your lap, dip your head, and make yourself "small." Repeat 4 times.

Run in place 8 times to a count of 4.

Nod your head 8 times.

Move your knees from side to side 8 times.

Touch body parts as you say the following: "Head and shoulders, knees and toes." Repeat. Then say, "Eyes and ears and mouth and nose. Head and shoulders, knees and toes."

Try to keep your knees straight while you bend over and touch the floor. The toddler can finish your fun session by running under your "bridge."

Materials: None

Practicing First Scooping

1

Goal:

For the toddler to improve fine motor skills by learning to scoop.

Experience:

Scooping is a very popular activity for children of this age. Scooping has 3 motions: scooping, maintaining the action, and releasing. Encourage the toddler to complete all 3 motions.

Show the toddler how to scoop, move to another container, and release the contents into another container. Encourage the toddler to scoop from one container to another on his own.

This activity can be done with divided buckets and dishes.

Variations: You can endlessly vary the scooping experiences simply by changing the type of scoop, container, or type of material being scooped.

Materials:

Wash pan, small container, divided dish, divided bucket, material to scoop (e.g., beans, macaroni), and scoops (e.g., ice cream, flour, large, small, light, heavy). A water table provides a good base for catching the spills of initial scooping activities.

Playing with Sticky Shapes

2

Goal:

For the toddler to further develop the pincer grasp.

Experience:

Show the toddler how to press forms onto a window or mirror. Invite him to try. Next, show the toddler how to press 2 or 3 forms together to make a line or picture on the window.

    This activity further develops the thumb and forefinger pincer grasp needed for so many fine motor tasks. It is also fun for toddlers!

Materials:

Colorforms-type material in sticky plastic, a window or mirror

Matching Lids and Jars

3

18–24 Months

Goal:

For the toddler to match lids to jars.

Experience:

1. Show the toddler the assortment of jars with their lids.

2. Take each one out of the basket, and one by one, remove the lids and randomly line them up in front of the jars.

3. Now try to put the lids back on the jars. Match each lid to a jar and nod your head yes if it is a match and no if it isn't. If yes, put the lid on with exaggerated motion. If no, try the next and so forth until all are matched.

This can be a very popular activity if you have selected a variety of jars.

Materials:

Simple, unbreakable jars and matching lids (at least three different jar–lid combinations), and a basket large enough to hold them all. Also, consider tins and pop-off lids from candy jars.

Transferring with Large and Small Spoons

Goal:

For the toddler to improve coordination by learning to spoon small items from one container to another.

Experience:

Pour macaroni into a wash pan and show the toddler how to spoon it into a bowl. Fill the wash pan full so it is easy to spoon from. Fill half of a divided bucket with macaroni and show the toddler how to spoon from side to side.

You can do the same with a clean, divided pet feeding dish.

When developmentally appropriate, provide a smaller spoon for the toddler to practice scooping from one container to another.

Use your imagination in setting up things for him to spoon from side to side in the pet feeding dish or from one separate dish to another.

It often works well to have children do their first spooning experiences at a water table because there are bound to be spills.

Materials:

Large and small spoon; divided bucket; pet feeding dish; wash pan and bowl; substances such as macaroni, navy beans, or puff balls; water table

18–24 Months

Stringing Large Beads

5

Goal:

For the toddler to learn the multistep fine motor task of putting large beads on a string.

Experience:

Show the toddler how to string a bead onto a plastic tube and slide the bead down to the end. This is a 3-step task of putting string through the bead's hole, pulling it out the other end of the bead, and then pulling the bead down the length of the tube or string. Help the toddler master each of the 3 steps. It might be easier if the toddler works with the plastic tube or string when it is lying on a table top rather than holding it in her hand.

1. Show the toddler how to thread each bead through the hole.

2. Pull the bead through the tube.

3. Slide each bead to the end, then add another.

4. Next, have the toddler string a bead onto a length of string. Be sure the plastic tip of the string is longer than the length of the bead and that there is a knot at the end of the string. Again, it might be easier if the toddler works with a piece of string that is lying on the table top rather than holding it in her hand.

Show the toddler how to take the beads off of the string or tube and put them away.

Materials:

Large beads with large holes, plastic tube or stiff plastic string, string with a plastic tip (such as a shoe string), basket to hold the beads and plastic or string

Using Funnels

6

Goal: For the toddler to scoop into a funnel.

Experience:

1. Working over a water table or sand pile, place a basin full of scooping material beside a funnel and container for catching the material.

2. Place the funnel on top of the container to catch the material.

3. Scoop, spoon, or use your hands to transfer the material from the basin to the funnel and show the toddler how to do this.

Variations: With funnel activities, it is also great fun for the toddler if you vary the material used for scooping. Also change the type of funnel to further vary the experience.

Materials: Scoop and/or spoon, funnels of different sizes, containers to scoop out of and funnel into, material to scoop (be sure material will pass through the funnel when moving quickly and won't clog up), a water table or other set-up for containing spills

7

Shelling Corn

Goal: For the toddler to use very precise finger motions.

Experience: Put ears of dried corn in a water table or in a divided bucket. Give the toddler a dish to hold the pieces of corn. Show her how to pick the corn kernels off of the cob one by one and drop them into the dish.

Note: *Watch the toddler carefully so she does not eat the kernels or put them in her ears or nose.*

Materials: Containers for the shelled and unshelled corn, ears of corn, water table

Cup-to-Cup Pyouring

Goal:

For the toddler to continue to develop wrist dexterity by pouring from one cup to another.

Experience:

Begin cup-to-cup pouring by using a solid object in a cup. Liquids will come later!

1. Show the toddler how to leave one cup on the table and pick up the other. The tendency for a toddler is to lift both cups and try to join them in the air. Show her that one cup must remain stationary.

2. Pick up the other cup and pour its contents into the stationary cup.

3. Encourage the toddler to pour cup to cup while keeping one cup on the table. Praise her attempts.

Note: *Watch the child carefully to make sure she does not swallow small materials.*

Materials:

Two matching cups or plastic glasses, material to pour between cups (a single bead or walnut works well), tray or basin to hold the cups, possibly a water table to catch spills

Putting Small Objects in a Container

1

Goal:

For the toddler to learn to put different kinds of objects into small containers.

Experience:

In previous container play, the toddler learned to put things in and take them out of containers. Most likely, she now knows the entire sequence: putting objects in the container, taking the lid off, taking objects out, and repeating the process. With this knowledge, the toddler can perform these processes independently.

This activity involves smaller objects and an opening that is the shape of the object, so it is basically a shape-fitting activity.

Encourage the toddler to complete the process of fitting the object through the hole in the top of the container, taking the lid off the container, and dumping out the object.

Materials:

Container, small objects that correspond to holes in top of container (e.g., puff balls and round hole, formica chips in a slit hole, clothespins in a milk bottle)

18–24
Months

Using a 3-Piece Shape Sorter

2

Goal:

For the toddler to recognize, sort, and fit 3 objects by shape.

Experience:

Be sure the toddler can put a circular object or square-shaped object into proper holes before you introduce this third shape.

1. Review the names of the square and circle and point to where they go in the shape sorter.

2. After seeing that he is ready for the triangle (or another third shape), present it.

3. Now, slowly draw your finger around the opening for the new shape. Tell him the name of the shape.

4. Offer him a turn.

5. Cut three different shapes in a coffee can or oatmeal box lid.

6. Supply shapes that fit in only one of the holes.

7. Encourage the toddler to sort objects by shape as he pushes them through the appropriate holes.

Materials:

A 3-piece shape sorter may be homemade or purchased. Those involving circle, square, and triangle shapes are preferable to circle, square, and rectangle sorters. You'll also need objects in the appropriate shapes.

Understanding *Part* and *Whole*

3

Goal:

For the toddler to understand part-to-whole relationships.

Experience:

Show the toddler an object with 2 halves combined, such as a barrel. Take it apart and put it back together. Offer the object to the toddler to take apart and put back together.

Follow a similar approach in taking apart a 2-part puzzle and putting it back together. Invite the toddler to watch you, and then ask her to do the same.

Show the toddler a picture of a familiar object or animal. Cover half of the picture. Ask the toddler to uncover the covered half.

These exercises will help your toddler think about part-to-whole relationships.

Materials:

Any object or puzzle divided into two pieces that make a whole, such as barrels, plastic eggs, and many puzzles. You may make your own puzzle by mounting a picture on cardboard, cutting it in half, and laminating the halves.

18–24
Months

Problem Solving

Goal:

For the toddler to problem solve using advance thought or trial-and-error effort.

Experience:

Present the toddler with a long necklace and a small box. Observe if the toddler rolls up or otherwise compresses the necklace in order to make it fit into the box. Let the toddler work with this task in a trial-and-error fashion if she doesn't immediately see what to do.

Cover 1 ring hole on a ring-and-spindle toy. See if the toddler sets the covered ring aside, which indicates she knows it won't go on the spindle. Again, if she doesn't anticipate the problem with the ring, let her use trial and error until the solution appears to her.

Play a game of releasing small cars down an incline for several days. After this, place a block on the "road's" path about halfway down. Give the toddler a car and see if she anticipates that the blocks need to be moved before the car will go down.

Think of your own games that also call on the toddler to anticipate a solution to a problem.

Materials:

Small box and long beaded necklace; ring-and-spindle toy with something to cover one of the rings; car, incline, block

Nesting 3 Cups or Boxes

5

Goal:

For the toddler to understand size relationships by successfully nesting 3 cups or 3 boxes.

Experience:

Line up 3 nesting cups and point to each while talking about its size. Show the toddler how to nest the 3 cups. Let him experiment with this. It may take him a while to correctly nest the cups.

Offer boxes that fit into each other. Follow the above directions with the toddler.

If these exercises are too hard, take away one of the objects, nesting the smaller container into the larger.

When the child has mastered nesting 3 cups or boxes, you may offer more cups or boxes to nest.

You may also turn the cups over to build a pyramid (e.g., tower of ascending-size blocks).

Materials:

Nesting cups, boxes, and/or towers (3 of each)

18–24
Months

Stacking Many Blocks

Goal:

For the toddler to combine many blocks to build a high tower, long train, or 3-block bridge.

Experience:

Now the real fun of working with blocks comes in! How tall a tower can the toddler build? How long a train of blocks can she line up one by one?

Alternate stacking blocks with the toddler—first you, then her, then you, then her. Gradually let her take over the construction. When a tower is done, let her knock it down! If more permanent towers appeal to you or the child, try building one out of Duplo blocks.

Blocks placed side by side in one long line also have great appeal. Ask the toddler to show you how long she can make a line of blocks. Pretend it's a train, or make one connecting Duplo wagons.

Show the toddler how to make a 3-block bridge.

These experiences help to build the toddler's visual-spatial skills through discriminating differences—a tower of 3 blocks is quite different spatially than a train of blocks or a tower, for example.

Materials:

Unit or alphabet blocks, Duplo blocks

Matching by Color

7

Goal:

For the toddler to understand the correspondence principle of matching objects by color.

Experience:

Show the toddler how to match objects by color, placing them in color-matched containers.

This activity may be done in many ways. The objects that may be matched by color are limited only by your imagination. You may also begin with 2 colors and increase to 3.

1. Cut off the tops of bleach or plastic milk jugs, rinse them out well, and tape them with masking or duct tape if the edges are sharp.

2. Line the edges with permanent markers in primary colors (red, blue, yellow). Create other color-matching containers.

3. Show the toddler how to drop small objects that match the color of each jug's edge. As you match the objects with their containers, nod your head yes or shake it no depending on the success of the color match.

Continue until all objects are sorted.

Note: *Always observe toddlers carefully to make sure they do not put small objects in their mouths.*

Materials:

Plastic bleach or milk jugs; red, yellow, and blue permanent color markers; small objects such as counting bears of colors corresponding to the markers

Telling Immediate Experience

8

Goal: For the toddler to gain a sense of time, beginning with *now*.

Experience: When you are playing with a toddler, ask her, "What are we doing now?" If she doesn't know, say something such as, "*Now* we are playing with playdough. Soon we'll put it away and have a snack."

Talk about what you are doing *now* throughout the day.

Materials: None

Bottle Painting

1

Goal:

For the toddler to learn a new way of painting.

Experience:

1. Begin by taping a large piece of paper to the table.

2. Demonstrate use of the bottle paints. A choice of two colors is easiest for the child and the least distracting.

3. Let the child experiment holding the bottle and dabbing or sliding it along the paper.

Materials:

Bottle paints with brushes or sponges on the ends (available commercially), art aprons or smocks, paper

Playing at the Sand Table

2

18–24
Months

Goal:

For the toddler to explore materials such as sand, rice, and oatmeal.

Experience:

1. Place a sufficient amount of sand, rice, or oatmeal in a small container such as a small washbasin or dish. To confine spills, put the small container in a water table or empty swimming pool.

2. Give the toddler scoops and spoons and encourage her to feel and pour the material.

3. Remind the toddler that the sand (or rice or oatmeal) stays at the table, and keep an eye on her until you're sure she's learned to not carry the material around the room.

Materials:

Sand, rice, or oatmeal; water table or empty child's swimming pool; scoops and spoons; dish or small wash basin

Playing with Playdough

Goal:

For the toddler to experience tactile activities such as pounding, poking, squishing, and rolling.

Experience:

1. Take a small ball of playdough and divide it between yourself and the child.

2. Demonstrate poking, pounding, squishing, and rolling.

3. Encourage the toddler to do these activities with his own playdough.

To enhance this activity, make your own playdough using the recipe in the materials list.

Materials:

Playdough, either purchased or homemade (see page 28)

Finger Painting

4

Goal:

For the toddler to become acquainted with finger paint and experience early self-expression through this medium.

Experience:

1. Tape large pieces of paper to the table and put an art smock or apron on the toddler.

2. Put a *small* amount of paint on the paper and demonstrate smearing the paint. You may want to let the child rub and squish the paint in her hands first to become familiar with its texture.

3. Encourage the toddler to smear the paint on the paper.

Please note that not all toddlers will enjoy touching the paint. Its texture may be uncomfortable or the toddler may not like to get messy, so he may not wish to try it. If he doesn't like it the first time, try again in a week or so.

Materials:

Large pieces of paper, at least 8½–14 inches in size, (butcher or finger-paint paper works best), finger paints, art smock or apron

Discovery 18–24

5

Goal:

For the toddler to experience air movement and the sensation of moving in and out.

Experience:

This activity requires several adults and is fun to do with a group of children. Spread the parachute or sheet on the floor or ground. Let the toddlers touch it.

1. Have the adults take the edges of the parachute or sheet and lift it up.

2. When it billows up, invite the toddlers to run underneath. Now move the parachute or sheet up and down. Invite the toddlers to run in and out. The toddlers will love catching the breezes as they run!

3. Spread the parachute or sheet on the floor and let two or three toddlers lie down in the middle. Now have the adults and other toddlers move the edges of the parachute or sheet up and down. (Don't try to lift the children up off the ground!)

The play is in the movement. The texture and color of the parachute or sheet will also add interest.

18–24 Months

Materials:

Parachute or large sheet (a parachute allows air to pass in and out more easily) and at least 3 adults

6

Taking a 5-Senses Nature Walk

18–24 Months

Goal:

For the toddler to explore a widening world.

Experience:

This experience is good for both groups and individual children. Travel to new outside places, such as nearby parks, duck ponds, or any place of interest in your neighborhood. These places can be "rediscovered" at different times of the year.

Take a paper bag and collect rocks, pinecones, leaves, and flowers. Help the toddler discover his outside world by stressing multiple senses: touching, smelling, hearing, and seeing. Use words to describe sensory experiences.

Another time, you might go on a "listening" or "smelling" walk.

Travel to an inside place such as a shopping mall or grocery store with the same sort of discovery attitude. Notice textures, colors, and sounds. The sense of taste may be used if you buy a special treat for a snack.

Use your imagination to think of worlds to discover, both inside and outside.

Note: *It's best to start out with short walks. Some children aren't used to long outings or to walking very far.*

Materials:

A bag for collecting items; a cart, wagon, or stroller (helpful but not necessary)

Painting with Water

7

Goal:

Experience:

For the toddler to learn a new way to experience water.

This activity builds on a toddler's love of water and is especially fun outdoors. If done indoors, have a lot of towels handy and work over a tile or water-resistant surface.

1. First, the toddler should put on an art apron. In warm weather, the toddler can wear a swim diaper or a bathing suit.

2. Put a small amount of water in the buckets.

3. Give the toddler a paintbrush, and let her "paint" waterproof objects such as plastic tables and chairs, walls, or a fence.

This is a great activity for groups of children, who can all paint together using separate buckets or sharing them.

Materials:

Water, small buckets (ice cream buckets or sand pail), 1- to 3-inch paintbrushes, art aprons

18–24
Months

8

Cooking

Goal:

For the toddler to experience cooking, using taste, smell, and touch.

Experience:

1. Choose a simple recipe, such as banana bread, pizza, or cookies. Have all of the ingredients prepared before inviting the toddler to help you.

2. Invite the toddler to wash his hands.

3. Let the toddler add pre-measured ingredients and stir.

4. When cooking with a young child, it is more important to focus on the child's learning process than the product. In other words, don't worry if things get messy or if the food doesn't turn out perfectly.

5. Let the child smell and taste the ingredients.

Continue to share the joy of cooking with the toddler on other days!

Materials:

A simple recipe, all of the needed ingredients, an apron

18–24 Months

Expressing Affection

1

Goal:

For the toddler to express caring feelings and give hugs to other children.

Experience:

Toddlers sometimes find it difficult to learn to express affection to other children when their partners do not cooperate; however, expressing affection is important.

Begin by complimenting the toddler on giving his teddy bear love when he hugs it.

When he is with another child and both seem to be sharing pleasurable feelings, ask him if he'd like to give the child a hug. Do this a couple of times and then watch to see if the children hug each other spontaneously.

Materials:

A soft bear or doll

18–24
Months

Expressing Emotional Control 2

Goal:

For the toddler to improve his ability to maintain emotional control.

Experience:

Toddlers may be prone to emotional outbursts, but it is not a good idea to accept frequent temper tantrums. Helping a toddler be in control (with some latitude) is a worthwhile objective.

When the toddler tries to express strong emotions in a calmer way, tell him, "Thank you for letting me know in a way that I can understand." Observe that you are reinforcing the expected behavior.

Notice when he seems to be struggling to regulate his feelings, and then provide support. Help him succeed. When he has an especially good day in regulating his emotions, give him a small reward or let him do a favorite activity.

Materials:

None

18–24
Months

Dealing with Fears

3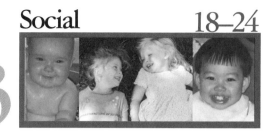

Goal:

For the toddler to confront his fears.

Experience:

As toddlers become aware of a bigger world, they often develop some fears. We can help by respecting these fears, and through gradual exposure, we may help them overcome many.

Begin by acknowledging a child's fear. Tell him you understand that it is scary to him.

Some fears are avoidable. If you can avoid a child's feared object for a while, do so. For example, if a child is afraid of loud sirens, you might not want to take him on a field trip to a fire station. Other feared objects may not be as easily avoided. For example, if the toddler is afraid of the dark stairs to your entry, think of ways to make them less scary by adding lighting, if possible. If you are always rushed when you go down them, try to be relaxed. Since most toddlers love climbing, perhaps it would be fun if he could take 20 minutes some day to crawl up and down the stairs with your supervision.

The point is to change the child's perspective of the feared item, and through gradual exposure and your support, make it seem less fearsome.

Materials:

Whatever the child is afraid of, such as a vacuum cleaner or the stairs to the basement

18–24
Months

Understanding *Mine*

Goal:

For the toddler to express a healthy sense of possession.

Experience:

Saying "mine" is a toddler's way of saying she believes she is a person who can claim objects that are separate from her. It's a healthy developmental sign.

When you're playing with a toddler who has a favorite blanket or doll, take your own blanket or object and say, "Annie's blanket" [or "Mommy's blanket"]. "This is mine." Then point to the blanket again and say, "This is…[wait for her to say "mine"]." If she doesn't say it, you can say, "Annie's" and then, "mine."

As you go about your day, when a toddler comes to you and asks for something of yours, you might say, "It's mine, but I'll share it with you."

To help a toddler with the conceptual part of ownership, identify the things that are clearly hers. Say, "This is yours. It's your blanket. Here's your coat. This is Annie's coat."

Materials:

Toddler's favorite toys, blanket, other possessions

Giving Things Back

5

Goal:

For the toddler to respond to requests to give an object to others.

Experience:

Another side of the "mine" idea is that some things belong to others.

When children squabble over a toy, note who had the toy first. To the one who appeared on the scene second, say, "This is Ryan's. You may have it when he's finished. Here, this one is Ashley's." Praise her when she gives the toy back.

When children are playing, you can identify what you see with them. "This is Ashley's bear now. She is playing with it. Ryan has the pegs now."

When children are playing with a divisible material such as playdough and a new child joins in, ask each child to give the newcomer a small piece. Thank them for giving some and show them that they all have enough to play with.

Ask one child to get another child's coat or blanket and to give it to its owner.

Materials:

Children's toys, blankets, coats, other possessions

18–24
Months

Putting Stickers on Body Parts

6

Goal: For the toddler to identify parts of the body.

Experience: Toddlers love stickers, so this is a fun way for a toddler to learn more about the parts of her body.

Ask the toddler to put a sticker on an elbow, tummy, hand, leg, and so forth. Next, ask the child to move the sticker to areas such as the wrist, knee, neck, and chin.

Materials: Stickers

18–24
Months

Using Adults as Resources

7

Goal:

For the toddler to use adults as a resource.

Experience:

It's important for a child to know when he needs help and where to get it. When a toddler has a problem and begins to cry, go to him and say, "Come and get me when you can't fix it. I will help you." Then, when the toddler does come for help, say, "You came to get me for help when you needed it. Good job. Now we can fix the wagon."

Another way toddlers will use adults as a resource is to show them something. Whenever a toddler takes your hand and tugs on it, go with her. She may have something to show you. If she does, spend some time with her to see what she wants you to see.

Materials:

Whatever the toddler is working on

18–24 Months

Knowing Self from Mirror Image

8

Goal: For the toddler to differentiate self from image in mirror.

Experience:

1. Sit in front of a mirror with the child. Place your finger on the child's nose. Say, "My finger is on your nose." Then remove your finger and place it on the nose of the child as seen in the reflected image. Say, "My finger is on the nose in the mirror." Invite the child to do the same thing, putting her finger on her nose and on her nose in the reflection. As she does this, she gains understanding of how she is different from what she sees in the mirror.

2. Ask her to touch her nose. Does she touch her own nose or the mirror image? Encourage her to touch her own nose. You may want to say, "This is Marina and this is a mirror. This is Marina's nose and this nose is in the mirror. Where is Casie's nose? Where is Casie's nose in the mirror?"

3. Play the game again, asking her to find other parts of her body that she can see in the mirror.

Materials: Mirror large enough to show a clear view of child's head and shoulders

18–24
Months

Bringing Things for Nap

1

Goal:

For the toddler to gain independence by being an active participant in the naptime ritual.

Experience:

When it is time for a nap, invite the toddler to get her blanket, toy, or another item. Then, encourage her to go by herself to her mat/bed with her things.

It is important to have her things in the same easy-to-get-to place every day and to keep her schedule as consistent as possible.

Materials:

Blanket, soft toy, mats, and whatever else is a part of the toddler's going-to-sleep routine

18–24
Months

Using a Spoon to Eat

2

Goal:

For the toddler to use a spoon successfully (with little spilling).

Experience:

Give the toddler foods that lend themselves to being successfully eaten with a spoon.

If the toddler begins messing with the spoon, put the utensil away and switch to finger food.

Once a toddler experiences success with a spoon, he will become more and more skillful.

Materials:

Easy-to-hold spoon, a dish with high sides

18–24
Months

Washing Hands and Face with Help

3

Goal: For the toddler to be an active participant in hand and face washing.

Experience:

Hands: Be sure the toddler can reach the sink or basin with a stepstool. Turn on the water and show him how to wet his hands. Rub some soap on his hands and show him how to rub them back and forth to make lather. Then show him how to rinse. Have a towel beside him so he can pick it up himself, and if you're using a paper towel, have him throw it away himself.

Face: Tell the toddler it's time to wash his face. If this is something he doesn't like, a warning will help him prepare. Invite him to step on the stool, wet the washcloth, and then rub soap on it. Tell him you will wash his face and then he may help you if he likes. Tell him to watch in the mirror. When you have washed him sufficiently, give him the washcloth and let him wash also. Remember, your goal is for him to wash his own face, so the time spent helping him understand the process will pay off in the future. Help him dry his face and show him where the towel goes.

At this stage, hand and face washing are likely to be carried out by you and the child together. Later, he will do these independently.

Materials: Sink, soap, towel, washcloth, step stool, appropriate dish for soap

18-24
Months

Zipping and Unzipping

4

Goal: For the toddler to gain skill using a zipper.

Experience: Purchase or make a frame for a zipper (available from toy supply stores or catalogs) that is closed on the bottom. Explain zipping and unzipping to the toddler and show him how each works. Let him practice on his own.

When the toddler puts on and takes off his coat, let him assist in the zipping and unzipping process. It will, of course, be a long time before he will be able to join an open zipper.

For now, he will enjoy being a part of the process, and he will gain confidence in working with fasteners.

Materials: Zipper frame, coat

18–24
Months

5

Undressing

Goal:

For the toddler to actively participate in the undressing process.

Experience:

When the toddler comes indoors in cold weather, ask her to take off her hat. Generally, a toddler will discover how to do this on her own. Offer her different kinds of hats to try on and take off in front of a mirror. Each hat feels a little different and will require a different tug to remove. She will enjoy looking at herself in the mirror with a hat on and watching herself pull it off.

When taking off a toddler's coat, pull one sleeve out and let her finish removing her coat independently. Soon she may be able to take it off entirely by herself.

Materials:

Hats, coat, jacket or sweater, mirror

18–24
Months

Learning First Outdoor Safety Rules

Goal:

For the toddler to come when called and to stay with you when on a walk.

Experience:

It's important that a toddler learn ground rules for safety when outdoors, two of which are to come when called and to stay with you on a walk.

Be very consistent in calling the child's name (or children's names one by one) on outings, such as when leaving the playground or the park. Praise the child/children for coming. A good way to begin this would be to make the period or event following the outdoor play period a pleasant one so that the children build positive associations between coming when called and what follows. Don't tell the child/children, "Come and get your treat." Expect the child/children to come, and when they do, provide the treat the first several times.

When on a walk, one of the easiest ways to keep a group of children safe and together is to use a walking rope. This is a rope long enough for the group of children to walk beside, with a loop for each child to grasp.

Later, practice taking a walk without the rope with the child (or children) and provide a lot of praise when your safety rules for staying nearby are followed.

Materials:

Walking rope

18–24 Months

7

Blowing Nose

Goal:

For the toddler to begin to take responsibility for using a tissue.

Experience:

Show a toddler the tissue box and invite her to take a tissue. Take an extra one. Go to the mirror and let her watch you wipe your nose. Ask her if she would like to try wiping her own nose. Show her where the tissue goes in the garbage.

The next time the toddler's nose is running, ask her if she remembers where the tissues are. Then ask her whether she would like to wipe her own nose or have you help her. Work toward having the toddler wipe her nose independently.

Demonstrate how you blow your nose, and ask the toddler to try blowing and wiping her own nose. Some children understand this at a very young age, whereas others don't for some time.

Compliment the toddler on her attempts to keep her nose dry.

Materials:

Tissues

Indicating When Wet and Dry

8

Goal:

For the toddler to begin awareness of toilet learning.

Experience:

For some time, you've probably been commenting on whether a child is "poopy" (or other preferred term) when being changed. You may ask, "Are you poopy?" when a child is playing. This is the time that some toddlers start to give you some sign that they understand what this means and will tell you when their diapers are soiled. If a toddler gives you any indication at all, praise her highly for her awareness and communication. Later, she may be ready to share the same awareness of being wet. Sometimes wearing cloth diapers intensifies the sensation of being wet.

It is now time to show your child what toileting is all about. Let her observe someone else using the toilet, and explain the process. Offer the toddler a chance to sit on the toilet. The first time she sits, she will probably not produce. Many children need some time to get used to the chair or toilet. Be relaxed and give this stage plenty of time.

Materials:

Diapers, possibly a small toilet chair

18–24 Months

Holding Telephone to Ear

1

Goal:

For the toddler to begin pretending skills by imitating a telephone conversation.

Experience:

In this activity, you may use a real telephone or a play telephone.

Offer the telephone to the toddler and pretend to talk to him. Ask questions. Supply answers with new words. Pretend to talk on your own telephone.

Materials:

Real telephone or play telephone

18–24
Months

Rocking a "Baby"

Goal:

For the toddler to pretend to rock a baby so as to add to her ability to "be like Mommy" and other adults. To foster feelings of nurturing and affection.

Experience:

When you know a toddler can rock by himself in a rocking chair, give him a baby doll and tell him the baby needs to be rocked. Say, "Can you rock the baby?"

Remind the toddler of songs he might sing to the baby or any other "baby activity" he might be familiar with.

Materials:

Child-sized rocker, small doll

18–24 Months

Sweeping/ Washing Dishes

3

Goal:

For the toddler to pretend to do household tasks.

Experience:

This experience fosters a toddler's wish to copy the work he sees being done at home. At this point, accuracy in work is not a goal.

When you are sweeping, give the toddler a broom and ask him if he would also like to sweep. At this stage, sweeping will be a back-and-forth movement with the broom.

Invite the toddler to wash dishes with you. Have him stand on a step stool or devise some means for him to reach the sink. Give him unbreakable dishes to wash, and show him how to rinse the dishes.

Note: *Control the water temperature so the child does not burn himself.*

Materials:

Child-sized broom, unbreakable dishes, waterproof apron, step stool

18–24
Months

Trying on Hats and Purses

4

Goal:

For the toddler to try on hats and purses, which is a first step in pretending to take on a different persona.

Experience:

Put on a hat and tell the toddler, "This is my hat. Would you like one? Here, do you want a purse, too?"

    After she puts on her hat and holds her purse, say, "Let's go look at our hats and purses in the mirror."

    Extend this experience with other available dress-up clothes.

Materials:

Several types of hats and purses, a mirror

18–24
Months

Pretending to Drive

Goal:

For the toddler to pretend to drive, like she sees adults in her life doing.

Experience:

Place a steering wheel toy in a large box and show the toddler the pretend car. Show her how to turn the steering wheel and invite her to drive the car.

If she doesn't understand that she is to turn the wheel, show her again and invite her to try once more.

Materials:

A large box, steering-wheel toy

18–24
Months

Pretending to Cook

Goal:

For the toddler to learn to pretend with a familiar activity, such as cooking, using more than one action.

Experience:

At this point, most pretend activities in a toddler's repertoire generally involve one action. The toddler may be able to pretend to use the stove or pretend to stir, but he probably won't do both.

1. Show the toddler how to put a pan on the pretend stove.

2. Invite him to cook with you.

3. Ask him if he is cooking.

4. Put a spoon in the pan and stir pretend contents.

5. Ask the toddler if he would like to mix some pudding.

6. Pretend to add ingredients to the pan and ask him to stir.

Materials:

Pretend stove, pan, spoon

Using Objects for People

7

Goal:

For the toddler to carry out more advanced pretend play.

Experience:

Toddlers' pretend play may now extend to understanding that tiny play people can represent people in the toddler's life.

1. Line up several of the people toys in front of you and the toddler. Say, "This is Mommy. This is Daddy. This is Barbara [or name of person in child's family]. They are all going on a bus ride." Put them on the play bus. Drive them around and say, "They have to get off now. Mommy, get off. Daddy, get off. Barbara, get off." Walk the people around a little.

2. Then, offer the toddler a different person and ask, "Who's this?" If she doesn't understand, review the names you gave the set of people. Ask her again. Play with it a little. If she still doesn't understand, ask her if she would like to put Mommy on the bus, Daddy on the bus, and so forth.

Often, when children understand the concept that the dolls can stand in for people they know, they become very excited and want to play the game over and over. Eventually, the toddler should begin to make original representations of the play people and not just repeat your representations.

Materials:

Small toys such as Lakeshore people or Fisher-Price people, toy bus or car

18–24
Months

Using Objects for Objects

8

Goal: For the toddler to begin abstract pretend play.

Experience: The toddler's pretend play could now be so advanced that he spontaneously substitutes an abstract object such as a block for another object.

Lift a block as if to drink from it and tell the toddler, "This is my drink." Ask him if he would like a drink and then give him a block.

You can make the blocks substitutes for all types of food, utensils, vehicles, and so forth.

Materials: Blocks

18–24 Months

24–30 Months

Beautiful Beginnings: A Developmental Curriculum for Infants and Toddlers   24–30 MONTHS

	1	2	3	4	5	6	7	8
Communication	Naming Things in a Basket	Naming Matching Cards	Saying First and Last Name	Talking About Details in Books	Asking and Answering Questions	Labeling Areas of Room and Objects	Reciting Nursery Rhymes	Singing Songs
Gross Motor	Exploring New Body Motions	Sliding Down a Big Slide	Swinging on a Swing	Jumping	Walking on a Balance Beam	Swinging at a Ball	Playing with a Hoop	Running Down a Ramp
Fine Motor	Washing Windows or Mirrors	Stringing Beads	Cutting with Scissors	Drawing Lines and Circles	Snapping and Zipping	Opening and Closing Jars and Lids	Pounding	Putting Together a 5-Piece Puzzle
Intellectual	Sorting by Color	Following 2-Part Commands	Understanding One and More	Understanding Up/Down and In/Out	Sorting by Shape and Identity	Nesting Cups or Barrels	Identifying Colors	Identifying Opposites
Discovery	Painting with a Sponge or Brush	Listening with Headphones	Gluing and Pasting	Exploring Playdough Forms	Dancing Outdoors with Scarves	Washing Objects	Finger Painting	Exploring Objects by Touch
Social	Naming Others	Showing Items to Others When Asked	Waiting for Turns	Matching Pictures	Identifying Body Parts	Sharing Show and Tell	Talking About Friends at Home	Responding to the Emotions of Others
Self-Help	Washing Hands at Appropriate Times	Table Washing	Waiting to Eat	Putting away Materials When Finished	Using an Apron	Using Utensils to Eat	Saying "Please" and "Thank You"	Beginning the Toileting Process
Pretend	Conversing on a Pretend Telephone	Caring for a "Baby"	Initiating Pretend Play	Pretending to Be Animals	Pretending About Transportation	Dressing Up	Having a Tea Party	Building with Blocks

Naming Things in a Basket

Goal: For the toddler to name objects.

Experience:

1. Place a number of household objects or small toys in a basket (e.g., ball, spoon, small dog, plastic doll, small animal, toy truck).

2. Ask the child to name each item as you take it out of the basket and place it in a row.

3. Now repeat the exercise, inviting the child to name the objects and to line them up by herself.

4. Repeat this experience with new objects to teach the child additional words.

Materials: Basket with small objects

Naming Matching Cards

Goal:

For the toddler to name objects in pictures, increasing her understanding of representations.

Experience:

1. Make a set of cards (i.e., flash cards) that have pictures of simple household objects or things in a child's world.

2. Laminate the cards and place them in a basket.

3. Remove each card from the basket one by one, and as you do so, name the picture and invite the child to repeat the name after you.

4. After completing this experience, point to each card and ask the child to tell you, "What's this?"

Materials:

Basket, laminated cards

Saying First and Last Name

3

Goal:

For the toddler to say her first and last name when asked.

Experience:

1. Ask the child, "What is your name?" to see if she can recite her first and last name.

2. Explain to the child that most of us have two names and that it is good to be able to say your first and last names.

3. Ask the child to identify others by first name and later by first and last names.

Materials:

None

Talking About Details in Books

Goal:

For the toddler to expand language skills by talking about details in picture books.

Experience:

1. When looking at a book with a 2-year-old, ask him to identify things in the pictures. Begin by asking him, "Where is [the dog]?"

2. Choose another simple item in the picture and ask the child to point to the item you have chosen.

3. Continue by asking him to identify other items in the picture.

4. Later, ask him to tell you what is pictured on the page by asking him, "What's this?"

Be sure to offer a variety of interesting picture books.

Materials:

The child's favorite books

Asking and Answering Questions

Goal:

Experience:

For the toddler to learn to ask and answer questions.

1. Play a game with the child in which you ask a question such as, "Where is your shoe?"

2. Wait for the child to answer. Then encourage the child to ask you a question.

3. Continue asking each other questions using phrases such as

   "Where is...?"
   "What is...?"
   "How big is...?"

Materials:

None

Labeling Areas of Room and Objects

Goal:

For the toddler to use pictures and labels in the environment.

Experience:

1. Begin by labeling the various areas in the learning environment. For example, you may have a block area, playhouse area, library, puzzle area, snack area, and so forth. Hang signs from the ceiling with words and pictures labeling what happens in that part of the room. To some extent, this can be done in a home as well as a center.

2. Arrange the materials so that every toy and object that the child uses has a place. As much as possible, include a picture of the object on the shelf to help the child learn where each thing goes.

3. Invite the child to get things off of the shelf in a particular area, and when she is finished, help her to examine the labels or pictures to determine where the items belong.

4. Encourage her to pay attention to the labels and pictures in the environment.

Materials:

Signs and pictures of the areas and materials in the room

Reciting Nursery Rhymes

7

Goal:

For the toddler to learn traditional nursery rhymes as another form of language expression.

Experience:

Choose two to three nursery rhymes that you and the child enjoy.

Throughout the day, recite one or more of these with the child. When the child becomes more familiar with each rhyme, encourage her independence by saying the first lines and letting her finish the rhyme, adding support whenever needed.

When the child recites a rhyme by herself, celebrate!

Continue reciting the nursery rhymes as much as possible, and add new ones to foster good memory and language skills.

Materials:

Books of nursery rhymes

Singing Songs

Goal:

For the toddler to sing children's songs.

Experience:

Choose two to three children's songs that you and the child enjoy.

Throughout the day, sing one or more of these songs with the child. When the child becomes more familiar with each song, let him try to sing the song on his own, adding support whenever needed.

When the child does sing a song by himself, celebrate!

Continue singing songs as much as possible, adding new ones to foster good memory and language skills.

Materials:

None

Exploring New Body Motions

1

Goal: For the toddler to explore new body movements.

Experience: Encourage the child to experience new motions with his body.

To begin, stand facing the child and ask him to swing his arms, bend, turn around and around, touch his toes, grip his hands behind his back, and so forth. Demonstrate each new action yourself and emphasize the action words you are using.

Variations:
Play "Simon Says." Again, as you are standing facing the child, say, "Simon says touch your toes," and so forth. Invite the child to be "Simon" and follow his lead.

Another variation on this game is to have the child face a large mirror while creating the actions.

Materials: None for the first variation. Large mirror (such as a dance studio mirror) for the second variation

Sliding Down a Big Slide

2

Goal:

For the toddler to slide down a big slide.

Experience:

When the child has achieved coordination to climb steps, position her at the top of a small slide and help her maintain balance in mastering the slide. Once she feels comfortable with this, give her the opportunity to slide down a larger playground slide.

She may want you to slide with her the first time or may prefer for you to catch her when she is part way down. Stay with the child for the first dozen or so times she slides down a larger slide to be sure she has mastered the steps necessary to slide safely.

If she is sharing a slide with other children, be sure she understands safety rules, such as waiting for her turn and giving other children time to get down the slide before she comes down.

Talk about this new adventure with her.

Materials:

Playground slide that is slightly larger than ones the child has played on before

Swinging on a Swing

3

Goal:

For the toddler to experience back-and-forth motions of swinging on a traditional swing.

Experience:

Most children love swinging. By now the child is probably able to master swinging on a sling, simple board, or metal-seat swing. Teach the child how to get on and off of the swing by himself. Give him gentle pushes and watch to see if he is able to swing straight back and forth and to hang on tightly. When he does, you may give him higher pushes.

Point out safety rules about swinging: Always hang on tightly and do not swing sideways or when others are walking in the area of the swing. Try different types of swings.

Memorize this fun poem by Robert Louis Stevenson called "The Swing." Chant it with the child while he is swinging:

> "How would you like to go up in the swing?
> Up in the air so blue?
> Oh, I do think it the pleasantest thing
> Ever a child can do!
> Up in the air and over the wall,
> Till I can see so wide,
> Rivers and trees and cattle and all
> Over the countryside—
> Till I look down on the garden green,
> Down on the roof so brown—
> Up in the air I go flying again,
> Up in the air and down!"

Materials:

Playground swings of different types

Jumping

Goal:

For the toddler to jump independently.

Experience:

If the child can jump off a very low surface and jump on a mini-trampoline with someone holding her hands or using a handle, she may now be ready to jump off of the ground, unaided.

Stand facing the child, holding the child's hands in your hands, and help her complete a freestanding jump. Then stand beside her and encourage her to jump up.

Some children find this motion quite challenging to master, so if the child is not able to do it, wait a few weeks and try again. She may jump while singing a song or playing a game. If she does have difficulty jumping, go back to jumping off of a surface about 4 inches high or jumping on a mini-trampoline with a handle for support.

Use fun phrases like "jumping frogs," "jump up," and "jump down."

Materials:

None for the basic jumping exercise; a surface about 4 inches high or a mini-trampoline with a handle for practicing jumping

Walking on a Balance Beam

5

Goal:

For the toddler to walk on a slightly higher balance beam.

Experience:

The child may now be able to walk along a very low balance beam, maintaining his balance.

Lay out a 2-feet by 6-feet board and ask the child to walk along it. You may need to hold his hands for balance, or he may be able to do this unaided.

If he is successful, elevate the board with two other low boards, one on each end of the longer walking board.

Use the language that relates to the child's accomplishment and experience (e.g., "You have good balance," "You are stepping carefully").

Variations: You can vary the challenge by laying out a more narrow board, by elevating the board, or by asking the child to walk in different ways (e.g., heel to toe, backwards).

Materials:

Wide and low board anywhere between 2-feet by 6-feet long, other narrower or longer boards, small boards to elevate the walking board

Swinging at a Ball

Goal:

For the toddler to hit a ball with a hand or bat, furthering eye–hand coordination.

Experience:

The child may enjoy batting at a very lightweight ball with his hands and arms or using a very lightweight plastic bat.

Toss the ball to him and encourage him to hit the ball as it comes to him.

You could also hang a ball from the ceiling and let the child practice swinging at it with his hand or bat.

Materials:

Lightweight balls of different sizes; a small, very lightweight plastic bat

Playing with a Hoop

7

Goal:

For the toddler to move through hoops, furthering her perception of her body in space.

Experience:

Lay down 1, 2, or 3 hoops in front of the child and encourage her to step from one hoop to the other. As she gains skill in stepping from one to another, make the game more challenging by spreading the hoops apart or by asking her to jump from one to another.

Variations: Here are some other games to play with hoops:

- Stand a hoop on edge, hold it securely, and invite the child to crawl through it.

- Place the hoops so that one is close by the child and the others are further away, so she has to step different distances.

- Throw beanbags into the hoops.

These games help the child to gain a concept of her body in space.

Materials:

Hula-Hoops, wooden hoops, beanbags

24–30 Months

Running Down a Ramp

8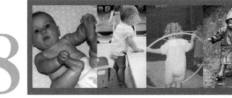

Goal: For the toddler to run downhill.

Experience: Set up a slight but sturdy incline for the toddler to walk and then run down. You may set up a small route for her to follow. For example, she may climb on a carpeted box and then run down the ramp.

As the toddler gains assurance, create a steeper incline. It is fun to vary this experience by going outside and running down hills.

Share the excitement she is probably feeling when she runs by talking and laughing about this adventure.

Materials: Ramp or small hills

Washing Windows or Mirrors

1

Goal:

For the toddler to wash windows and/or mirrors to improve fine motor skills.

Experience:

1. Invite the child to help you wash windows, or a mirror if windows are not an option.

2. Go to the sink and put a small amount of water in a bucket and a spray bottle. Have a squeegee handy.

3. Take the bucket and spray bottle to the designated area.

4. Model the following: Spray the window with three squirts of water. Pick up the squeegee. Begin to scrub using the sponge side with large movements, from left to right. Turn to the squeegee side and clear the window of water, using a top-to-bottom motion. Continue until the window is clean. Occasionally rinse the squeegee in the bucket of water. Use the towel to wipe your hands.

5. Now invite the child to try.

6. When finished, empty the bucket and spray bottle in the sink and put the supplies back in the appropriate places.

Variation: Try shaving cream or foam soap.

Materials:

Bucket, water, squeegee, spray bottle, mirror or window, towel

Stringing Beads

2

24–30 Months

Goal:

For the toddler to improve eye–hand coordination skills by stringing beads.

Experience:

1. Place the wooden beads and the shoelace in a basket.

2. Invite the child to string beads.

3. Place the basket on the table and remove the shoelace from the basket.

4. Tie a knot at the end of the shoelace and lay it down horizontally on the table.

5. Choose a bead and feed the shoelace through the bead, taking your other hand and sliding the bead to the end of the shoelace where the knot is. Continue until all of the beads are laced.

6. To remove the beads, slide the first bead off the shoelace and place it in the basket. Repeat one at a time until all of the beads are back in the basket.

7. Roll up the shoelace and place it in the basket.

8. Invite the child to try. Provide support and encouragement as needed.

Note: *Watch the child carefully to make sure he does not swallow any materials.*

Materials:

Basket; 6 to 8 large, wooden, colored beads with holes for string; shoelace or string with one end finished and the other knotted

Cutting with Scissors

3

Goal:

For the toddler to learn to cut using scissors, an important fine motor skill.

Experience:

Get a piece of paper and the pair of scissors. Have the child hold the paper in one of her hands and the scissors in the other hand. Place your hand over her hand that is holding the scissors and show her how to cut the paper.

Continue cutting the paper together with the scissors. Once the child feels comfortable with this motion, let her cut the paper by herself.

Note: *You may want to begin this exercise using child-friendly scissors that have blunt ends and a loop to squeeze instead of holes for the thumb and forefinger.*

Materials:

Child-friendly or regular child scissors, paper

24–30
Months

Drawing Lines and Circles

24–30
Months

Goal:

For the toddler to begin representational drawing.

Experience:

1. Take out a large sheet of paper and invite the child to draw with you.

2. Ask the child to choose a large crayon or marker.

3. Begin by showing the child how to draw a straight line, going from the top of the paper to the bottom or from the left to the right.

4. Now, let the child try drawing a line any way he chooses.

5. Next, model making a circle, starting at the top of the page and circling to the right. It is not necessary for the child to copy your movements exactly, but you are modeling the beginning of writing and reading as you go left to right and top to bottom.

Materials:

Paper, large crayon or marker

Snapping and Zipping

Goal:

For the toddler to learn the fine motor skills of snapping and zipping.

Experience:

1. Get a snap frame and invite the child to use it with you. Place the frame on the table.

2. Using your left hand, grasp fabric to the left of the frame. Using your right hand, pull the snap head from its mate. Continue until all snaps are unsnapped. Lay the left side open, then the right side.

3. To resnap, close the left side. Close the right side. Beginning at the top, use your left hand and place your index finger under the mate of the snap head. Using your right hand, place the snap head on top of its mate. Use your thumb to snap in place. Continue in the same manner to the bottom. Announce, "The snap is snapped."

4. Now, invite the child to try, assisting whenever necessary.

When the child is ready to learn to zip, repeat the same procedure with the zipper frame.

1. Using your left hand, grasp fabric at top left of the zipper head. Using your right hand, take the zipper pull of the zipper head and pull down to the bottom. Separate the left half from the right half. Open the left side, then the right side.

2. To rezip, close the left side. Close right side. Insert the tab of the non-zipper into the zipper head. Using your left hand, hold the ends taut. Using your right hand, zip to the top. Announce, "The zipper is zipped."

3. Now, invite the child to try, assisting whenever necessary.

Materials:

Snap frame, zipper frame

Opening and Closing Jars and Lids

Goal:

Experience:

For the toddler to learn to open and close jars and lids.

1. Gather a variety of jars with lids. Try to find ones that are very easy to open (e.g., plastic peanut butter jars, Tupperware or disposable containers, other containers with easy-to-open lids).

2. Begin with one big and one little container with matching lids. Show the child how to place the lid on the container. Let him try.

3. When he has successfully completed matching and applying the lids to the two containers, add more jars and lids.

This is often a very popular activity among 2-year-olds, and it builds on other experiences that ask children to match jars and lids.

Materials:

A variety of jars with easy-to-screw-on lids

Pounding

Goal:

For the toddler to learn to pound a peg.

Experience:

Select a plastic pegboard and hammer. Place the pegboard in front of the child. Holding the hammer, demonstrate how to pound the board. Now invite the child to try.

If you have a woodworking area in your room or home, let the child practice hammering using his plastic hammer.

A more advanced exercise is to invite the child to pound golf tees into foam blocks. Provide this activity if the toddler seems to be ready for a greater challenge.

Materials:

Plastic pegboard, plastic hammer, wood blocks, foam blocks, golf tees

Putting Together a 5-Piece Puzzle

Goal:

For the toddler to learn to put together a puzzle with several pieces.

Experience:

1. Select puzzles with simple, large pieces. Make sure all puzzles are complete, discarding any with missing pieces. Keep the puzzles in an accessible puzzle rack.

2. Invite the child to choose a 5-piece puzzle from the puzzle rack.

3. Ask the child to sit with you at a small table or on the floor. Model taking the pieces out of the puzzle one by one and placing them next to the puzzle frame.

4. Demonstrate putting the pieces back into the frame one by one. Take a moment to observe the completed puzzle.

5. Invite the child to try. If the child is having trouble, work with two or three puzzle pieces at a time.

6. Show the child how to return the puzzle to the puzzle rack.

Materials:

5-piece puzzle, puzzle rack

Sorting by Color

1

Goal:

For the toddler to learn to observe and group objects by color.

Experience:

1. Put colored felt in the bottom of muffin tin cups. Begin with two colors: red and yellow.

2. Find objects that match the two colors.

3. Show the child how to match by color, placing the yellow objects in the muffin tin with the yellow felt and the red objects in the cups with the red felt.

While you are doing this activity, use color words and language of comparison, such as "same," "not the same," "different," and "alike."

Expand this experience by adding a piece of blue felt to another of the muffin tins and find blue objects.

Materials:

Muffin tin, felt, small objects

Following 2-Part Commands

2

Goal:

For the toddler to carry out a 2-part command. This activity teaches the child to remember and sequence actions.

Experience:

Give the child a fun, 2-part command or direction. For example, ask her to first take the lid off a box and then put a ball in the box.

Other 2-part commands could include

- "First, take off your shoes and then put them by the door."

- "Please open the cupboard and then take out a bowl."

- "Pick up a ball and then give it to Mary. Thank you."

Remember to use language such as "first," "second," and "then." This is also a good time to model politeness, using "please" and "thank you."

Materials:

None

Understanding *One* and *More*

3

Goal:

For the toddler to learn about concepts of *one* and *more*.

Experience:

Place one Cheerio (or other small object) in front of the child. Offer it to the child as you say, "Here is one Cheerio." Next, offer the child a handful and say, "Here are more Cheerios."

This experience helps the child develop a beginning concept of quantity, teaching that "more" is different from "one."

Note: *When using non-edible materials, watch the child carefully to make sure he does not swallow them.*

Materials:

Small objects such as Cheerios

Understanding *Up/Down* and *In/Out*

24–30 Months

Goal:

For the toddler to learn the orientation concepts *up*, *down*, *in*, and *out*. This helps the child learn concepts and words that will help her to orient herself in space.

Experience:

Toss a ball or beanbag into a box and then dump it out of the box. As you do this, say, "Let's toss the ball *in* the box; let's dump the ball *out* of the box."

Variations:
"Let's throw the ball *up*; let's throw the ball *down*."

"Put the baby *in* the bed; now take her *out* of the bed."

Materials:

Ball, beanbag, box, baby doll, doll bed

Sorting by Shape and Identity

5

Goal:

Experience:

For the toddler to sort by shape and identity.

1. Find 3 small shapes or objects that can be easily outlined. Make a set of 3 cards each with one of the 3 shapes clearly outlined on each card.

2. Place the shapes or objects and their corresponding cards into a basket.

3. Show the child how to match the shape with the appropriate outline on the card. She may match by considering the shape or by identifying what is represented (e.g., a dog) or both.

While doing this activity, use language such as "same," "different," "These go together," and, if appropriate, name shapes such as "square," "rectangle," and so forth.

Materials:

Basket, objects, cards, markers to outline objects, or shapes that match objects in the basket

24–30
Months

Nesting
Cups or Barrels

Goal:

For the toddler to continue to observe and sequence according to size.

Experience:

By now, you may have had the opportunity to introduce the toddler to 2 nesting cups or barrels. Now, you can bring out 3 or 4 nesting cups or barrels. Show the child how 1 cup fits inside the others. Then let him repeat the action.

If this concept is difficult, go back to only 2 objects. When he has mastered two, offer more cups or barrels.

This teaches the child to observe and sequence. Many future tasks will require him to sequence by size and order.

Nesting cups or barrels

Materials:

Identifying Colors

7

Goal:

For the toddler to identify 1–8 colors.

Experience:

1. Gather a set of small objects in a can or basket. Use only primary colors, 2 colors at a time.

2. Lay out 2 objects in a row. Ask the child, "Which one is red?"

3. Continue, using other objects and colors as is appropriate to the individual child.

4. Throughout the day, ask color questions; for instance: "Whose shoes are red?" or "Which ball is yellow?"

Materials:

Small can or basket with primary-colored objects

24–30 Months

8

Identifying Opposites

Goal: For the toddler to learn about opposites.

Experience:

1. Place objects in a can or basket to illustrate the concepts of

   - *rough/smooth*
   - *hard/soft*
   - *big/little*

2. Invite the child to explore the objects and feel the textures while you provide the word that frames the concept. For example, say, "This is rough. This is smooth." (Examples of rough objects include an emery board, a pumice stone, or a rock. For smooth objects, try using a smooth stone or a ball.)

   Variations: For additional opposites that can't be illustrated with objects, such as *hot/cold* or *fast/slow*, use pictures or actions to make the concepts real and concrete.

Materials: Basket with objects or pictures depicting opposites

Painting with a Sponge or Brush

1

Goal:

For the toddler to learn to paint with a sponge or brush in order to experience the wonders of making beautiful marks.

Experience:

1. Make painting very simple for 2-year-olds. First, teach the child to put on his own apron.

2. Clip a piece of paper to an easel and protect the floor underneath with papers or plastic.

3. Begin using a sponge on the end of a paint stick.

4. When the child has mastered this form of painting, advance to painting with a very wide brush and one color of thick tempera mixed with liquid soap (for easy removal of spills). Use a paint container that has a lid with an opening for the brush.

5. When the child is finished, always write his name and the date on the paper. Tell him what you are doing.

6. Teach him to wash his hands and to put the apron back on the hook when done.

Materials:

Easel, paint, paper, clips, paintbrush, paint container with lid, apron

24–30 Months

2

Listening with Headphones

Goal:

For the toddler to learn the beauty of listening intentionally to music.

Experience:

1. Select an audiotape or CD of music the child enjoys listening to. Insert the headphones into the audiotape or CD player, and invite the child to listen.

2. Teach him to sit quietly and listen to the music.

3. Designate a chair or corner for listening activities.

4. Teach him to put the headphones back in their proper place and to turn off the music when completed.

Materials:

Headphones, audiotapes or CDs, chair

24–30 Months

Gluing and Pasting

3

Goal:

Experience:

For the toddler to use glue and paste.

1. Provide the child with a glue stick and pieces of paper.

2. Show him how to apply glue to the paper and join the pieces of paper together. You may also use paste for this activity.

3. When finished, teach the child to wash his hands and put his completed product up to dry.

4. Remember to sign his name and the date.

For fun, vary the types of paper you use.

Materials:

Glue, paste, pieces of paper

Exploring Playdough Forms

4

Goal:

For the toddler to explore playdough using tools and to further the child's ability to use tools according to their purposes.

Experience:

1. Put the playdough, cookie cutters, and a small rolling pin in a basket.

2. Invite the child to get his apron. Show him how to roll out the playdough and cut pieces with the cutters.

3. Show him how to put the dough, the cutters, and the apron away when finished.

4. Later, for added interest, you may want to add other items to the basket. For example, you could add a small butter knife for cutting the playdough.

Materials:

Playdough (see page 28), cookie cutters, rolling pin, apron

Dancing Outdoors with Scarves

5

Goal:

For the toddler to dance and to move her body in space.

Experience:

1. Collect scarves or make them out of fabric scraps, using lightweight fabric.

2. Go outside with the child on a breezy day. Demonstrate holding the scarves up in the wind. Show the child how to securely hold onto one corner and allow the wind to dance with the scarf.

3. Model making large, sweeping movements with your arms, turning around, and holding the scarf low and high.

4. Encourage the child to explore the space around her with the scarf.

5. You can play a game by calling out specific actions: Move the scarf fast, slow, high, low, or just let her explore.

6. You can also dance with scarves.

Materials:

Lightweight scarves

24–30
Months

Washing Objects

6

Goal:

For the toddler to expand his encounters with water and pretend play.

Experience:

1. Protect the floor with a plastic sheet.

2. Put soapy water in a basin and have the child put on his apron.

3. Give the child objects to wash. Show him how to wash the objects and lay them on a towel to air dry. Later, you can add a dish brush or washcloth as part of the wash and rinse.

4. When through, teach the child to put his apron back on the hook, drain the water, and wipe up any spills.

Note: *Always supervise the child carefully when engaging in water play.*

Materials:

Plastic sheet, basin, water, soap, apron, objects, towel, dish brush, washcloth

7

Finger Painting

Goal:

For the toddler to explore a different way to finger paint, to feel the sensation of finger painting on paper, and to create a product.

Experience:

1. Begin by laying papers or plastic on the floor for protection.

2. Whip soap flakes with water and add a little tempera paint if you want color.

3. Cover a table with plastic or select a table with a laminate surface. Attach paper to the surface.

4. Invite the child to put on an apron. Show him how to "paint" with his fingers.

5. Cleaning up is easy because the "paint" is soap. Allow the child to help you with cleanup as much as possible.

6. When the child is finished, write his name and the date on the paper. Tell him what you are doing. Teach him to wash his hands and to put the apron back on the hook when done as part of this activity.

Materials:

Soap flakes, paint, paper, apron, plastic sheet

24–30
Months

Exploring Objects by Touch

8

Goal: For the toddler to further develop and rely on the sense of touch.

Experience:

1. Prepare a box with a space just big enough for the child's hand to fit through. Place familiar objects in the box.

2. Invite the child to put her hand into the box and identify the objects by touch.

Materials: Prepared box, familiar objects

24–30
Months

Naming Others

1

Goal:

For the toddler to be aware of people around him by identifying people by name.

Experience:

Ask the child to point to various people in the room. Ask him, "Where's Justin?", "Where's Abbie?", and so forth.

Change the game by asking, "Who's that?" Point to various people in the room as you are doing so and ask the child to identify each one by name.

Materials:

None

Showing Items to Others When Asked

Goal: For the toddler to expand sharing skills by passing objects back and forth.

Experience: Ask the child to show you something she is playing with. Ask her questions such as

- "May I see your bear?"

- "Will you show it to me?"

- "May I hold it?"

Variation: Play another version of this game by asking the child to show a toy to others in the room. Ask her, "Will you show Heather your truck? I think she'd like to see it. Will you let her hold it?"

Materials: Familiar toys that the child likes to play with

24–30 Months

Waiting for Turns

Goal:

For the toddler to develop the patience to wait for a turn.

Experience:

While the child is waiting to play with a toy or for a turn in an activity, explain the idea of taking turns. You can say, "Now it's Eduardo's turn, your turn will be next. Wait for your turn." When it's the child's turn, say, "Now it's *your* turn."

Turn taking is an important part of many social skills. This activity helps a child learn to delay gratification and to wait for his turn. It will also help him build an understanding of how to play games and learn the rules of social situations.

Materials:

Toys that children are currently playing with

Matching Pictures

Goal:

For the toddler to identify important people in photographs to increase her awareness of people in her life and her relationship to them, and to remember these people when they are not present.

Experience:

1. Gather or provide photographs of people in a child's life (e.g., mother, father, sister, teacher, home visitor, the children in a child care classroom). Because the photographs will be used in a project, use duplicates, not originals.

2. Glue the photographs on a piece of cardboard in 3 rows of 5. Draw heavy black lines between the pictures so that the completed item looks like a Tic-Tac-Toe board.

3. Now, cut duplicate photographs the same size as the squares on the board. Back them with cardboard and laminate them.

4. Invite the child to match each photograph of an important person in her life with one on the board. Encourage her to name each person as she does this and to talk about that person.

Materials:

Duplicate photographs of people in the child's life, cardboard, glue, laminate, black marker

Identifying Body Parts

Goal:

For the toddler to develop self-awareness by identifying more body parts and their functions.

Experience:

Ask a child to point to various parts of his body. Ask, "Where is your head? Elbow? Leg? Nose?" and so forth.

When a child has an ailment or injury, identify the part of his body that hurts (e.g., "You have a scratch on your knee").

In general, encourage the child to be aware of his own body. As he matures, ask him to tell you what each part of the body helps him to do. For example, his legs help him to run fast. His eyes help him to see. His hands help him to pet the dog.

Materials:

None

24–30 Months

Sharing
Show and Tell

6

Goal:

For the toddler to participate in Show and Tell or other ways to share verbally with others in a small group.

Experience:

At home, during mealtime conversations in which each person has a chance to contribute, encourage the child to show and talk about things she has discovered or created.

At the child care center, in small groups of 3 or 4 children, give each child opportunities to talk about what he or she wants to show. When a child brings something to Show and Tell from home, it becomes an important and enjoyable way for her to connect her home and center environments.

A fun way to find Show and Tell objects at a center is to take a walk and give each child a bag for found objects. When you return, invite each child to share what she found and name it; for example, a leaf, stick, or rock.

Materials:

Found, discovered, created, or other important objects

24–30 Months

Talking About Friends at Home

7

Goal: For the toddler to begin to develop friendships.

Experience: Having friends helps the child to develop social skills and to expand his circle of important relationships.

Encourage the child's budding friendships. If at home, invite children over to play for short periods of time. Have enough materials for both children to play with little conflict.

If the child attends a child care program, find out who he shows interest in there. As you see him show signs of true affection and interest in other children, encourage him to talk about his friends.

Materials: None

24–30 Months

Responding to the Emotions of Others

8

Goal:

For the toddler to develop empathy.

Experience:

Notice if the toddler is responding when another child is crying or laughing. She may bring her blanket or "binky" as comfort if she sees another child crying. Or she may begin laughing or smiling if another child is laughing.

When you see these expressions of empathy, you can comment on the appropriate response, "His blanket makes him feel better when he is sad," or simply nod your approval. Similarly, the toddler may respond to the feelings of a character in a book (e.g., sad bunny) and offer a gesture or comment.

If you do not see the child offering empathy, show her your own responses. Modeling your emotions and these activities help children to develop empathy. Don't worry if you do not see signs of empathy at this age; true empathy develops later. However, you can nurture its beginnings by encouraging appropriate emotional responses to the feelings of others.

Materials:

Picture books in which clear emotions are portrayed

24–30 Months

Washing Hands at Appropriate Times

1

Goal:

For the toddler to wash hands at appropriate times.

Experience:

Establish a procedure for hand washing before and after the child eats (and after toileting). Use a low sink or a step stool to help the child reach the basin. At this stage, it is important to demonstrate hand washing and to help the child to learn to wash his hands at the appropriate times.

1. **Washing:** Invite the child to wash his hands. Show him how to turn on the water. (Adjust water temperature to avoid burning.) Help him to immerse his hands in the water (filling the sink or letting the water run), rotating his palms up and down. Pick up the soap (or push the pump if using a soap dispenser). Model rubbing hands together to create lather, then let him try. Show him how to wash his palms, the back of his hands, and between his fingers. Immerse both of his hands in the water again. Take his hands out of the water and gently shake them over the sink.

2. **Drying:** Pick up the towel and dry both hands. Set the towel aside, or throw paper towels away. Use a sponge to clean up any spills and squeeze the sponge out; then put it away.

3. Take a moment to admire how clean his hands are.

Always allow plenty of time after each meal or toileting for this important self-help ritual to be completed. Encourage the child's independence in this task.

Materials:

Sink, step stool, sponge, water source, pump or bar soap, towel or paper towels

24–30 Months

Table Washing

Goal:

For the toddler to develop the cleanup skill of washing a tabletop.

Experience:

Invite the child to help you wash the table. Have him put on an apron. Fill the bucket with an appropriate amount of water and bring all the materials to the table. Model the following for the child, inviting him to participate after each step:

1. Pick up the sponge and moisten it in the water. Squeeze to remove excess water. With long, smooth, circular strokes, dampen the table by generally working from left to right and top to bottom.

2. Now take the brush, dip it into the water, and stroke the brush over the soap 2 or 3 times. Continue to add soap as necessary.

3. After the entire surface is scrubbed, immerse the brush and swish in water to rinse. Shake excess water from brush. Wet the sponge in the bucket and squeeze it. Starting at the top left-hand corner, wipe the table with long, smooth strokes. Rinse the sponge in the bucket when necessary and squeeze.

4. When all of the soap has been removed from the table surface, wipe once around the edges (sides) of the tabletop. Rinse sponge. Examine the table to make sure all of the dirty spots have been removed. Comment on the clean table.

5. Open the drying towel on the table. Place a hand on top of the towel and dry the table, again using a circular motion (generally left to right, top to bottom). Fold or discard the towel.

6. Empty the pail. Help the child hang up the apron. Return supplies to appropriate place.

Materials:

Apron, bucket, small towel, scrub brush, soap and dish, sponge

24–30 Months

Waiting to Eat

Goal:

For the toddler to follow a mealtime routine. Learning this routine teaches the child to delay gratification and to approach meals with decorum and respect.

Experience:

Teach the child to prepare for meals by following a simple routine: wash hands, find her place at the table, and sit patiently with her hands in her lap while meal preparation routines are observed and all are seated.

Select a place at the table that is always her place so she knows where to go. Try using a special place-mat that shows her where to sit.

Materials:

Placemat

Putting away Materials When Finished

Goal:

For the toddler to gain a sense of mastery of and pride in the environment by learning how to put materials in their proper places.

Experience:

Arrange the environment so that every toy and object that the child uses has a place. As much as possible, include a picture of the object on the shelf to help the child learn where each thing goes.

Invite the child to get an object off the shelf, and when she is finished, help her to see how to put it away in its proper place.

Learning this routine also gives adults a feeling of order and mastery.

Materials:

Labels for areas and materials, pictures of toys and objects to tape to appropriate place on shelves, adhesive tape

24–30
Months

Using an Apron

5

Goal:

For the toddler to gain independence and a sense of mastery by knowing how to put on, take off, and put away an apron.

Experience:

1. Provide the child with a plastic apron to use for water play, painting, and other messy activities. Select a style that the child can put on and take off by himself.

2. Hang this on a hook that is easily accessible and near where it will be used.

3. Teach the child when to use the apron, how to put on the apron independently, and how to take it off and put it away when he is finished.

Materials:

Plastic apron

Using Utensils to Eat

Goal:

For the toddler to use a spoon and a fork for eating.

Experience:

If the child uses her fingers, gently encourage her to use the spoon or fork as appropriate. Reintroduce the use of a spoon, then a fork. Model and demonstrate how to hold them. Make it as fun as possible.

Be sure to select foods that work well with a utensil during this stage so that the child experiences success.

If passing food is part of the lunch routine, help the child learn how to pass a small plate or bowl of food (after placing her utensil down to pass the food).

Materials:

Child-size fork and spoon, foods that work well with utensils

24–30
Months

Saying "Please" and "Thank You"

7

Goal:

For the toddler to say "please" and "thank you" when appropriate. Learning to be cordial builds a child's sense of confidence, independence, and participation.

Experience:

Encourage the child to say "please" and "thank you" throughout the day. Mealtime is a good opportunity to teach courtesy. For example: When asking for seconds, encourage the child to ask by saying "please," and then "thank you" when he receives the helping.

If passing food is part of the lunch routine, help the child learn how to pass a small plate or bowl of food and to use "please" when asking another to pass it, again responding with "thank you" on receiving it.

Materials:

None

24–30 Months

Beginning the Toileting Process

8

Goal:

For the toddler to become familiar with using the toilet. This set of activities will help the child become familiar with toileting in preparation for actual toilet learning.

Experience:

When the child shows some interest in using the toilet, show her what it is for. (You may have already done some of these steps.) The child may indicate to you that she would like to try to use the toilet, or she may only be ready to be introduced to it at this point.

If at home, secure a small toilet seat or a step stool so that the child can use the toilet easily. If the child has siblings or is at a childcare center, allow the child to observe others using the toilet.

Show the child how to wipe front to back and how to flush the toilet. Remember to introduce hand-washing as part of the routine.

Some children are motivated to use the toilet when they see undergarments (e.g., "big-girl pants") that children wear when they are able to use the toilet independently.

Materials:

Toilet, step stool to reach the toilet and sink, hand-washing supplies, undergarments

24–30 Months

Conversing on a Pretend Telephone 1

Goal:

For the toddler to have a pretend telephone conversation. This activity allows the child to represent something not present and to do so with a 3-part sequence. The sequence helps the child to build a longer attention span.

Experience:

Most 2-year-olds are very interested in telephones. Give the child a toy telephone and pretend to talk to him. Encourage him to begin with "Hello." Next, have some exchange, such as "How are you?" (Listen for the child to answer.) End with "Good-bye."

Using a second play telephone, have a pretend conversation with your child.

Materials:

One or two small pretend telephones

Caring for a "Baby"

Goal:

For the toddler to pretend to care for a baby. To develop his ability to hold a symbol in his mind.

Experience:

1. Give the child a small baby doll to play with. Encourage him to hold the baby in a caring way. You may tell him he is caring for his baby "like Mommy and Daddy" or someone else he knows who has a baby.

2. Next, give him a small blanket and show him how to wrap the baby.

3. Expand the pretend play by giving him a doll's bottle and showing him how the baby can drink its bottle.

4. Encourage the child to talk about the care he is providing.

Adding steps to the pretend play helps the child to build complexity in his play and develop a longer attention span.

Variations: Rock the baby, pat the baby, put the baby to bed, sit the baby in a highchair, feed the baby with a spoon, dress the baby, and so forth.

Materials:

Doll baby, blanket, doll accessories

Initiating Pretend Play

3

Goal:

For the toddler to *initiate* pretend play, which encourages planning skills and a sense of mastery.

Experience:

At this age, many children are able to begin pretend play on their own. Help the child to plan ahead for the pretend play. For instance, if the child looks for the baby doll (or any other object used in pretend play), ask him if he needs the blanket or the bottle.

You can help a child to initiate additional steps in his pretend play by planting questions about what's next. You can extend the play by making suggestions, but then back out and let the child choose whether to carry out the suggestion.

Materials:

Doll baby, blanket, doll accessories

24–30
Months

Pretending to Be Animals

Goal:

For the toddler to build complexity in pretend play by adding ideas such as animal-related themes to pretend play.

Experience:

Bring out a basket of several small, plastic animals and farm or zoo toys as support.

If the child "walks" the animal, you might show her how to lead the animal to feed. Watch for the child's ideas and follow her lead.

Later, you might encourage her to take the animal for a ride or to lay the animal down for a rest or to move it to another pen.

Materials:

Plastic animals and other toys that extend pretend play (plastic fence, barn, zoo cages, and so forth)

Pretending About Transportation

5

Goal:

For the toddler to bring more complexity to pretend play by using transportation toys.

Experience:

Bring out a basket of several vehicles and small people to put into the vehicles. Follow the child's lead and respond to his comments as you play with him. For example, if the child is driving around a car, show him how to put a person in it and ask, "Who is that driving?"

Watch for a possible next step in extending the child's play (e.g., bring out a small house and ask if he wants to drive the car to the house).

Materials:

Small vehicles such as cars, trucks, airplanes, boats, and other support toys for transportation pretend play

24–30
Months

6 Dressing Up

Goal:

For the toddler to extend pretend play using "going outdoors" dress-up clothes.

Experience:

1. Bring out a basket of dress-up clothes such as hats, scarves, mittens, and small coats.

2. Encourage the child to put on outer garments. Let him take the lead in putting these on.

3. If he indicates that he is pretending, encourage this. He might say, "Go outside." You might join in the game and ask, "You are pretending to get ready to go outside. What else do you need to put on to go outside?" You may pretend by going to the door or by going outside and coming back.

4. Expand the child's language by discussing the weather and what she might need to wear outside.

Materials:

Hats, scarves, mittens, coats, boots, other dress-up clothes

24–30 Months

Having a Tea Party

Goal:

For the child to extend pretend play by having a ritualized event such as a tea party. It promotes the child's ability to sequence and gives her a sense of mastery as she imagines herself acting like a grown-up.

Experience:

Bring out a tray with small cups, a pitcher, and small plates. Invite the child to sit at a small table in a small chair. Invite the child to pour a cup of pretend tea and to eat pretend cookies.

You may also choose to set up this tea party with some water in the pitcher and/or small, real cookies.

A tea party provides a great opportunity to talk to the child. Also, children enjoy pretending to eat.

Materials:

Tray, small cups, pitcher, small plates, table, small chair, plastic and/or real cookies

24–30
Months

Building with Blocks

Goal:

For the toddler to pretend using blocks. This experience expands the child's ability to use a "neutral" object, such as a block, to stand in for or symbolize something else.

Experience:

Bring out a basket or tray of blocks. Follow the child's lead and listen and respond to her language as she begins building.

If she says she is building a house, you might comment on that, and at the right moment, help her to extend the idea by adding a garage for a car or a room for a baby.

Try to understand the child's idea. What is she using the blocks to stand for or symbolize? If the idea of pretending with blocks has not occurred to the child, you can gently suggest that a block might be a car; two together might be a train.

The child might not always want to use the blocks as pretend objects, but may do so some of the time.

Materials:

Blocks of any kind

30–36 Months

Beautiful Beginnings: A Developmental Curriculum for Infants and Toddlers   30–36 MONTHS

	1	2	3	4	5	6	7	8
Communication	Using 3- and 4-Word Sentences	Using Names and Pronouns	Using Action Words	Guessing Sounds	Carrying on a Brief Conversation	Asking Questions	Singing and Listening to Music	Reading Books
Gross Motor	Tossing a Beanbag	Playing Follow the Leader	Hanging Upside Down	Bouncing a Ball	Completing an Independent Somersault	Jumping Up	Moving Through an Obstacle Course	Pedaling a Tricycle
Fine Motor	Filling a Pitcher	Scooping Using Containers	Folding	Tonging	Stringing Small Beads	Basting	Drawing	Completing an 8-Piece Puzzle
Intellectual	Naming Colors and Shapes	Identifying Gender	Identifying Things by Function	Sequencing	Locating Objects by Color or Shape	Following Directions	Understanding One-to-One Correspondence	Playing "What's Missing?"
Discovery	Playing to a Beat	Flying a Kite	Growing Things	Expanding Water Play	Playing with a Tent	Playing with Puppets	Painting with a Small Brush	Following Art Directions
Social	Making Choices	Expressing Feelings with Words	Recounting Details of an Incident	Taking Turns	Talking and Listening in a Small Group	Playing Jointly	Identifying and Talking About One's Body	Matching Names with Pictures
Self-Help	Knowing a Daily Routine	Washing Hands Independently	Using the Toilet	Taking Clothes Off and Putting Them On	Wiping Up Spills and Sweeping	Brushing Teeth	Preparing Simple Foods	Setting the Table
Pretend	Pretending with People Toys Using 2–3 Steps	Visiting the Doctor Using 2–3 Steps	Pretending to Be Animals	Playing House over Time	Pretending with Other Children	Playing Grocery Store	Playing Post Office	Extending Pretend Play

Using 3- and 4-Word Sentences

1

Goal: For the child to create longer sentences.

Experience: As a child communicates, he will begin forming longer sentences. With 2-word sentences, such as "Mommy go," you may supply additional words: "Mommy go to work." This helps the child to "fill in" his implied meaning with words. The child will learn to use longer sentences to express the important meanings he wants to convey.

When reading and talking with the child, pay particular attention to his sentences and the concepts he is communicating. Help him expand his sentences during everyday conversations.

Materials: Books

Using Names and Pronouns

2

Goal:

Experience:

For the child to understand simple pronouns.

Play a game with the child as she learns the meaning of names and pronouns.

Ask her to complete commands and refer to her as "you" and to yourself as "me." "Could you bring the bear to me?"

Ask her to take things to different people whom you identify by name; follow up with the appropriate pronouns: "Give this to Susie; give it to her."

Materials:

None

Using Action Words

3

Goal:

For the child to use action words to expand the number of verbs in her vocabulary.

Experience:

Tell the child what you are doing using a variety of action words (e.g., "I am *brushing* my hair. Would you like to *brush* your hair?").

Play games using action words by asking the child to jump, run, reach, climb, roll, and so forth.

When reading to the child, discuss the action of the characters in the book. Invite the child to repeat the verb you choose. You could also ask her to find the character that is carrying out different actions.

Materials:

Books

Guessing Sounds

Goal:

For the child to identify sounds without visual cues.

Experience:

1. Invite the child to close her eyes. Then, ask her to "listen very carefully" to identify different sounds.

2. Introduce a variety of sounds to the child when her eyes are closed. (You might want to put a blindfold on the child if that would make the game more fun for her.) You could use musical instruments, household objects such as pots and pans, tape-recorded sounds, or other familiar sounds in the child's world to play this sound game.

Materials:

Variety of objects that make sounds, blindfold

Carrying on a Brief Conversation

5

Goal:

For the child to be able to carry on a brief conversation.

Experience:

By this age, most toddlers are now ready to engage in conversations using words and short sentences. Listen very carefully to what the toddler is telling you. Try to go back and forth having a real dialogue.

It is important to have conversations of *all* types. During snack and meals, take the time to engage the child in conversation. This is an opportunity to teach him to listen to other speakers as well as to be the primary speaker. Model careful listening.

Materials:

None

Asking Questions

Goal:

For the child to ask a variety of questions. This helps a child learn more about forms of speech.

Experience:

Encourage children to raise questions of all kinds.

"**When** is Daddy coming home?"

"**Why** did you put on your coat?"

"**How** did you do that?"

When a child asks a question, respond to her quickly with brief, clear answers. When reading to the child or in conversation, ask *when* and *why* questions about the content.

Materials:

None

Singing and Listening to Music

7

Goal:

For the child to continue to learn from and enjoy music.

Experience:

Singing: Sing with the child on a regular basis (you have probably been doing this for some time already). It is important to learn new songs and teach them to the child. Sing them together often.

Listening: Listen to music with the toddler whenever possible. Introduce a wide variety of music (e.g., classical, jazz, country).

Playing: Have a basket of musical instruments readily available to you and the child to enhance your music time together.

Materials:

Variety of recorded music on CDs or audiotapes, children's songbooks, musical instruments

30–36
Months

Reading Books

Goal:

For the child to continue to learn from and enjoy picture books.

Experience:

Read picture books every day to the child. For a child between 2 and 3 years old, you can now read books that have a clear story line (e.g., *The Very Hungry Caterpillar* by Eric Carle).

Discuss the story with the child. Ask her questions, such as "What did the caterpillar do?"

Young children love to have stories reread to them. If you are rereading a story, ask the child to recall the story line or details about the story before you read it: "Do you remember what the bear does next?"

What a delight to help the child discover the joy of books!

Materials:

Variety of books with a brief story line

1

Tossing a Beanbag

Goal:

For the child to learn to throw underhanded and over-handed with accuracy.

Experience:

1. Make several small cloth bags and fill them with dried beans or lentils.

2. Sew the bags up to make beanbags.

3. Show the child how to toss the beanbags at a target. Examples of targets include an empty, stable bucket; a circle taped on the floor; or a stable basket.

4. Ask the child to stand behind a line and show her how to throw the beanbag underhanded and over-handed.

5. When the child is throwing with accuracy, move the line back a few inches and have her try again.

Materials:

Materials to make beanbags such as cloth, beans, and lentils; targets; heavy tape

Playing Follow the Leader

30–36
Months

Goal: For the child to follow directions in action songs using gross motor movements.

Experience: Purchase a CD or audiotape of children's action songs. Follow along to the actions with the child. For example, the recording may direct the child to "touch your head" or "stomp your foot." Do these things with the child and then watch to see if she is able to do this independently. The child will learn to listen and take action.

If this is too difficult, play Follow the Leader with the child yourself first, and let the child follow a simple series of your actions until she masters them.

Materials: CD or audiotapes of action songs

Hanging Upside Down

3

Goal:

For the child to learn to hang by the knees on playground equipment.

Experience:

1. Begin by inviting the child to put his head on the floor while standing. This gives him the beginning feeling of being upside down.

2. Now, move to a jungle gym or hanging bar. If the child is comfortable, invite him to hang from his knees while you hold onto him.

Note: *Be sure there is sufficient padding beneath the bars for this exercise. An adult should stay near the child at all times while he is learning this new ability.*

Materials:

Jungle gym or hanging bar with padding underneath

Bouncing a Ball

4

Goal: For the child to bounce a ball.

Experience: Give children plenty of opportunities to practice bouncing a ball. A child will develop coordination and a sense of timing through this experience.

1. Play catch with the child using a bouncy rubber ball that is about 8 inches to 10 inches in diameter. The child is probably already familiar with throwing the ball.

2. Now add a variation to ball play by inserting a bounce.

Variation: Invite two children to play with each other in this way.

Materials: Rubber ball

Completing an Independent Somersault

Goal:

Experience:

For the child to complete a somersault independently.

For a while, you may have been helping the child complete a somersault. Now, perhaps she is ready to do this by herself. Show the child how to put her head down and turn over into a somersault without using any props, such as the ball or wedge.

Initially, you may need to help her roll her legs and torso over.

It is important to give the child many novel and exciting ways to move her body; a somersault is one novel way for her to move.

Note: *Be sure to observe the child carefully to avoid neck injury.*

Materials:

None

Jumping Up

6

Goal: For the child to jump up off the ground.

Experience: If the child is able to successfully jump off a low step, now invite him to jump *up* from the ground.

You may need to give the child the sensation of jumping up off the floor by holding his hands and giving him a lift.

You will find children usually love learning new ways to move and experience the joy of their bodies in motion.

Materials: None

Moving Through an Obstacle Course

7

Goal:

For the child to move through an obstacle course.

Experience:

Set up an obstacle course with boxes to crawl through, tables and chairs to crawl over and around, and other safe items found in the child's environment.

Invite the child to make her way through the course. Children build confidence by reaching a goal despite obstacles.

Take this opportunity to use language such as "over," "around," "through," "under," and "You found a way."

When reading to the child, point out how characters in books continue in spite of barriers.

Materials:

Boxes; chairs; tables; other safe items to build an interesting, fun obstacle course

Pedaling a Tricycle

8

Goal:

For the child to learn to ride a tricycle using reciprocal pedaling skills to propel the tricycle.

Experience:

1. Secure a small tricycle.

2. Invite the child to sit on the tricycle.

3. Show him how to turn the pedals to make the tricycle move. You may need to push him with his feet on the pedals in the beginning.

4. Go very slowly until he has the feeling of pushing his feet in a circular motion to make the tricycle move.

Materials:

Small tricycle

Filling a Pitcher

1

Goal:

For the child to learn to pour liquid from a pitcher. This experience will help the child to pour his own beverages.

Experience:

1. Choose a small or medium-sized pitcher (about one quart) with a good handle that the child can easily grip.

2. Tape or draw (using a permanent marker) a line marking *half full* on the inside of the pitcher.

3. Demonstrate how to hold the pitcher with one hand on the handle and the other under the spout.

4. Set the pitcher on the counter beside the faucet. Turn on the water just enough to get a small stream. (**Note:** *Adjust the water temperature so that the child cannot be burned.*) Point to the line inside the pitcher and demonstrate filling it to that level.

5. When the child has mastered this, show him how to pour the water into the sink, using one hand to hold the pitcher and the other for support under the spout.

6. Show the child where the pitcher is stored, and return it when finished.

Materials:

Pitcher, tape or marker

30–36 Months

Scooping Using Containers

2

Goal:

For the child to improve his ability to scoop from one container to another. The child will enjoy the pattern of this experience while gaining more precision with her hand muscles.

Experience:

1. Purchase scoops of different shapes and sizes and containers with two sides, such as pet-feeding dishes or cleaning buckets. Use a dry substance, such as beans or macaroni, for the scooping material. Place materials on a tray.

2. Invite the child to do some scooping. Demonstrate using the scoop to transfer the substance from the left to the right side of the container.

3. Now show the child how to scoop all of the material back to the other side. Look around the tray for any loose material and place it in the appropriate container.

4. Invite the child to try the activity.

5. When she is finished, show her how to return the materials to the shelf.

Materials:

Scoop; divided container; rice, beans, or other dry substances that are easy to scoop; tray

30–36 Months

3 Folding

Goal:

For the child to learn to fold along a stitched line, improving precision in fine motor skills.

Experience:

1. Using colored thread, stitch along the half line of a square white handkerchief, and then stitch along the quarter lines of the handkerchief.

2. Place the handkerchiefs in a basket and put the basket on a shelf in the child's play area.

3. Invite the child to get the basket and show him how to lay the handkerchief flat on the table.

4. Next, show him how to fold it along the stitching, first at the half line, then the quarter line.

5. Show him how to put the folded handkerchiefs back in the basket neatly and return the basket to the shelf when he is finished.

Materials:

Basket, handkerchiefs with half- and quarter-fold lines stitched

30–36 Months

Tonging

30–36 Months

Goal:

For the child to improve thumb and forefinger pincer grip by using tongs to pick up objects.

Experience:

1. Bring the container and tongs to a table. Invite the child to join you.

2. Pick up the tongs and show the child how to grasp them, using your thumb and forefinger pincer grip. Pick up the substance from the left container and move it into the right container. Continue until the left bowl is empty.

3. Now, move all of the cotton balls (or other objects) back to the first container. Check around the container for any loose materials.

4. Invite the child to try. When she is finished, invite her to return the materials to the shelf.

Materials:

Tongs; divided container; cotton balls, wooden blocks or other objects that can be grasped easily with tongs

Stringing Small Beads

Goal:

For the child to improve fine motor skills by stringing small beads.

Experience:

If a child has mastered stringing large beads and does not put small toys in her mouth, she may now be ready to string small beads.

1. Select 6–8 beads and a good string with one end finished and the other knotted. Put these in a basket on a shelf in the play area.

2. Show the child where to find the beads and then provide support and encouragement as she strings the small beads, using the same procedure as with the large beads.

3. When she is finished, tell her that she may pull the beads off of the string and return them to the basket on the shelf. Alternatively, the child may want to display her accomplishment.

This activity takes great concentration but is fun for the child to complete.

Materials:

Small beads, string, basket

Basting

Goal:

For the child to use a baster or eyedropper to transfer liquids. This experience is good for further developing the thumb and forefinger pincer grasp.

Experience:

1. Put colored water in one side of a divided container.

2. Bring the baster and divided container to the table. Invite the child to participate.

3. Demonstrate how the water is drawn up into the tube by squeezing the baster or eyedropper. Transfer the colored water from the left bowl to the right bowl until the left bowl is empty.

4. Reverse the procedure, going from right to left.

5. Demonstrate using a sponge to clean up the spills around the bowls.

Materials:

Divided container (or two identical containers), colored water, baster or eyedropper, sponge

7

Drawing

Goal:

For the child to represent ideas, people, animals, or objects by drawing.

Experience:

Many parents and teachers are eager for the child to draw a picture that is "of something." The child will begin to represent reality in his drawings; one day he may tell you that "this picture is a baby" or other person, place, or thing.

Attend to what the child says about crayon, chalk, or paint marks. What you see may look like scribbles; however, regardless of what is there, the child reaches an exciting milestone when he uses *representational thinking* (i.e., designates a symbol to represent an idea, person, or object) in his drawings.

To support this budding interest, respect the child's idea and do not offer suggestions on how to make it look more like what he tells you it is. Also, do not overwhelm the child by asking too many questions about what it is.

Write the child's label for the picture when you write his name and date on the creation.

Materials:

Paper, pencil, chalk, crayons, or paint and paintbrush

30–36 Months

Completing an 8-Piece Puzzle

8

Goal:

For the child to complete even more complex puzzles.

Experience:

When the child is able to successfully complete a 5-piece puzzle, she is ready for more complex puzzles.

1. Select puzzles with simple large pieces that are complete (always discard puzzles with missing pieces). Keep the puzzles in a puzzle rack that the child has easy access to.

2. Invite the child to try to put the puzzle together. Show the child how to take out all of the pieces and lay them in a row for easy access. The child may be able to spontaneously complete the puzzles, but if not, you can only take out 2 or 3 pieces at a time.

3. Show the child how to return the puzzle to the puzzle rack.

Materials:

8-piece puzzles, a puzzle rack

30–36 Months

Naming Colors and Shapes

1

Goal:

For the child to identify and name 1–8 colors and 1–5 shapes.

Experience:

1. Bring out a basket that has a number of different objects (e.g., small bears of different colors such as red, blue, yellow, green, orange, purple, black, white, and brown) and a set of objects of varying shapes (e.g., circle, triangle, square, rectangle, and oblong). It is best to use objects that are the same in every way except for color or shape.

2. Ask the child to point to the "red one," "the square one," and so forth.

3. When the child is able to identify the correct color or shape, make the task more difficult by asking him to name the color or shape.

Materials:

Basket with different colored objects and shapes

Identifying Gender

2

Goal:

For the child to correctly identify boys and girls.

Experience:

Children determine who is a boy or a girl or a man or a woman in a variety of ways, and they tend to have concepts of gender by this age.

Tell the child whom in her world is a girl or a boy, then ask her to tell you who is a girl or boy.

You may also point out gender when reading to the child.

Tell the child how boys and girls are different and the same. Try to avoid gender stereotypes; for example, point out that girls don't always have long hair and that some boys play with dolls.

Materials:

Books with boys, girls, men, and women

Identifying Things by Function

3

Goal:

For the child to learn about function and be able to identify a variety of objects by what they do.

Experience:

Bring out a basket with a number of different types of tools and objects that do different things, for example, a hammer, toy saw, and toy screwdriver, or another basket with an airplane, car, buggy, tricycle, and wagon.

Pointing to different objects, ask the child, "Which one flies? Which one do we drive on the road? Which one do you ride in? Which one do you pull? Which one do you build things with?"

When reading to the child, make sure to include language that explains, "what things do" whenever possible. Ask the child to tell you, for example, "Where is something on the page that you can ride in?"

Materials:

Baskets with small objects that serve a purpose such as small tools, toys, a hairbrush, or a toothbrush

Beautiful Beginnings: A Developmental Curriculum for Infants and Toddlers by H. Raikes and J. Whitmer. Copyright © 2006 Paul H. Brookes Publishing Co., Inc. All rights reserved.

Sequencing

Goal:

For the child to sequence by size.

Experience:

1. Lay out materials that are sequenced by size.

2. Ask the child to show you which comes first, second, third, and so forth.

3. If the child is able to sequence, you can then say, "This one is biggest. This one is next biggest. This one is littlest." It is best to routinely begin with the largest and work toward the smallest.

The child will enjoy doing this on his own after he understands how to use the materials appropriately.

As a follow-up, when reading to the child, ask him to show you the little (or small), big, and bigger items on the page and talk about sequence in stories (e.g., small, medium, and big bear in Goldilocks story).

Materials:

Sequencing materials such as tower with rings, nesting cups, Montessori pink tower, or Montessori brown stair

Locating Objects by Color or Shape

5

Goal: For the child to identify objects by color and/or shape.

Experience: Ask the child to locate something in the room by color or shape. Ask questions such as, "Find the red toy" or "Find a square book."

When the child masters this task, identify two characteristics. Ask him to "Find a red, square toy" or "Bring me a purple, round pillow."

The child will learn how to observe and generalize what he sees in his everyday environment.

For follow-up, when reading a book, ask the child to pick out shapes and colors.

Materials: Items usually found in a classroom or home

6

Following Directions

Goal:

For the child to follow 2- and 3-stage directions in sequence.

Experience:

Give the child 2 tasks to complete that should be done in close physical proximity to each other. For example, you might say, "Go upstairs and put the socks in the drawer" or "Get the paper and then shut the door."

Another way to help the child learn to sequence directions is to ask her to remember what happened earlier in the day. For example, ask, "What did we do today? We put on our coats and then we went outside."

When reading, discuss with the child what characters did in the stories and the sequence. Use the language of sequencing: "first," "then," "next."

Materials:

Books

30–36 Months

Understanding One-to-One Correspondence

Goal:

For the child to understand one-to-one correspondence and beginning concepts of quantity.

Experience:

1. Give the child 1 Cheerio and then another, counting as you give them to him. "Here's 1 Cheerio; here's another Cheerio; that's 2."

2. Next, lay out 2 blocks and 2 other small objects. Line up the blocks with the objects so that the child sees correspondence in quantity. The child will learn beginning concepts of quantity.

One-to-one correspondence can also be taught when reading by pointing out 1 and 2 objects on the page.

Materials:

Cheerios, blocks, small objects, books

30–36
Months

Playing "What's Missing?"

8

Goal:

For the child to remember 3 items and to keep an image in mind.

Experience:

1. To play this visual game, bring out a basket with 3 objects that the child is familiar with.

2. Lay them out in a row.

3. Take 1 away. Ask the child, "Which one is missing?" "Which one is gone?"

Variation: When reading, put your hand over 1 object on a page and ask the child to tell you which one is missing or hiding under your hand.

This teaches the child to observe and keep an image in her mind.

Materials:

Basket with 3 objects, books

Playing to a Beat

1

Goal:

For the child to use instruments or to march following the beat of music. Listening to music frequently will help the child to become attuned to rhythm in music.

Experience:

Give the child or children rhythm instruments (shakers, knockers, rhythm sticks, and tambourines) and sing a tune that they are familiar with. You may also play an audiotape or CD. Invite them to shake or strike their instrument in time with the music.

The child or children may also enjoy marching and moving to the beat.

Invite the child to clap the rhythms with you.

Materials:

Rhythm instruments, recorded music

30–36 Months

2

Flying a Kite

Goal:

For the child to fly a kite, discovering the lift from air and wind.

Experience:

Take a simple kite to an open space or playground and let the child help you get it up into the breeze.

Call the child's attention to the feel of the wind and talk about how the breeze keeps the kite up in the air. Enjoy!

Materials:

Kite, wind

30–36
Months

Growing Things

3

Goal:

For the child to experience the excitement of caring for a growing or living thing and to learn responsibility for a task that must be performed regularly.

Experience:

1. With the child, gather materials to plant seeds.

2. Invite the child to help you plant the seeds in small cups. You may want to plant seeds in a clear cup so the child can see the roots as they grow.

3. Water the plant, and put it in a sunny place.

4. Invite him to observe the changes in the plant each day.

If you have a pet, you may also invite the child to help care for it.

Materials:

Plastic cups, seeds, soil, a sunny window

30–36
Months

Expanding Water Play

Goal:

For the child to continue to experience joyful learning through water play.

Experience:

Children this age love to play in the water. Provide many opportunities with a lot of variety for water play. Bring objects to the water table, sink, or basin and let the child practice pouring and floating. Let the child play with objects that sink and float. Encourage play in a small wading pool.

Note: *Never leave a small child alone when playing in water.*

Materials:

Water table, sink, or basin; objects that sink and float; cups for pouring; small wading pool

5 Playing with a Tent

Goal:

For the child to play in a tent, discovering the fun of playing in new enclosures.

Experience:

Provide a small tent and invite the child to take her toys inside the tent to play or to play with the tent in any way she enjoys. Small children love to crawl in and out of tents and other structures.

Use vocabulary on related concepts such as *inside* and *outside*. Talk about how much fun it is to be in a cozy, private place. When reading, ask the child which characters are inside and which are outside.

Materials:

Small tent

Playing with Puppets

6

Goal:

For the child to experience puppet play to discover how a puppet can provide another form of expression.

Experience:

1. Obtain several hand puppets. You may want to select characters with whom the child is familiar.

2. Show the child how the puppet can "talk" and invite him to talk with the puppet. Show how the puppets can take on actions, such as how they comfort one another and wave good-bye.

3. Let the child experiment with the puppets. The child may want to make his puppet talk to yours.

4. A next stage in puppet play is to use puppets to help the child express his feelings.

5. Show the child how to put the puppets away when he is finished.

Materials:

Several hand puppets

Painting with a Small Brush

7

Goal: For the child to paint with more detail by using a small brush

Experience:

1. The child may now be ready to paint with a small paintbrush. Prepare the paint (mixed with soap) and easel, cover the floor, and select paint cups with lids as before.

2. Invite the child to get his apron.

3. Select only 1 paint color until the child has mastered all of the steps of dipping the brush in and out of the paint cup.

4. Allow the child plenty of time to lose himself in artistic work. Encourage him to experiment. Some children will make a single stroke; others will cover the entire paper.

5. Write his name and date on the picture and hang it up to dry.

Remember that there is no right way for a child to paint a picture and no need to make a picture "of something." It is not helpful to insist that the child tell you what it is.

Materials: Small paintbrush, paints that mix with soap, paint cups, apron, paper, easel

30–36
Months

Following Art Directions

8

Goal:

For the child to have a new art experience. Exposing children this age to a wide variety of art experiences will help to develop creativity and imagination.

Experience:

Bring in a new art medium. Do not tell the child what to make. Invite her to follow directions to learn how to use the materials.

For example, you may have a project that involves gluing small pieces of wood or Styrofoam together. Teach the child to watch while you show how to dip the glue stick, how to cover the wood or Styrofoam with glue, and how to press the pieces together. The child will then learn how to create something on her own.

Remember, once you have demonstrated how to use the materials (e.g., the glue stick), allow the child to create her masterpiece however she chooses.

Materials:

Materials needed for a specific art project

30–36 Months

Making Choices

1

Goal: For the child to improve decision-making abilities.

Experience: Two-year-olds are good at making choices and need many opportunities to practice. Sometimes, however, a child doesn't have a choice and must follow a rule. For example, a child might not have a choice about whether to put on her pajamas. But you can give her the choice to wear her "blue ones" or her "bunny jammies." It is important to make complying with simple rules fun but matter of fact. Give her choices within the parameters of what she *can* do.

Whenever possible during the child's day, ask her "Would you rather...?" and "This *or* that?" giving her practice in making up her own mind and developing thinking and reasoning skills. Keep it simple. Two choices are enough for most 2-year-olds.

Materials: None

30–36
Months

Expressing Feelings with Words

Goal:

For the child to express feelings in words. Being able to talk about feelings helps the child to gain control and emotionally regulate himself.

Experience:

Helping a child express his feelings using words is an important developmental goal.

When the child seems to be angry, sad, disappointed, lonely, or happy, name these feelings for him.

When reading, discuss the feelings of the characters with the child.

Materials:

Books

30–36 Months

Recounting Details of an Incident

3

Goal:

For the child to tell the details of a past event. Being able to remember and tell about past events contributes to the child's sense of mastery and the ability to understand social and other events in his life.

Experience:

Encourage the child to recount details of a recent event. Select an event involving people. Encourage the child to tell you what happened. Use language such as "before," "just happened," "after," "then," and "next."

When reading, stop to discuss what just happened in the book. Also encourage the child to think about what might come next.

Materials:

Books

30–36
Months

Taking Turns

Goal:

For the child to learn *how* to share materials. In this experience, the child learns about waiting, turn taking or sharing, and completing an activity.

Experience:

If a child wants a toy that another child is playing with, teach him to ask to have it "when you are finished." Be certain the child receives the toy when the first child is finished. The child may sometimes be the one who gives the toy to another when he is finished, or he may need to be supported in following through to give the toy to the waiting child. (It is a good idea to have duplicates of the most popular toys for children this age rather than insisting that children always share.)

A good time to emphasize sharing is when children are working on their own projects but can also share materials. For example, when working with playdough, provide enough materials for every child to have one tool (e.g., a rolling pin, a cookie cutter, a plastic knife). Invite children to exchange the tools. You will find that secure children are often generous with others—sharing naturally—and you can quietly compliment children on sharing behaviors. Use language such as "when finished," "wait," "next," "done," "your turn," "his turn," and "share."

When reading, stop to discuss what the characters are doing. If a character is taking turns, waiting, or exchanging materials, point that out.

Materials:

Books, everyday toys and materials, blocks or other materials suitable for more than one child to play with

30–36 Months

Talking and Listening in a Small Group

5

Goal:

For the child to talk freely and listen in small groups.

Experience:

A child can be encouraged to express herself when with a small group of children or during family gatherings. Ask the child questions or employ a type of Show and Tell approach in which each person speaks or shows an item. Encourage the child to speak so that others can understand her, pay attention to other speakers, and encourage other speakers to listen fully when she speaks. With practice and successful interactions, the child will learn to speak with confidence.

A second important lesson is for the child to learn to listen to other children and to respectfully take turns to speak. This can be difficult when the child has such important things she wants to say. Draw the child into a conversation with another child and gently encourage the two children to take turns. When another child is telling a story, encourage the first child to listen carefully. Encourage the child to ask questions of the speaker. Compliment the child or children on listening well, especially when they are able to do this without cues. Help them find common conversation topics and themes.

When reading stories, point out when characters express themselves and when others are good listeners.

Materials:

Books and items to discuss

30–36
Months

Playing Jointly

Goal:

For the child to play cooperatively with another child for a short time.

Experience:

We can expect children this age to play together for a short time. Set up block play, making sure there is room for at least two children. If the children are building while engaged in parallel play, ask them if they can build a tower together by taking turns adding blocks to the tower. Encourage one child to offer pieces to the other child to put on the tower. Use words such as "cooperating," "sharing," "working together," "playing together," and "building together."

Block play is a good way to encourage joint play, but encourage joint play in other areas of play as well.

When reading stories, point out when characters are working and playing together.

Materials:

Books, blocks, or other materials suitable for more than one child to play with

Identifying and Talking About One's Body

7

Goal:

For the child to gain greater body awareness, to be able to describe her body, and to discuss its states, when appropriate. The child's self-concept grows as she understands her own body.

Experience:

Continue to help the child know her body and its wonderful functions. Now, help her describe internal states as well as to name the features. If she has an "owie in her head," identify it as a possible headache. Talk about her "squinting her eyes" when the sun is bright. Note her shiny hair and her smooth skin.

As always, many of these concepts can be emphasized during book reading with the child. Talk about characters' bodies and what they are like.

Materials:

Books

30–36
Months

Matching Names with Pictures

Goal:

For the child to view photographs and name familiar children. This activity helps the child to become more aware of children around him.

Experience:

By now, the child should be aware of all of the children in his environment and be able to identify them by name.

    Collect pictures of the children the child knows. Arrange these on a board with squares to match to pictures (e.g., Tic Tac Toe board, Lotto board), or make laminated cards. Ask the child to say each child's name as that child's picture is held up.

    When first names are mastered, ask for first and last names. As names are mastered, you may add by asking the child to remember something about each child, such as something the child likes or the child's hair color.

Materials:

Pictures of children, board with squares to match to pictures (e.g., Tic Tac Toe board), or laminated cards

30–36
Months

412

1

Knowing a Daily Routine

Goal:

For the child to know and follow a daily routine, which helps the child feel secure and safe and will remove many potential conflicts over change and what to do next.

Experience:

A child's ability to follow a consistent routine each day is important. Help the child to know a routine and invite her to tell you what comes next. Also let her help you get the materials for the next stage in the chosen routine.

Remember, 2- to 3-year-olds often have trouble changing activities, so be sure to give cues before the next step in the routine. For example, you might give a 5-minute notice before it's time to clean up for lunch.

Here is an example of a routine for home and center that many children this age can learn:

Get up, get dressed, diaper or toilet, have breakfast, clean up, put on coat, ride in the car using a car seat, arrive at center, hang coat and put things away, greet teacher and friends, play, sit during circle time, diaper or toilet, have a snack, play, clean up, go outside, eat lunch, clean up, nap, diaper or toilet, snack, greet parents, say goodbye to teachers and friends, ride home, arrive at home, diaper or toilet, play, dinner, play, clean up, bath, story, bedtime.

At home and at the center, it is important that all of the adults in the child's life are as consistent as possible with the child's routine.

Materials:

Cubby or a consistent place for child to put items for each period in the daily routine

30–36 Months

Washing Hands Independently

2

Goal: For the child to wash hands independently.

Experience: Set up the materials for hand washing so that the child can do it "all by herself." By this time, you might have already taught the child to wash her hands with help.

Use a low sink or a step stool; place soap in an unbreakable soap dish or use liquid soap with an easy-to-use pump. Set water temperature and water volume so that the child cannot burn herself.

Invite the child to wash her hands by herself. Remind the child of the steps she has learned about how to wash hands:

1. Wet hands and turn off water.

2. Soap, lather both front and back of hands.

3. Put soap back.

4. Rinse and turn off water.

5. Pick up the towel and dry both hands and in between fingers.

6. Hang up the towel, or throw it away or recycle it (if disposable).

7. Wipe up any spills with a sponge.

8. Squeeze the sponge and put it away.

In the beginning, make sure to praise the child for coming close to following the steps "all by herself."

Materials: Sink, water source, sponge, step stool, bar or liquid soap, cloth or paper towels

30–36
Months

Using the Toilet

3

Goal:

For the child to use the toilet independently.

Experience:

By now, perhaps the child has shown some interest in learning to use the toilet. When you think it is time for toilet learning and the child has indicated she wants to do this, give her the chance to use the toilet on a very regular basis throughout the day.

Follow a toileting routine regularly and emphasize the child's growth in using the toilet. Every family likes to select its own terms for the toileting process, so find out more about them and use them consistently. Keeping the process consistent between home and the center, as much as is possible, will aid in the child's success. Make sure you teach the child hygiene practices such as washing hands.

Many children will delight in their ability to use "big boy" or "big girl" pants. Small rewards and a lack of pressure or shame help this process to go smoothly.

Remember, some children learn to use the toilet very quickly and others take longer. Do not become angry or stressed about the child's failures; this will only make it more difficult for the child to learn. Keep the emphasis positive and stay relaxed about the process. If the child has many accidents, considering postponing the toilet learning process for a later date.

Materials:

Toilet or potty chair, toilet paper, sink, water, sponge, step stool, bar soap, cloth, paper towels

30–36
Months

Taking Clothes Off and Putting Them On

Goal:

For the child to take clothes off and put them on.

Experience:

Be sure the child has clothing that is easy for him to put on and take off by himself. This is a time for pants with elastic bands versus buttons or suspenders.

Encourage the child to take off his own clothing at appropriate times, for instance, when coming in from a walk, when preparing for a bath, or when preparing to toilet.

Later, offer him opportunities to put on the same clothing, which is a more challenging task. Work on one garment at a time.

Materials:

Clothing such as jackets, pants, hat, socks, shoes, shirts

30–36
Months

Wiping Up Spills and Sweeping

Goal:

For the child to clean up spills.

Experience:

Invite the child to help you clean up.

Get the broom and dustpan and model how to use them, making sure to use the broom in short, sweeping motions as you gather the material into the dustpan. Now, let the child try. Return the dustpan and broom to their proper storage place.

Also allow the child to help you clean up using a sponge, such as cleaning off a table or wiping up a spill on the floor. Model for the child how to wet and wring out the sponge and rinse it clean.

Materials:

Small broom, dustpan, sponge

30–36
Months

Brushing Teeth

6

Goal: For the child to brush teeth independently.

Experience:

1. Give the child a small toothbrush with a small dab of toothpaste on it.

2. Take out your own toothbrush and place a dab of toothpaste on it. Say to the child, "Now, you are big enough to brush your teeth by yourself. I will show you how I do it. I brush my back teeth, I brush my front teeth, and I brush inside and outside all of my teeth. Now, you brush your teeth."

3. Invite the child to look in a mirror while he brushes to be sure he is brushing all of his teeth.

4. Invite the child to rinse out his mouth and put away his cup (or discard a disposable cup).

5. Show the child how to rinse out the toothbrush and put away the toothbrush. Show him also how to put away the toothpaste.

6. Talk to the child about being able to brush his "own teeth every day."

Materials: Toothbrush, small tube of toothpaste, drinking cup, a place for storing the toothbrush

30–36 Months

Preparing Simple Foods

Goal: For the child to prepare simple foods.

Experience: Young children enjoy learning to prepare food.

1. Begin with simple food preparation such as spreading peanut butter on a piece of bread or cracker.

2. Invite the child to help you.

3. Wash your hands and the child's hands.

4. Pick up a blunt butter knife and take out a small amount of the peanut butter. Spread it on the piece of bread or cracker. Remind the child, "We don't lick the knife."

5. Put the lid back on the peanut butter container.

6. Place the snack on a napkin or plate and invite the child to eat it. Use a sponge to wipe up spills or crumbs.

7. Invite the child to spread peanut butter on his own cracker or bread, following your steps.

Other possible food preparations could include banana cutting, bread cutting, tortilla spreading, or tortilla rolling.

Materials: Bread, crackers, or tortillas; peanut butter; banana; butter knife; sponge; napkin or plate

419

Setting the Table

8

Goal:

For the child to set a table, continuing to participate in her own self-care.

Experience:

1. Invite the child to help you set a table.

2. Begin by having him set out placemats. Help him count the people to ensure that he has the right number. Then have him place the plates in the appropriate places.

3. Next, show him where to place the glasses and let him put one by each plate. Demonstrate where the napkins and then the utensils go.

By placing the items on the table one at a time, the child also is beginning to learn one-to-one correspondence.

You might also create placemats that outline where utensils are placed.

Materials:

Plates, napkins, child-safe utensils, placemats

30–36
Months

Pretending with People Toys Using 2–3 Steps

Goal:

For the child to carry out advanced pretend play using small people toys.

Experience:

1. Use toy sets with small people characters such as Little People by Fisher-Price. Play with the child to make these people complete two or more steps. For example, make them go to bed and then wake up and drive to school.

2. Ask the child to give the people names to represent people in the child's world. Ask, "Who is this? Grandma? Who is this?" Encourage the child to call one of the people by her own name.

3. Ask the child to take the people through a third action. This activity can be used to help the child gain mastery over issues related to people and their interactions, but for the most part, it is just plain fun.

Materials:

Toys with people characters and accessories

30–36
Months

Visiting the Doctor Using 2–3 Steps

Goal:

For the child to pretend playing doctor to expand the child's pretend-play possibilities and to familiarize the child with a visit to the doctor's office.

Experience:

Begin by setting up a few props seen in a doctor's office (e.g., stethoscope, play thermometer, doctor satchel). Pretend you are both visiting the doctor. Use language typical of a doctor visit that the child knows.

For a 2-step pretend, "see" the doctor and "get checked." Later, you can add a third step and then more steps. You could have the child listen to your heart, check your ears, take your temperature, and so forth. The child may want to pretend with a parent or enjoy being the doctor to check her teddy bear or doll.

You can read books about going to the doctor or dentist to expand the child's pretend-play possibilities. This is especially good to do before the child needs to visit the doctor.

Materials:

Play stethoscope, play thermometer, doctor satchel

30–36 Months

Pretending to Be Animals

3

Goal:

For the child to pretend to be an animal.

Experience:

Many children love pretending to be animals they know, such as dogs, cats, pigs, and cows. They enjoy moving like these animals and making the sounds the animals make. Animals can do all of the things the child likes to do, such as sleep, play, and eat. It is especially fun for a child or a group of children to pretend that they are doing these activities as animals they know.

It is also fun to introduce children to new kinds of animals and to ask them to try to imitate these animals, talking about the sounds they make, places they live, and what they eat.

Read books about animals and their habitats to expand the child's thinking about possibilities.

Materials:

Animal books, masks, props to suggest animals

Playing House over Time

Goal:

For the child to continue to expand his thinking and understand his own routines by playing house over several play periods.

Experience:

By now the child may have several actions related to playing house.

You can continue to expand the child's thinking by helping him act out play actions that may span more than a day. For example, the "mommy and daddy" can get up, eat breakfast, go to work, come home, eat dinner, go to bed, wake up again, and so forth. This helps the child better understand not only his own routines but also how to execute a play plan that has several pieces and involves remembering the play themes over time.

Materials:

Typical play house items

Pretending with Other Children

5

Goal: For the child to pretend with another child.

Experience: By now, children may be able to assume simple roles in which one child becomes the baby, one child becomes the mommy or grocer, and another becomes the shopper.

If the child has not already brought other children into her pretend play, help her to do so.

Make sure that the roles the children choose are very simple.

Materials: Pretend play items

425

Playing Grocery Store

6

Goal:

For the child to pretend playing grocery store.

Experience:

Take a field trip to a grocery store.

Set out boxes and cans, plastic fruits and vegetables, a cash register with play money, bags, and a grocery cart. Invite the child to "shop" for groceries.

Read books about grocery stores and food preparation to give the child additional activities for pretend play.

Materials:

Boxes and cans, plastic fruits and vegetables, a cash register with play money, bags, grocery cart

7

Playing Post Office

Goal: For the child to pretend playing post office—another pretend theme representing adults in the child's life.

Experience: Take a trip to a post office.

Set up a simple post office, with paper for letters, envelopes, small boxes, and "stamps."

Encourage the child to pretend mailing a letter or package.

Send a real letter to a relative or friend and encourage that person to write back to the child.

Reading books about letters and the post office can provide the child with additional play ideas.

Materials: Paper, envelopes, small boxes, "stamps" (e.g., stickers)

30–36
Months

Extending Pretend Play

8

Goal: For the child to extend pretend play to many areas.

Experience: Pretend play can extend into any area of the child's life. You can take a field trip, read stories, and then set up activities for pretend play for any interest or experience the child may have. Some examples of settings include a restaurant, beauty shop, clothing store, zoo, farm, pumpkin patch, construction site, fire station, or train station.

Read and talk with the child about the magic of the larger world that the child is so curious about. Let the world become more real by bringing it into the pretend play area.

Materials: Specific materials needed for each area

30–36 Months